Love the Way You Lie

BOYS OF RIVERSIDE

GRACIE GRAHAM

This is a work of fiction. Names, places, characters, and events are fictitious in every regard. Any similarities to actual events and persons, living or dead, are purely coincidental. Any trademarks, service marks, product names, or named features are assumed to be the property of their respective owners and are used only for reference. There is no implied endorsement if any of these terms are used. Except for review purposes, the reproduction of this book in whole or part, electronically or mechanically, constitutes a copyright violation.

Copyright © February, 2023 by Gracie Graham

All rights reserved.

To my husband, who has witnessed both the joy and agony of my writing and encourages me through it all.
Thanks, babe.

Chapter 1

MACKENZIE

Sometimes I imagine what it would be like if I were dead.

Weightless. Floating in the dark. Mind blank.

I imagine what my father's life would be like with me gone and wonder how much better it would be without the constant fear that tragedy could strike again and take me away, too. Sometimes I conjure up images of heaven. But mostly, I imagine the nothingness of it all. The stillness. Ever since the accident, I'm not sure what I believe about the afterlife anymore, so these dreams are dependent on my mood. They're constantly changing shape, although, I'd *like* to think there's more after this life–that my mother's someplace else, looking down on me.

I slide into the seat of my car. The leather is hot, and my shirt instantly sticks to my back. Pressure fills my chest, and my stomach turns with the overwhelming urge to vomit, but I push it back down.

Closing my eyes, I clench my hands around the steering wheel and breathe. It's all I can do to keep from bolting as blood pounds in my ears. Once I'm able to open them again, I grip the keys in my hands a little tighter while the four-leaf clover key chain dangles from my fist, mocking me.

I want to put the keys in the ignition, turn the radio up and pull out of my driveway with the music pumping like I used to; not a care in the world. I want to place one hand on the steering wheel while I cruise down the interstate, the wind whipping through my hair.

But I can't.

I can't bring myself to start my car, any more than I can will myself to remember.

The rumbling of an engine behind me breaks through my ominous thoughts and I jerk my head up, glancing in the rearview mirror to see my dad's cruiser.

Busted.

I wipe my damp palms on the front of my jeans and get out of the car at the same time he does. We share our dark hair, but that's where the similarities stop. His is streaked with silver, but the hazel eyes staring back at me are unlike my own because the ice blues eyes I inherited from my mother are cool and crisp like polar caps.

His belt hangs on his hips. Only the butt of his gun and the radio are visible as he slams his car door closed. The static sound of the dispatcher fills the quiet air as she relays a message to one of the officers before Dad has a chance to click it off. And when he takes a step toward me, his expression transforms instantly. His worry is revealed by his frown, creased forehead, and the crow's feet by his eyes.

"Mackenzie," he starts, his gaze flickering to my car, "everything okay?"

"Uh, yeah. Just . . ." I hook a thumb back toward the car with a sigh, "seeing if anything's changed."

"Has it?"

I shake my head, disappointed in myself, and the sympathy in my father's eyes nearly cripples me. "All in good time," he says, placing a hand on my shoulder and giving it a squeeze.

"Right." I offer him a smile that doesn't quite fit.

It's almost been a year, I want to say. But I don't. Because he doesn't need a reminder, and because the passing of time changes nothing. I haven't been able to drive since the accident—can barely even bring myself to sit behind the wheel.

"Anyway, I thought maybe we'd order a pizza, rent a movie or something. What do you say? I even bought some of that red licorice you like from the Sugar Shack on my way home."

My smile fades from my face. "Dad, it's Friday . . ."

He rocks back on his heels, his thumbs hooked in his belt, and I can tell he remembers but is trying to find an excuse, any excuse, to keep me here tonight—at home. Where I'll be safe.

"You promised, Dad," I remind him.

He exhales and runs a hand over his face, then stares off into the distance, gaze trained on the front door where the same floral wreath Mom put up a year ago still hangs. "Yeah, I know I did." He pauses as if the next words out of his mouth cause him pain. "But are you sure you're ready for this?"

I've been *ready,* I want to scream. *It's you who isn't.*

But I swallow my thoughts because I don't want to upset him. "It's just a party," I argue.

"Just a party today. But you start school on Monday and the squad agreed to let you back on with little notice, it'll mean practice nearly every day. You have a lot coming up. Maybe a party is pushing it." He nods as if agreeing with himself. "I think it's best if you just stay in."

"Dad," I step forward and grab his hand. "Please? Graham will be there. He'll watch over me."

I say it because I know he loves Graham; we've been best friends for six years. When your father is the chief of police and has a daughter who nearly lost her life, it means he doesn't trust many people. But he trusts Graham. And it doesn't hurt that the Scotts are the most prominent family in Riverside.

"Why don't we see how the week goes. Then after the game Friday night, if you want to go out, we'll discuss it, yeah?" He taps me underneath the chin, and I hate it. It's one of the many things he does to make me feel like a child.

"But—" I start, but he's already turning toward the door.

"We'll get pineapple and ham," he calls over his shoulder, and I know it's supposed to be a peace offering because it's my favorite, and he hates it.

Two hours later, I'm curled up on the couch next to my father while a slapstick comedy plays on the screen. An open pizza box sits on the coffee table in front of us, along with two empty cans of Coke, a visual reminder Mom's not here. We never used to eat in the living room when she was alive. Although, we hardly ordered fast food either. A lot of things are different these days. Mom always used to cook these huge three-course meals and always insisted we ate at the kitchen table. "The food just tastes better," she used to say.

"Don't let her fool you," my dad would reply. "She just doesn't want pasta sauce on her sofa cushions." Then he'd wink at her and smile.

But we hardly use the massive dining room anymore. Dust collects on the gleaming surface of the polished cherry table.

When my phone buzzes, I slide it out of my pocket and check the screen. Another text from Graham.

Graham: *You coming???*

Dad was supposed to drop me off at school thirty minutes ago, where Graham was waiting. No doubt he's wondering where I'm at.

I glance over at Dad, who's half asleep. Every once in a while, his eyes blink closed before he jerks them open again, trying to stay awake for the movie, and though I hate that he kept me from going out, I can't find it in me to be angry. So I reply:

Mackenzie: *Can't. Dad went back on his promise. He thinks I should stay in since school starts Monday.*
Graham: *WTH. Do you want me to talk to him?*
Mackenzie: *No. I don't want him to worry.*
Graham: *Kenz.*

I can practically hear his disapproving tone over the line. *He can't shelter you forever*, he always says. *He's smothering you. He kept you cooped up in that house for too long. What's he going to do when you leave for college; go with you?* All things he regularly says. All equally accurate. But when it takes more than four months to even step foot in a car again without having a panic attack, going places is kind of challenging.

When I don't answer right away, he texts back again.

Graham: You know you're ready. You've BEEN ready.

Mackenzie: I know.

And I do. I really do. I was ready months ago, but Dad just doesn't seem to understand that. He's petrified the moment he lets me out of his sight, the world will come crashing down.

Disappointed doesn't even begin to describe the way I feel about sitting at home tonight when I'd promised all my old friends I'd be at the field party. I need this time to reconnect before the start of school on Monday; this slow entry back to a social life before I'm plunged into the thick of it headfirst.

Mackenzie: *You'll just need to have fun without me.*
Graham: *Sneak out.*

Graham's text draws me up short and I straighten on the couch, still as stone.

Mackenzie: *What? Are you serious?*
Graham: *Dead serious. I'm doing a beer run with Jace, and he's being a dick about stopping for you. Dude's just scared shitless your dad will catch us with a keg in the pickup. I should've taken my car. But if I call you an Uber, will you meet us?*

I chew on my lip and glance over at my father who snorts, then opens his eyes again and stares at the TV screen, squinting. He was called out at two a.m. and worked through the day, which means the second his head hits the pillow, he'll be out like a light, especially if he thinks I'm tucked away in bed. Safe.

When I don't reply right away, Graham texts once more.

Graham: *Come on. My cousin is supposed to show, too. You can meet him.*

I bite my lip. He says this as bait because he knows I'm curious about his cousin. Supposedly, they'd been close when they were little and lost touch over the years. But come Monday, the bad boy from Shaker will officially be playing football for Riverside.

My stomach clenches in the face of indecision. If I stay here, I'll miss out. And I'm desperately tired of missing out. All I want is to remember what it's like to be a normal teenager again without this dark cloud of tragedy hanging over me. But if I sneak out late at night, and Dad catches me, he'll come down on me hard. I can kiss my future freedom goodbye. Right now, my dad trusts me; it's the rest of the world he doesn't trust—life, fate, everything he can't control. Am I really willing to risk that?

I exhale slowly, mulling over my choices when I hover my fingers above the keypad on my phone.

Decision made, my pulse jumps as I type.

Okay. Give me an hour, and Dad will be in bed.

I thank my driver, then step out into the warm evening air where a symphony of katydids and crickets surrounds me. My nerves are like a livewire as I begin to climb the bluff that overlooks the field beside Crow's Creek, trying to focus on the beauty of the property. It's part of a long stretch of farmland and hunting grounds, just outside of town. At one time, it belonged to Jace Taggert's grandparents, but after they died, his parents took it over and kept the large log cabin on the property for weekend getaways. Still, it remains mostly vacant, which makes it the perfect place for Rebel football parties.

My sandals sink into the soft earth as I crest the hill. Any minute, I expect to hear the sound of a radio blaring and my peers' laughter. I anticipate Graham sweeping me into his arms like he always does when it's been more than a day since I saw him last. He has a way about him that always makes me feel special, and the picture I conjure makes me all the more excited to see everyone.

But it's eerily quiet, save for the sounds of nature all around me, and when I plant my feet at the top and survey my surroundings, my heart stutters in my chest. Weeping Willows cast shadows on the field in front of me, which is startlingly empty.

I blink several times to ensure I'm seeing right, yet nothing changes.

No one is here. How can that be?

My heart kick-starts in my chest and pumps into overdrive as I ignore the prickling sensation creeping up my spine and make a move to grab the purse by my side. When I grasp nothing but air, I cast a glance to my shoulder and hip. *It's not there.*

I stare at my side, dumbstruck, before I realize I must've left it in the Uber after I touched up my makeup. Which means I'm more than ten miles from home in the middle of nowhere without a phone. Without money or a way to get home.

Shit.

Chapter 2

GRAHAM

I listen to Kenzie's phone ring over the line for the billionth time, but when she doesn't pick up, I slam my cell down on the hood of Jace's truck. *Why the hell isn't she answering?*

Jace, who's on his third beer, eyes me over the rim of his cup. "I take it that means you still can't get a hold of her?"

"This never would've happened if we'd just picked her up in the first place," I roar, taking my anger out on him.

"And risk the chief catching us picking up his princess with a keg in the back of my truck? Yeah, no thanks. I like my spot on the team, thank you very much."

I glare at him even though I know he's right. I like Kenzie's dad. He's a good dude at heart, and even though he's too overprotective, I understand it. I would be, too, if I lost my wife in a car crash that also nearly took my daughter. But if I was a gambling man, I'd bet everything on the fact the patrol car suddenly cruising the country roads around Crow's Creek is on account of him. My guess is he tipped off the local PD because in the two years we've been partying up there, they've never set up a DUI checkpoint on those roads. It's in the middle of nowhere with no bars, which means the only reason they'd be there is to bust someone in particular—us.

When the officer pulled us over, I thought Jace might wet his pants. The only thing between him and the keg in the bed of his truck was an old tarp and a couple of bungee cords. So the minute he let us go, Jace took it as a gift from God and hightailed it the hell out of there, then sent everyone a text with a change of location.

Ever since, I've been trying to get a hold of Kenzie but can't. Even the dumbass Uber driver isn't picking up.

"I should've stayed," I mumble to myself. I should've asked Jace to drop me off so I could wait for Kenzie, instead of assuming I'd be able to get a hold of her once we settled in our new spot. "I'm going after her," I say, wrenching the door to Jace's truck open to the sound of his protests. "Relax, dude. I won't put a scratch on your precious baby."

"Fine." Jace hovers in front of the driver's side window. "But no freaky shit in the back seat."

I flip him off.

"He wishes," Teagen, our tight end chimes in, so I flip him the bird on my other hand, grateful I have a spare, then hammer the gas as I back out, spinning the tires and smiling at the knowledge I've successfully skyrocketed Jace's blood pressure.

Once I'm back on the road, I call Kenzie again. It goes to voice mail, so I curse and double check my texts to make sure I haven't missed anything. Ten minutes pass when a loud *POP* breaks the silence, and the truck jerks to the right, then slows down.

"The hell?" A thunking sound fills the air in answer, and I growl. "You've got to be freaking kidding me right now."

I sigh as I steer the truck to the side of the road, knowing what I'll find before I even get out to inspect the tire. Sure enough, it's flat as a pancake, so I crouch underneath the bed to check for the spare and find . . . nothing. There's only an empty void of space where the tire should be.

"Shit!" I shoot to my feet and kick the rim with my foot, then roar at the pain.

I rake a hand through my hair. All I can think about is Kenzie alone at Crow's Creek, wondering where everyone is. With any luck, she'll realize no one's there and have the Uber take her straight back home. It could be why the driver isn't answering, though it doesn't account for why she hasn't picked up any of my calls. Unless she's pissed at me. After all, this is her first night out alone, and for all she knows I've stood her up only an hour after I proposed she sneak out to meet me.

I imagine all the things that could happen if Kenzie is stranded and decides to walk home or to the nearest residence, which is miles from Crow's Creek.

She could have a panic attack.

A flashback.

She could get hit by a car.

Some crazy asshole could pick her up.

A million different scenarios fight for precedence. None of them good.

I clench my jaw so hard, I think it might crack as I grab my phone off the driver's seat and dial Jace. When he doesn't answer, I try each of the guys. But none of them pick up because they're either half-trashed already, or the music is too damned loud for them to hear their phones.

As I tuck my phone back in my pocket, I catch my reflection in the truck window. My sandy waves are mussed from running my hands through them, my green eyes wild in the moonlight, and I swallow as I contemplate my options.

Call a tow and wait. Or walk back to the party and borrow someone else's ride, which will take longer than I'd like. Both options mean a lot of time passing before I know Kenzie's whereabouts and if she's okay.

Unless I call Chief Hart, her father. He always answers. Being on-call is part of the job. Surely, Mackenzie has made it back home by now. I could simply call and tell him I have a bad feeling and have him check on her. If anyone could understand that, it's him.

But if she isn't there . . .

He'd never let her out of his sight again. He'd make her quit the squad before school even started. He'd never trust her with me again.

I shudder and squeeze my eyes closed so hard I see spots.

My hands fist at my side as I war with myself on what to do.

When I blink them open, I punch the side of the truck. Pain radiates through my arm, but it feels good. It grounds me.

And then I turn and head back the way I came.

Chapter 3

MACKENZIE

I NEVER SHOULD'VE COME. This is my retribution for sneaking out. You reap what you sow, and I must've done something awful in my former life because if the past is any indication, karma loves to make me pay.

I turn to head back down the hill, unsure of what to do about my current predicament, when a shadow behind one of the huge willows moves. It comes closer, creeping toward me until the moonlight illuminates the dark form and a man takes shape.

I freeze and step back, but he continues his advance until he's close enough I can make out all his features. Close enough to realize he's the most beautiful boy I've ever seen. Thick, dark hair frames a face sculpted from stone. With high cheekbones, a prominent jawline under full lips, and espresso eyes, I sense he's every bit as dangerous as he is beautiful, and when he speaks, his deep baritone does nothing to contradict this theory.

"What are you doing out here?"

"I can ask the same of you, can't I?" I say, hating the way my voice shakes. "This is private property."

Amusement sparks in his dark eyes. "Ya don't say. Is it yours?" He takes another step closer and my heart races as a knowing look flickers through his gaze and more details come to my attention. He's wearing a black T-shirt and jeans, and what

I thought were long sleeves at first glance, turn out to be tattoos. Ink covers his right arm from the wrist up. And when he lifts one hand to tuck an unlit cigarette behind his ear, I get a glimpse of a muscular bicep.

He purses his lips as his gaze travels over me, like he's trying to decide what he wants to do with me before he smiles, and I shiver in response. If I scream, there's no one to hear me for miles. I imagine the headlines, *Slain Teen Found in Crow's Creek is Chief Hart's Daughter!*

It would kill my father, absolutely destroy what's left of him.

"Are you here for the party?" I ask, hoping he says yes.

He glances at the nothingness around him. "Pretty sad if this is how you Riverside kids party."

"I'll take that as a yes."

"Take it however you want, sweetheart." He grins.

I'm not your sweetheart, I want to bite back, but with the way he's currently staring at me, I'm too scared.

"I better get going," I say and turn, stumbling back down the hill toward nothing while my heart pumps a thunderous beat. I'm only hoping I can put some distance between myself and this stranger, who I can feel in my bones is trouble.

"Where's your ride?" he calls from behind.

Like I'd tell you.

I ignore him, but before I even make it to the bottom of the hill, his hand is on my arm, spinning me around. "You're walking?"

Again, I say nothing. I have no idea who he is and I'm not about to reveal that I'm completely and hopelessly alone with no way out of here.

He lifts his eyes from mine, then nods to the gravel parking strip below. "No point in pretending. I saw you get dropped off, so I know you don't have a ride. You'll get yourself killed walking on these back roads."

"I'll be fine," I say, and yank my arm from his.

He raises his hands in surrender and takes a step back. "Suit yourself."

"Who are you, anyway?" I narrow my eyes at him. Though I know I should leave, I feel an inexplicable urge to ask the question. "Do you know Jace?"

"Jace . . ." he drawls like he has no recollection of the name. "You mean, the cocky bastard who thinks his shit-ass stats as a receiver make him Riverside's MVP? Or is it one of the others who think they can make State on their own?"

"They're good guys," I snap, giving myself away. "And, Graham, our quarterback, *will* take us to State this year."

"Defensive, huh?" His eyes rake over me, and I can't help but feel like he sees beneath the tough-girl front I'm putting on to the scars below. "Let me guess. One of them is your boyfriend. Jace, maybe?"

"What? No." I cross my arms over my chest. "They're my friends." Or, at least, most of them *were*, before I disappeared for nine months. "Graham, the quarterback, is my best friend, actually."

Shit. Why did I just say that? Why am I telling him anything when I have no idea who he is?

A smirk curls the corners of the stranger's mouth. "Bet he loves that."

I tense. "What's that supposed to mean?"

"Guys with friends that look like you don't really want to be *just* friends."

My cheeks burn at the insinuation. He has no clue what he's talking about. Graham's the *best* best friend a girl could ask for, and he's never once indicated he wants anything more.

"You know nothing about me."

"Oh, I know exactly who you are." He takes a step closer, and his gaze rakes down my body once more. "You're Mackenzie Hart."

I suck in a breath, and his eyes brighten when he sees his words have hit their mark. "How did you know?"

He laughs, a raspy sound inside his chest. "I've heard all about you, princess. Gorgeous. Dark hair. Big blue eyes. Pouty lips and a body made for sinning. The chief's daughter, which is only one of the reasons you're untouchable. The way they talk about you, it's like they've immortalized you. The only thing is, now that you're right in front of me"— his gaze flickers from my face, down my body and back again—"I can't for the life of me figure out why."

I press my mouth into a tight line as anger boils beneath the surface of my skin. His words cut deep, but it's not his dismissal that gets me, it's the other things he's said. About everyone at school immortalizing me. I've been absent from the outside world—my friends, school—for so long, I've practically become a legend. Like I'm not even this real person but some fictional creature inside a storybook. Just a girl everybody once knew. The one they talk about and pity. The one whose mom died and nearly died herself.

I still remember waking up in the hospital. The wall of flowers beside my bed. Cards. Balloons. Stuffed bears. Like a memorial for the dead, only instead of dying like I was supposed to, I woke up.

I swallow over the ache in my throat, because there's no way in hell I'm losing it right here, right now, in front of this random guy, who clearly thinks too highly of himself and very little of me. The one whose body language and words indicate he hates everything about me and my friends.

I tilt my head and stare directly into his eyes, unwilling to back down. "So you've heard about me. You know the guys, and you're here, which means you must've been invited to the party, same as me. But, you're also clearly out of the loop since we apparently missed the memo that it was canceled. But I've never seen you before . . ." I trail off as my wheels start spinning.

He brings his hands together for a slow clap and takes a step closer, until there's only an arm's length between us. "Observant little thing, aren't you? Too bad you still don't have a clue."

I can feel the air change. How it turns thick and charged. Like all we'd need is a lit match for it to go up in flames.

"Tell me your name." I demand, pulling my arms tighter across my chest.

"I'm not good at following orders." One corner of his mouth curls, and there's something about the way he says it that sends a frenzy of butterflies rioting inside my chest when all I should do is turn and run. "Tell me, does Daddy know you're out here this late at night all alone?"

I blanch, giving myself away.

"How cute. If it's rebellion you want, I have a few more ideas." He winks, and my insides curl.

"I have zero interest in adding another notch to your belt," I snarl before I turn and hurry down the bottom of the hill toward the gravel turnoff, wondering if he'll follow or let me go.

My feet crunch over the rocks, face flaming from anger and something else I can't place—embarrassment, maybe? Somehow, I'm shamed by this boy I don't even know. But my insides scream. I have no ride. No way to get home except on foot, which will take at least five hours, maybe more. My father will be up for work by then. Not to mention, traversing these dark country roads is pretty much a death wish.

I'm totally and irrevocably screwed.

"You want a ride?" His voice draws me up short and I freeze. The last thing I want to do is to accept favors from this creep. My heart pounds in my chest at the thought of being trapped in such close proximity to him, and the only thing more unsettling than that is I have no idea whether it's fear or excitement driving its frantic pace.

I glance over my shoulder. He's still standing in the same spot, twirling his unlit cigarette between the fingers of his right hand while he watches the indecision play over my face. His facial expression, even his words are indifferent about the idea of giving me a ride, but the way his body tenses as he waits for my answer says otherwise.

"I won't beg, princess."

"I don't see your car." I glance around me as the words leave my mouth, looking for his ride. "Actually, can I just borrow your phone? Maybe I can call—"

"Your BFF?" he mocks. "What's his name again, *Graham*?"

"Jealous?" I arch a brow.

He barks out a laugh. "I barely even know you. But it's not surprising you'd assume as much."

"What's that supposed to mean?"

He lifts a shoulder and drops it. "Just that girls like you think you're something special, that every man with a pulse wants them. But I've got news for you, princess"—he closes the gap between us and dips his head to my ear so he can whisper—"I don't want you. But if I did, you'd know it."

I swallow and step back before my knife-like gaze meets his again, because somehow I believe him.

He reaches into his pocket and pulls out his phone, then hands it to me as I sigh with relief. My hands shake as I dial Graham's number, glancing up at the dark-eyed stranger to see him watching, and I get the feeling he notices everything. Just like the confirmation in his eyes when Graham's voice mail picks up.

My stomach drops as I hand the phone back, thoughts racing with my available choices when he places a finger under my chin and lifts my face to his. For one crazy moment, I think he might kiss me and the butterflies are back, swarming inside my hollowed-out chest, before he rasps, "Come on."

He drops his hand and turns as if I'll blindly follow like a good little girl and do as I'm told.

"I didn't accept your offer."

When he glances over his shoulder, he simply barks out, "let's go," like I'm an inconvenience. Which I guess I am.

My thoughts churn, knowing I shouldn't accept a ride and partly confused as to why he's even offering me one considering how he seems to dislike me. But if he wanted to hurt me, wouldn't he do it right here? We're as isolated out here as humanly possible.

Besides, he's my only option, and I know it.

Based on his growing smirk, *he* knows it, too.

I draw closer to him, so I can see his face, search his expression for his intentions in the hope my gut will speak to me.

He cocks his head to the side, letting me get my fill, as if he knows I'm searching his face for an answer. If I walk, I'll most likely get home too late, *and* risk getting hit and killed on the side of a dark and windy road in the process. Either that, or someone I don't know will try and pick me up which could be worse. Accepting a ride from him is a risk. My father would have a coronary if he found out I hitched a ride home with a stranger, let alone a tattooed stranger who has danger written all over him.

My gaze lingers over the ink on his arm.

But if it means getting home in time, assuming he doesn't try and . . .

While I'm debating my options, he places his hands on my shoulders and leans toward me, the scent of pine and cedar surrounding me. "Relax, sweetheart, I wouldn't dream of touching you," he whispers.

I shiver, goose bumps playing along my arms. When he pulls away, his dark eyes glitter in the moonlight, and I find myself answering, "Okay, fine. I'll take a ride."

I catch the briefest flash of a smile before he turns and heads up the bluff without a word, leaving me to wonder if I'm supposed to follow. Shifting my weight on my feet, I fidget, but just when I'm about to head after him, the soft purr of an engine rumbling in the distance draws me up short.

I pause as the sound grows closer. Until I feel the vibrations inside my chest, and the sight of him straddling a sleek motorcycle—all chrome and black and every bit as dangerous as he is—appears around the side of the bluff and comes to a halt in front of me. Reaching behind him, he grabs a helmet from the back of the bike and holds it out to me.

My mouth drops open as I stare at the machine beneath him and point. "You expect me to ride that?" I ask, hearing and hating the fear in my voice.

"Scared?" He laughs. "That's cute."

Either he doesn't know as much about me as he thinks he does, or he's more of an asshole than I thought. Because anyone who knows about my past would probably think twice before offering me a ride on this death machine.

I swallow, saying nothing as he rolls his eyes. "Hop on, doll. You won't break."

"You're a jerk, you know that?" I spit.

His eyes shimmer in the dark, as if the insult turns him on. "Never said otherwise." Then, leaning toward me, his dark and menacing eyes lock with mine as he murmurs, "Come on. I swear I won't bite. At least, not much."

He's goading me, I know he is. And it must work, because I inhale a ragged breath and say a little prayer for help, or mercy, to a God I'm not sure exists.

Then I accept the helmet, swing my leg over the motorcycle, and wrap my arms around his waist.

Chapter 4

ATLAS

Mackenzie Hart's reputation precedes her thanks to the Riverside gossip chain but seeing her in the flesh is like a kick to the gut. She's so beautiful it takes my breath away.

I remind myself to breathe as I hold the helmet out, watching the indecision warring inside her head. I really don't give a damn whether she takes me up on my offer of a ride or not. She's the last girl I'd ever make a move on, just like I'm sure I'm the last guy she'd bring home to Daddy. No doubt she's weighing up the odds on whether I'll lay my hands on her or not, as if I could do anything I wanted to her right now.

Every emotion plays out in detailed precision over her gorgeous features. There's a war in her ice-blue eyes, and conflict pinches her almost angelic face as she purses her rosebud mouth. One thing is for certain: this girl has zero poker face. But what she doesn't know is she really has no choice in the matter, because there's no way I'm letting her walk all the way home, alone, at this time of night. She'd be ripe for the picking for any creeper who comes along, that's if she doesn't get herself killed on these windy, country roads first. I might be an asshole, but even I have to draw the line somewhere. Just when I think I might have to grab her and strap her to the back of my bike, she accepts the helmet and slips it on.

She pauses beside me, eyeing the machine beneath my thighs warily. It's almost as if sliding onto the seat behind me is as big of a death wish as going to war, but I see the moment she makes her decision. Her ice blue eyes darken to sapphires under the moonlight, flickering with a fear so palpable it raises the hair on the back of my neck. Before I can say anything, she inhales a sharp breath and straddles the bike behind me, wrapping her arms around my waist so tightly my smile fades.

Her hands tremble when she clenches my shirt, as if holding onto me with a death grip might somehow save her from falling into the abyss of whatever the hell it is she's so afraid of. Her father. This bike. Me. The hell if I know, but damn, if I don't enjoy feeling like I'm part of the solution instead of the problem for a change.

The thought makes my heart clench inside my chest, so I shut it down, throttle the engine, and peel off without warning. It's a jerk move, considering she's clinging to me like a lifeline already. But it's a necessary one. Because I need something to obliterate this foreign feeling—the sting of want behind my ribs. I've just met this girl—I don't even know her—and already she's gotten under my skin.

I focus on my speed, the darkened roads spreading out before me like an inky snake, and the wind whipping through my hair, stinging my cheeks. I focus on anything but the girl behind me, whose sweet scent I can't decipher drifts toward me as I ride, all the way until we reach the outskirts of Riverside.

I come to a stop light and turn my head to where the side of her face is currently pressed into my back. For someone who seemed to detest me only moments ago, she sure doesn't mind me now. "Where to?"

"Do you know Pine Grove? It's a block behind the—"

"I know where it is," I snap. It's hard not to know everything and everybody in this town, it's so damn small. I've only been here a couple of weeks and already I know all there is to know. Riverside is divided into two sections. The haves and the have-nots. As it so happens, Dad and I have new digs in the form of a nice rusted-out trailer in a park surrounded by, you guessed it, the have-nots. Smack dab in the middle of farmland, as if the locals couldn't bear to have us closer to town.

Pine Grove, however, is on the haves' side, in the heart of town. I know because I've passed the housing complex every single day for the last two weeks on my way to practice. A couple blocks over is the wealthiest subdivision in all of Riverside. It's full of doctors, lawyers, and businessmen—the town's elite—including the town's claim to fame; the infamous former quarterback for the Pittsburgh Steelers, Cal Scott, my uncle.

I continue down the interstate until I reach the heart of town, then make a right, where I slow down as I cruise through the first neighborhood toward Pine Grove. I'd be lying if I said I wasn't a little bit curious to see what the Harts' castle looks like.

"You can drop me off down here at the stop sign," she says, her warm breath tickling the side of my face as she talks. "I'll walk the rest of the way."

No way am I letting her off to walk alone, even here, but I don't argue with her. Instead, I stop where she instructed, and when she swings her leg off the bike and steps down, I meet her eyes as she hands me the helmet. "Let me guess, you're afraid of getting caught with me?"

"More like I'm afraid of getting caught at all." The words slip from her lips, her expression completely unguarded, and it's the most honest she's been all night.

"I'll walk you then," I say, hating the feeling of relief coursing through me that it's not me she wants to avoid, because I have zero business with a girl like Mackenzie. Or any girl, for that matter. I don't have the time or energy for attachments.

Swinging down from the bike, I sit the helmet on the back of it to the sound of Mackenzie's protests. "No. Really, that's not necessary. I'll be—"

I ignore her, tuck my hands in my pockets and start walking down the road, her voice trailing after me as I go. Finally, she gets the idea that I'm not backing down and catches up to me. "Don't you ever listen?" she asks, scowling into the night.

"Don't you?" I shoot back. "After all, I'm not the one sneaking out after dark, now am I, princess?"

"Don't call me that." She crosses her arms over her chest, which amplifies her already ample rack.

When she catches me staring, I grin. "Why? I call it like I see it."

"I'm not . . ." She trails off, shaking her head and grumbling something under her breath before she glances back up at me and tips her chin up in defiance. "I'm not the spoiled, privileged brat you seem to think I am."

"No?" I quirk a brow.

"No."

Her sandaled feet move at twice the pace to keep up with my long stride, so I slow down a little to make it easier for her. "So, you're telling me you aren't sheltered and spoiled? That people don't put you on a pedestal?"

"Not because—"

"And that you don't get absolutely everything you want?"

"Not everything," she murmurs.

I catch the words, even though I'm pretty sure she never meant for me to hear them. I glance over at her, watching. "Name one thing you want that Daddy won't give you?"

She halts in her tracks and stares me down. "More freedom. My mother and my memory. Not that he can give me that, even if he wanted to, but . . ." She sighs and runs a hand through her hair while I stare into the abyss of her eyes, trying to decipher her words like they're the freaking holy grail.

But then she turns away from me and starts walking again, her posture rigid, and I can tell without even asking she won't expound on it any more than I should want her to, so I change the subject to something benign. "Let me ask you something . . ."

"Do I have to answer?"

"You claim you're not spoiled, but I find it hard to believe, knowing who your father is, that a girl like you, from a neighborhood like this, doesn't have a car."

Seconds pass before she says anything, and just when I think she might not answer at all, she says, "That's not a question."

"Why didn't you drive yourself to the party, princess?"

"There you go with the condescending nicknames again." She grumbles before she peers over at me, but I pretend like I don't notice, feigning indifference. It really doesn't matter to me if she answers my question or not; the truth is I really want to know for reasons I can't explain.

I slide out the unlit cigarette from above my ear and twirl it around the fingers of my right hand. I don't really smoke. In fact, I'm not a fan of vices as a general rule. But I don't often leave home without one. I keep a pack of smokes as a reminder of what I'm not. Of what I refuse to become. An addict like my pops. Not that there's anything wrong with a cigarette now and then. There are worse things to get hooked on. My pops is hooked on booze and pills. His father before him OD'd when he was seventeen, and my great-grandfather was an alcoholic. Substance abuse runs in my blood. Addiction might as well be a family trait. It would come easily for me. I know this without a doubt. Just like I know football is my answering prayer. And I don't need a reason to say yes to any of it.

"You really don't know, do you?" she asks, grounding me back to the moment. When I glance over at her, she adds, "About me?"

"You seem surprised."

"I guess I am, since you clearly knew who I was even though we've never met. *Everyone* knows." She shakes her head and bites her lip like she still can't believe I might be in the dark about whatever it is she's referring to.

"I don't have much taste for idle gossip. Never have. In small towns like this, I find what they lack in entertainment, they make up for in talk, even if it's all bullshit."

"Isn't that the truth," she whispers it so softly, I wonder if I imagine it.

"I've heard about you, sure. But I judged you based on what I know for a fact. Your father's the police chief, and he takes his role real seriously. Gave my pops and I a little welcome when we rolled into town," I say, remembering how he pulled up to the curb in his cruiser and stared. Eventually, he got out and said in no uncertain terms, that he expected we wouldn't be trouble and I'd go to school and keep my head on straight. "You're a cheerleader. Pretty. Popular. Spoiled. And from what I hear, untouchable."

"Pretty and spoiled aren't facts."

"From where I'm standing, they might as well be."

For a moment, I expect her to argue, but instead, she surprises me and says, "You're probably the only person in this whole town who doesn't know."

"Know . . .?" I wave the hand holding the cigarette. I'm not sure what frustrates me more. Her evasiveness or my desire to know what the hell she's referring to.

"About the accident." Her voice is thick, and I watch her closely, saying nothing as she pauses once more and turns to me. "Last year, I was in a bad car crash. I haven't driven since."

I nod slowly, suddenly understanding her hesitation with the bike. "Have you ever ridden before?" I gesture back to where we left my old Harley and she shakes her head.

I should feel bad for forcing her on it, but I don't.

"It wasn't as bad as I thought it would be," she says, and the corner of my mouth twitches.

I roll my eyes. "Is that why you were trying to squeeze the life out of me?"

"I was not." She laughs and swats at my arm, and the sound nearly brings me to my knees, it's so beautiful. And melodic. Like church bells on Sunday morning.

"How close are we?" I ask, lifting my eyes from her to the large, cookie cutter homes surrounding us.

"I'm about six houses down."

I nod and we continue to walk until she slows to a halt at a large brick house with a long, paved driveway and a colorful wreath hanging on the door.

"This is home," she says.

"And how did you sneak out? Through the front door?"

She shakes her head and motions toward an old gnarly tree. Its thick, twisted branches reach toward a second-story window.

"Mackenzie Hart, you rebel, you. Although, I have to say, the bedroom window and tree are a bit cliché."

"We have a security system. It beeps when you leave," she says, her tone defensive.

"Of course you do."

She shoots me a knowing look, which I ignore. "My father would hear me if I went in and out the door."

"How much trouble would you be in if you got caught climbing this thing into your window?"

A tiny puff of air escapes her lips as she stares up at the tree. "A lot. Not just for sneaking out, but because my father would be terrified I'd fall and break my neck."

"He's overprotective." I deduce.

"That's one way to put it."

"Not surprising, all things considered."

"Maybe." She sighs sadly and her shoulders sag a little, either in frustration or defeat. Maybe both. "But it gets tiring after a while, being treated like a porcelain doll. As if any wrong move might make me crack."

I file this information away for later use.

"This driving thing . . ." I say as pieces of the puzzle click into place. "Is he a part of that, the reason you haven't got back behind the wheel?"

Not that it's any of my damn business. Not that I should care. And I don't. But I'm curious.

Mackenzie's face pinches and she bites her lip before saying, "I don't know . . . maybe a little."

"You need to fix that."

"Trust me, I know."

"Well, you're not going to do it in the backseat of an Uber, I can tell you that."

Her head snaps toward me, and I see some of her well-guarded composure fall. "Don't you think I've tried?"

"I don't know. Have you?" I shove my hands in my pockets, preferring the anger flashing in her eyes to the look of despair from moments ago. For some reason, this girl gets under my skin. And I don't like it.

"Yes. I have."

I step toward her, face tightening with determination. "So what's holding you back?"

"Um, let me see . . ." She taps her chin. "I don't know. How about *everything?* Fear. The unknown. Guilt—"

"Don't give me any of this survivor's guilt bullshit. You lived. You're here. A survivor. Now act like one and live your life. Get your ass behind the wheel and push through it because you're grateful to be alive. Unless you're not."

Her mouth contorts into a cruel smile. "It's that easy, is it? Just start the car, push the pedal, and go?"

"Pretty much, yeah," I say, pissed for reasons that escape me. "Can't get past your fears without pushing through them."

Why the hell did I care?

A mirthless laugh escapes her lips. "My initial thoughts about you back at Crow's Creek were right. You really are an asshole."

"Better an asshole than a coward."

Her nostrils flare and her fists clench at her sides. For a moment, I expect her to hit me. Part of me wants her to. Because I need her to remind me why I need to stay far, far away when we start school on Monday.

"I'm not a coward. I know the truth, and I've accepted it, even if it kills me a little inside every time I think about it."

I lean closer until her scent washes over me, sinking into my bones like some kind of drug and I register what she smells like. Apple blossoms. "And what truth is that?" I whisper.

"I killed my mother."

Chapter 5

MACKENZIE

My heart pounds in my chest as the shock registers over his stupidly handsome face. And maybe I am a coward, because I don't wait around for his reaction to my admission. Instead, I turn and reach for the low hanging branch on the gnarly maple and boost myself up the first limb. Climbing carefully, I reach for another and climb for several seconds before I glance over my shoulder and see he's gone.

Disappointment washes over me so quickly I barely recognize it, though I'm not sure what I expected. For him to wait for me to get safely inside? For him to come after me and catch me if I fall?

How stupid. I don't even know this guy, and the little I glimpsed of him tonight—whoever he is—proves him to be crass and insensitive.

I finish my climb and shimmy myself to the end of the long limb that extends toward my window, then slip my fingers beneath the crack in the windowpane and slide it the rest of the way open. With practiced precision, I turn and slip my legs inside, butt-first until my feet hit the plush carpet of my bedroom floor.

I close the window behind me and dust off my hands as I try to rid myself of all thoughts of the dark-eyed stranger, but I can't seem to shake him. He was callous and rude and maybe even a little dangerous. I should want no part of him. Yet it's taking everything inside of me not to head back down the tree to find him on the street and force him to concede, to admit I'm right while single-handedly telling me I'm not to blame for my mother's death. Because for some reason, coming from him—someone who has zero problem telling me what he thinks of me and who doesn't treat me with kid gloves—I might actually believe it.

I peer down at the yard behind the thick pane of glass as if he might reappear. My gaze scans the area below as my thoughts drift back to the day I woke in the hospital. My father's face was the first thing I saw. He gasped in palpable relief when my eyes blinked open, and he called for the nurse. I'd come to find out later, I'd been in a coma for a week. It's like my brain knew what awaited me when I woke. Regardless, I wasted no time as I asked, "Where's Mom?" The last thing I remembered was sitting next to her in the car. Everything else was blank.

I saw the answer before he even opened his mouth. Brow creased, mouth flat below watery eyes, he shook his head. "I'm sorry, Kenz."

"No." My throat closed. I didn't want to hear the next words come out of his mouth, so I squeezed my eyes shut as if I could will them away.

"She didn't make it. I'm sorry, honey," he finished.

Pain enveloped me, so thick and stifling, I couldn't breathe. It sank into my bones, penetrating the marrow and bruising my insides. "I was driving, wasn't I?" I whispered.

Dad swallowed, and it was all the answer I needed. I closed my eyes and went back to sleep as tears slipped down my cheeks.

A chill ripples through me as I brush the memories away and take one last look in the yard, then turn. I'm being ridiculous.

Moving to my bedroom door, I crack it open and listen for any sounds or signs my father might be awake but hear none. Relieved, I shut it closed again and spin around, my gaze catching my reflection in the mirror of my vanity. Wide-eyed and a little bit breathless, I stare at myself in the moonlight when a dark figure emerges from my bedroom closet.

My first thought is of the stranger; he somehow followed me inside.

Time slows.

My eyes widen and a scream tickles the back of my throat. I open my mouth to let it rip, when the figure darts toward me and a hand clamps over my mouth.

Chapter 6

GRAHAM

"Shhh." I press my palm firmly against Kenzie's mouth as the scream dies in her throat. "What the hell, Kenz. You wanna wake the whole neighborhood, or what?"

Her heart beats frantically against my chest, and though I loosen my grip on her, I hold her a moment longer as the sound of my voice sinks in. Finally, her breathing slows about the same time my fear abates and I've convinced myself she's solid and real and safe where she belongs.

The second I release her, she spins and launches herself into my arms. I hold her for a moment, pressing a kiss to the top of her head before I lean back and take her face into my hands, staring into her eyes. Something's upset her. I can see it in her blue gaze and the way she's drawn her mouth into a straight line, and I assume it's the fact she thinks I bailed on her, but I can't be sure.

"I am so, so sorry, Kenz," I say, just barely suppressing the urge to run the pad of my thumb over her full, lower lip.

That's how it is with Mackenzie and me. She's forever tempting me, and I'm forever holding back, afraid to cross the line.

"Where were you?" Kenzie asks, a hint of tension in her voice.

"County police set up a checkpoint outside Crow's Creek when we got there. They even stopped Jace and me on our way to the field with the keg in the back of the truck. Jace got spooked, and I don't blame him. They were looking to bust us."

"But that doesn't make any sense. Why would they be all the way out there . . ." she trails off before recognition lights up her eyes. "My father."

I nod. "That was my thought, too."

Kenzie sighs and steps out from the canopy of my arms, and I regret the distance instantly. "He didn't want me going to the party, so he added a little insurance just in case I decided to head out there, after all." She reaches up to her head and runs her hands through her hair, while I allow her the time and space for her thoughts to breathe. "That's just like him," she says, a hint of anger behind her words.

She bites her lip for a moment before she glances back up at me and asks, "He never really had any intention of letting me go, did he?"

I reach out and take her hands in mine, bringing them to my lips where I place a chaste kiss on them. "I'm sorry, Kenz. I know how much you were looking forward to it, and I'm also sorry I wasn't there for you. I figured it wasn't a big deal and once we got set up at the new spot, I'd be able to call you and let you know the change of location. I kept calling and you never answered."

Her face twists. "I left my phone in the Uber."

"You scared the crap out of me when I couldn't get hold of you." I give her hands a little squeeze before I drop them and brush a dark lock of hair from her face. "I tried to come get you, but Jace's truck blew a tire, and he didn't have a spare."

"For as much as he worships that thing, you'd think he'd have five."

I crack a smile because everyone knows Jace is obsessed with his ride. "I did a burnout when I left for you. You should've seen his face."

She chuckles, and the sound of it sobers me. *What if something had happened to her tonight?*

"You're lucky I didn't call your father," I say, gently tracing her cheek with the pad of my thumb. "Because I thought about it."

Her eyes widen. "Thank God you didn't."

"It would've been worth it to ensure you were okay."

"Do you *want* to see me in school on Monday?"

I do. More than she knows because I've had a fantasy all summer about us walking the halls together, of finally making her mine. Her wearing my jersey on game day. Her holding my hand. Her kissing me every morning in front of her locker. Being my prom date—the queen to my king.

And so much more . . .

"So, what happened?" she asks, breaking through my train of thought.

"By the time I got back to the guys and borrowed someone else's car, you weren't there. I sped all the way back here. It's a miracle I didn't get a ticket. I just about went crazy when you weren't here either, but I told myself to wait. That you were smart and wouldn't do anything reckless. Thank God I didn't have to wait long. You must've been right behind me."

"I probably would've beat you here, but we parked more than a block away and walked because I didn't want to risk waking my father."

"*We*?" I frown and take a step back, sinking down onto her bed. "So, you did get a ride. Was it a different Uber?"

She shakes her head and avoids my eyes as she says, "No. It was this guy—"

"You got in the car with some random guy?" I nearly choke out. My brows rise to my hairline.

"Well, he goes to our school. I guess he didn't get the memo about the change in location either."

"Who was it?" I frown. Everyone I can think of was invited and accounted for. They knew about the change of venue. Except for Kenzie.

"Um . . . I kind of never got his name?"

My eyes bug out of my head. "You didn't get his name? So, you *didn't* know him?" I stand up abruptly. "Kenz, for all you know—"

"Listen, I'm here, right?" She steps forward, takes my hands in hers and squeezes. "I'm fine. Home safe. Everything worked out. No worries."

"I take back what I said about you not doing anything reckless," I grumble.

She grins and turns away from me, heading to her dresser where she pulls out an old pair of sweats and a shirt—an old Riverside Rebels T-shirt I once left in her car.

I pace behind her, moving from her bed to her desk where I stare at the acrylic paperweight I made her years ago. "So, this guy didn't come onto you? He just offered you a ride and that was it?" I ask, because something about it seems off.

She cocks a dark brow, a hint of amusement dancing in her eyes, and I nearly growl at her to just answer the question already.

"No. And even if he had, my daddy taught me a thing or two. I can handle myself. Police chief's daughter, remember?"

I chuckle under my breath and lift my gaze to the ceiling to say a prayer of thanks, even if I am being a little overprotective. Or possessive. I'm not sure which. But it's hard not to be when your best friend is as captivating as Kenzie is.

"But something good did come of tonight, actually," she continues.

"Oh?"

She reaches for the hem of her sweater, which I take as my cue to turn around, her voice sounding out behind me. "He made me realize that it's time. I need to stop being a coward and face my fears."

I stare at the wall to the tune of rustling fabric and squeeze my eyes closed until I see spots, trying not to imagine what she looks like without her clothes on. Because Kenzie in a bikini is heart-stopping. Kenzie naked . . . well, let's just say I have a vivid imagination.

"I'm finished," she murmurs, and I turn back around, internally patting myself on the back for my gentlemanly restraint.

My gaze soaks her in. Somehow, she's even more appealing in old sweats and a baggy T-shirt—or maybe it's just that it's *my* T-shirt that I like so much.

Swallowing, I force my thoughts back to something less indecent and focus on what she just said, "You're anything but a coward, Kenz."

"Am I?" Anger flickers in her eyes. "Because I keep saying I want to remember that day so badly. Yet anytime my thoughts get anywhere near it, I take a detour. I bail."

"Damn, Kenz, it was traumatizing. You lost your mother. You nearly died. The authorities said it was a miracle you survived."

I try to keep my voice down, but it's hard. My throat bobs as I remember that day, the intangible fear that consumed me as they rushed Kenz to the hospital. For twenty-four excruciating hours, I thought I might lose her—we all did—and it nearly killed me. Even after they stabilized her, she didn't wake up for days.

I remember pacing the hospital waiting room. The combined scent of astringent and cleaning spray stinging my nose. The sound of the overhead speakers. The beeping of the machines hooked up to her frail and broken body. Most of all, I remember thinking what would I do without her. How dull and meaningless my life would be. I hated myself for never telling her how I really felt.

Yet here I am nearly a year later, and I still haven't done a damn thing about it.

But that's about to change.

This year will be different.

I'll let Kenzie reacclimate to everyday life at school and reacquaint herself with her friends, and once she's thriving, I'll tell her. After all these years, I'll make my move.

"I don't blame you one bit for not wanting to dwell on the accident," I say, not because I think it's what she needs to hear, but because it's true.

"You want the truth?" she asks, crossing her arms over her chest, her expression both earnest and vulnerable. "I'm scared to remember. I was driving. I know it was my fault, and I'm absolutely petrified that if I remember the details of it; the last things we said to each other, our last moments together, and what I was doing a split second before I crashed, I'll come undone. Unglued. What if I can't handle the truth? What if it's worse than I could ever imagine?"

"What if it's not?" I murmur, tipping her chin up so she meets my eyes.

She scrutinizes my expression as if searching for a truth no one can give but her, and my heart breaks as I pull her into my arms once more, tugging her tightly against my chest where she belongs.

I want to dip my head down to meet her mouth so badly. To brush my lips against hers, to taste her fear and chase away the anguish etched in the lines of her face. But I won't. I can't take advantage of her when she's this vulnerable. This fragile. So instead, I do the only thing I can. I run my hands through her hair and down the length of her back, comforting her, whispering, "It's not your fault, Kenz. No one blames you. It was an accident."

A moment passes before she answers, "I wish I believed you."

MACKENZIE

I wake with a jolt, my breathing heavy. The sheet beneath me is damp with sweat, along with my pajamas. I know it was just a dream. The same one I always have. The one where my mother is trapped in my car. Blood trickles from her scalp, down the side of her face, and I am helpless. I can't move, can't call for help. All I can do is sit and watch as the life fades from her eyes.

I have no idea if this image of her is real or a figment of my imagination. I can't remember the crash any more than I can remember the moments that led up to it. All of it's a blur. But something about the dream seems off. The details don't quite match. Mom's face is distorted and her voice sounds strange. Instead of being in my car, we're in someone else's.

But I'm crying. I'm always crying.

I inhale through my nose, thinking about that morning. I came down for breakfast and . . .

Everything after is a mystery, except for what I've been told about the crash. I can't conjure the sequence of events if I tried. Lord knows I have.

I swallow and sit up, pressing a clammy hand to my forehead as my pulse evens out. Sun streams through my bedroom window and my legs ache to run. I have no idea what spurred the dream. I haven't had one in a while, and my best guess is talking about the crash with the boy I met last night triggered it.

I get up, barely taking the time to yank my hair into a ponytail and throw on a sports bra under my T-shirt before I slip on my sneakers and head down the stairs.

My shoes squeak over the hardwood floor as I make my way into the kitchen where Dad stands in front of the coffee pot dressed in his uniform, filling a travel mug with his favorite dark brew.

"Good morning," he says, eyeing me as he pops the lid on. "You're up early."

"I'm going for a run."

"Everything okay?" he asks, though his eyes tell me he already knows it's not.

He's too smart for his own good, too observant. Perks of having a police chief for a father.

"Yeah." I head to the cupboard beside the sink and grab a sports bottle, then fill it with water. "Just had a bad dream is all."

He nods as if he understands, and I wonder if he does. I wonder if he dreams about her, too. "You're taking Goliath?"

As if being summoned, the massive German shepherd prances from the living room into the kitchen and sits between us. Goliath is all sleek, black fur and cocoa eyes—so much sweeter than his dark, wolf-like appearance leads you to believe. Dad bought him for me a few months after the crash when he had to return to work, so I'd have company *and* protection. His greatest fear suddenly became losing me. Even now it rules every decision he makes and everything he does. It's why he refused to allow me back at school the last couple of months of my junior year, even after I begged and pleaded.

"Of course," I say, a little snippier than intended. Goliath is the whole reason I'm even allowed to run alone. Taking him is a given. After the accident, I'd gone through a rough patch at home. For the first month, I refused to get out of bed. I had zero desire to return to the real world. The holidays made things worse. Yet, just before Christmastime, Graham made me go for a run with him; he literally forced me out of bed, laced up my sneakers and shoved me out the door.

I still remember the feel of the cool morning air in my lungs. The way they burned with exertion. How my body ached and my muscles cramped after lying in a hospital bed, and doing the same at home for weeks. My heart knocked so hard against my ribs I thought I might collapse. But for the first time since waking up from the coma, I felt alive, really and truly alive again.

After that day, it became my coping mechanism. For a while, I was running two maybe three times a day. Rain, sleet, snow, it didn't matter. It got to the point where I'd whine because Graham was at school or practice and Dad was at work and I had no one to go with me. So, we settled on Goliath, one of the force's retired K9s. Dad says if he can't protect me, nothing can. I'm inclined to believe him. I once watched a video of Goliath taking out two assailants at once with nothing but his powerful jaws.

"Is this about the party last night?" Dad asks suddenly.

"What?" My head jerks toward him, ripping me from my thoughts, and for a moment, I'm thrown. How does he know?

"Look, I'm sorry. I should've let you go. I know that. I guess it's just hard letting go, after . . . after everything."

I exhale, relieved when I realize he has no clue I snuck out, and the tension in my spine dissolves.

"You forgive your old man for worrying, right?" He pulls me into a bear hug, placing a kiss on the top of my head and I nod. "Good." He steps back, and picks up his coffee. "Be safe and watch out for cars," he says to me, then he glances at Goliath. "You protect her, you hear?" Goliath's ears perk up like he knows exactly what my dad is telling him. "I'll see ya later," Dad calls out, heading for the front door.

"Bye!" I yell, then glance at Goliath. His eyes are only a couple of shades lighter than his fur, and the way he's staring at me, like he sees right through me, reminds me of *him,* the boy from last night.

A shiver crawls up my spine.

"Ready, buddy?" I murmur, reaching down and rubbing his furry chest. He lifts a paw in answer. "Let's go, then."

He follows me down the hall toward the front door where I grab his leash from the hook, then head outside with him trailing along. I start out at a slow pace, allowing my muscles to warm up, but I can tell Goliath wants to fly and stretch his legs. Sometimes I think he loves running as much as I do.

Keeping to the sidewalk, I head down our street and onto River Road, a long stretch of homes with large yards, manicured lawns, and three-car garages, which leads to Boyd Park—my favorite place to run—before I pick up the pace.

The knot in my gut loosens with each slap of my shoes on the pavement, and as the minutes pass, my thoughts become a little clearer.

I'm not sure what the future holds for me next year when I graduate. Before the accident, I assumed it would be college. Now, I'm not so certain. But regardless of what I choose, I know I don't want to live at home forever. I need to move out after high school. I need my independence more than anything, which means I can't rely on people to take care of things for me. I can't be chauffeured around like I'm still fifteen and waiting for a driver's license.

But it's a little hard to be self-reliant when I have yet to face my biggest fear. And that starts with remembering what happened the day of the crash. Until then, I'll always have this question hanging over my head. This lingering doubt. It's the unknown that haunts me.

Could I have prevented it? Could I have saved her? And more importantly, was it my fault?

Every time I ask Dad about that day, he shuts down. It's become clear he doesn't want to talk about it. Sometimes I wonder if he's yet to fully face his grief because he's been so busy caring for me.

I tried the therapist route, but it didn't last long. I attended several sessions before she asked me to walk her through that fateful morning, in a relaxed state, in an effort to recall what happened. Needless to say, I freaked and never went back. And Dad didn't make me.

I could ask Graham for help, but he won't push me. He'll be more concerned about my wellbeing than helping me accomplish my goal, and all it'll take is one mental breakdown, like the one I had in the psychologist's office, and he'll back down.

I need someone ruthless.

Someone who doesn't care how painful the memories might be, or how sharp my grief is. Someone who won't back down. The kind of person who will pursue the truth at all costs because they have nothing to lose if it breaks me.

My mind conjures dark eyes and a cruel smile, and suddenly, I know without a doubt who can help me. Suddenly, I've never been more certain of anything in my life.

I need *him*.

There's only one problem.

I don't even know who he is.

Chapter 7

GRAHAM

Coach dismisses us from practice, leaving me and the boys to amble off the field. I pause by the bench and take a sip of water. My legs ache so bad from conditioning, I'm not sure what's worse: that or the beating I took to my ribs when Yano, the best damn defensive lineman anyone could dream of having, sacked my ass.

Coach ripped him a new one for that, then laid into me next.

"Just so you know, I found a scratch on my truck." Jace sidles up next to me and smirks.

I fight the urge to flip him off because Coach is still watching and the last thing I want to do is run the bleachers. "You're lucky that's all you found on it, considering you left me with no spare."

"Maybe if you'd learn how to drive, you wouldn't need a spare." He grins.

"Or we could've picked Kenzie up like I wanted, and then I also wouldn't have had to spend my Saturday afternoon tracking down the Uber she left her phone in."

Jace snickers. "Duty calls, right?"

I shoot him a dirty look, which he ignores.

"I assume all is good with your girl, then?"

I nod. "Yeah. She's good." *Even if she did make a poor decision and accept a ride with a complete stranger.* "How good?" Jace wiggles his brows, and I shove him before he jogs off to catch up with Teagen.

I watch as they high-five, then make their way toward the locker rooms. Those two are forever giving me shit for my crush on Kenzie and the fact I still haven't made a move.

When I turn back around, I spy my cousin wiping the sweat from his eyes with a towel and nod in his direction. "You've been doing well."

He steps closer and peers out at the emerald turf. "I'm getting a helluva workout, that's for sure. You guys really know how to tear it up."

"You ready for Friday?" I watch him closely, waiting for his answer. After all, I'm the team captain, the quarterback. It's my job to make sure he's prepared.

Initially, when my father told me Atlas would be coming to play for Riverside, I'd been skeptical. The dude has a reputation that precedes him when it comes to football. He's one of the best wide receivers in the state. Heck, even Jace got a little nervous when he found out he was joining the team. Because he also has a penchant for trouble—suspensions, shoplifting, assault, and juvie, to name a few. The last thing I need for our team is trouble.

So far though, he's kept his head down and worked hard. He's not overly friendly with the guys, but he's not an ass either.

And I can work with that.

"I'm always ready," he says, lifting his water bottle to his lips. "The big question is whether Coach will play me or puss out and put Peters in. I heard his parents are already throwing a hissy fit at the prospect of me starting."

"I think you've got this. But it wouldn't hurt to hang with the guys more, get to know them. Coach likes camaraderie on the field," I say, because he hasn't made much effort outside of practice. Jace mentioned his absence at Crow's Creek just this morning.

Atlas shrugs. "I'm here to play football."

"Right, but you could've come to the field party."

"I planned on it but got held up."

Sure you did. Though in his defense, it was probably a good thing considering I don't even know if anyone called to tell him we'd changed locations.

"What about school? You ready to start somewhere new?"

"I liked my old teammates, and I'll miss them. But I'm not sorry to see Shaker in my rearview mirror," he says, referring to his old school, and I can't blame him. From what I've heard of Shaker, it isn't exactly the best educational institution.

"Well, we're here for ya, man. On and off the field." I clap him on the arm. "Just let me know if you need anything, all right?"

"Actually, there is one thing." He stops and turns to face me. "You got something going with Mackenzie Hart?"

My stomach bottoms out at the mention of her name, because there could only be one reason he's asking.

The temptation to lie balances on the tip of my tongue. But I don't want it getting back to her that I'm spreading rumors and risk messing shit up before it's even started. "We're friends. Why?"

His gaze shifts away and the tight feeling in my chest increases. "No reason."

MACKENZIE

I sit across from my father at the large kitchen island while he sips his coffee, my nerves causing me to choke down the plate of eggs he's made me. I've waited for this day all summer like a child on Christmas morning—with unadulterated anticipation. Part of me thought it would never come. Or, rather, my father would change his mind and force me to homeschool like he did last spring.

When I glance up to see him watching me, a part of me is still afraid he'll bring down the hammer at the last minute. But so far so good, which is why I'm eating breakfast and preparing for my first day back—the first day of my senior year—like the first day of kindergarten, with equal parts excitement and fear. The only thing keeping me grounded is reminding myself of my mission. To find the boy from Saturday night and ask him to help me. And, okay, if I'm being honest with myself, a part of me is intrigued by Mystery Boy more than I'd like to admit.

"Now, remember, if you need anything, anything at all, I'm just a phone call away," Dad says. His knuckles whiten as he clenches the mug of coffee in front of him.

"I will. Promise."

"I'll be here all day."

I smile. Dad took the day off "just in case." "I'll be okay," I reassure him.

"I know," he says, even though he doesn't; I can tell by the way his smile stretches like cinched plastic—a little tight and a bit forced. "And you're sure Graham's picking you up?" he asks, cocking his head as he looks through the giant picture windows in the living room, as if he's expecting Graham to be waiting there.

"Positive. He just sent me a text to say he's on his way," I lie, because my father will freak if he realizes I lost my phone.

"I hope he didn't send it while he was driving," he says in his cop voice.

I barely resist the urge to roll my eyes. I understand why Dad is nervous about letting me go; the last time he said goodbye before I left for school, I wound up in the hospital and Mom was in a body bag. But still . . . his protectiveness and his fear are stifling.

"He wasn't driving," I say with as much patience as I can muster. "He only lives a couple of minutes away. He texted on his way out the door."

"Right. Okay," Dad says, idly rubbing the back of his neck just as the sound of an engine rumbles outside. I peek over my shoulder to see Graham's blue corvette come to a stop in front of our house.

"That thing's a death trap," Dad mumbles under his breath as I hop off my seat and grab the book bag resting on the stool beside me, then sling it over my shoulder. If he thinks Graham's car is a death trap, I'd hate to hear what he thinks of the bike I rode on Friday night.

"Hey, aren't you going to finish your eggs?" he hollers.

"I'm not hungry," I call out at the same time the doorbell chimes.

I swing it open to find Graham standing in front of me, wearing a pair of dark jeans and a shirt that hugs the hard planes of his chest. One arm is braced against the doorframe, a bouquet of sunflowers tucked under the other.

He straightens when he sees me, a huge grin curling the corner of his lips as his eyes rake down my legs, exposed by the short hem of my baby blue sundress. "Dang, Kenzie Hart, don't you look fu—"

"Like a fine young woman?" Dad's voice cuts in behind me, and I nearly die a little inside.

Although, if Graham's expression is any indication, he beats me to it.

His face turns ashen as he straightens to address my father while I giggle behind my hand. "Chief Hart, good morning, sir."

I glance back to see Dad's lips twitch and I know he's enjoying this interaction with Graham a little too much. "It is, isn't it?" He lifts his mug to his lips and takes a sip as he glances outside as if to survey just how fine a morning it is.

"Uh—" Graham's gaze shifts to me as if unsure of what to do and I roll my eyes at him.

"Are those for me?" I ask, motioning toward the flowers.

"Oh, right. Yes, of course." He takes a step closer and hands them to me. "For your first day back."

I catch a whiff of his aftershave; it's like inhaling a piece of the forest on a warm autumn day, and when he meets my eyes, I realize just how vibrant they are, like staring into a peridot gemstone.

A low fluttering starts in my stomach as I take the flowers and say thanks, then hurry off into the kitchen to place them in a vase of water.

I reach below the kitchen island, my hands hovering over the crystal vase—my mother's favorite—before I swallow over the lump in my throat and push it aside, instead choosing the blue one in the back.

I fill it with water and place the flowers inside, quickly arranging them as I push back the nerves rising to the surface. I've been trying my best to ignore them ever since I went to bed last night. Of course, I've seen some of my friends and classmates since the accident last year; some came to visit me immediately after I woke up in the hospital, but my encounters with them have been sparse to say the least. This morning, I'll face everyone for the first time all at once, and if I'm being honest with myself, the idea of it terrifies me. Just because you want something so badly, doesn't make it easy.

I can hear Graham and my father talking at the door, so I leave the flowers, pick my bag back up, and head toward them once more just as my father says, "Take good care of her today."

"You know it, sir."

"And you're driving her home after practice?"

"Yes, sir."

"If anything changes, let me know." He points to Graham, who nods.

"Ready?" I interrupt. Dad loves Graham—at least as much as any father can love his daughter's male best friend—but no doubt he gave him the third degree before this morning.

Graham reaches out and takes my hand, guiding me down the stairs just outside the door as he waves goodbye. Once we're out of earshot, I glance over at him and smile. "You can relax now."

Graham shakes his head. "You could have told me he was standing there."

I stop at the passenger side of Graham's car and lean over the hood, resting my arms on its cool surface. "How was I supposed to know he was right behind me?"

Graham arches a brow and opens his car door, and I know what he's thinking. I should've known because he's been hovering all morning and fretting over this day for weeks.

"Right." I laugh.

I open the passenger door and slide inside, taking a moment to smother the instantaneous bubble of fear that balloons inside my chest. Inhaling, I glance over at Graham, and as if he knows I need a distraction, he stares at the front door again and says, "Look at him."

I peer through the windshield to where Dad stands like a sentinel in the doorway.

"I've been friends with you for years, have come around how many times, and the man still scares the ever-loving shit out of me."

I snort and buckle my seatbelt as Graham does the same, knowing Dad is watching to make sure we do.

"He has that way about him." I sigh and wave to him at the same time Graham places my phone in my lap.

I stare down at it in shock.

"I charged it for you," he says as he backs down my driveway.

"How—"

"Tracked down the Uber." He shrugs like it's no big deal, and the only thing stopping me from throwing my arms around him and planting a big kiss on the side of his sweet face is my father's eyes boring holes in us as we leave.

"You ready for this?" he asks, glancing over at me while he drives. He lifts his hand off the center console and moves it toward me, almost as if he might place it over mine, then pauses midair and rests it on the steering wheel instead.

I inhale through my nose, trying to sound confident when I say, "Totally."

"You really do look gorgeous, you know." His gaze flickers to my dress. "I'm not just saying that."

"Thank you. You don't look so bad yourself." I grin and turn my eyes to the scenery passing by my window, my cheeks heating from the compliment. "It's your cousin's first day, too. Is he ready?"

Graham stiffens, and I wonder if maybe something happened. "I think so. I talked with him briefly at practice yesterday."

"How's that going?"

"Practice?" He glances over at me. "About as good as you'd expect. Peters isn't too happy with the new addition, of course."

"You still think Coach is going to replace him?"

"That's the plan. Coach would be crazy not to. I mean, Atlas's stats are amazing. No one can argue with that. He's probably the best receiver in the state. His talent was wasted at Shaker."

"And how do you feel about it?" I ask, because I know how loyal Graham is to his teammates. Ever since he got word that his cousin was moving back to the area, he'd been conflicted about the news. He and Atlas used to be close until Atlas moved away, and it's been years since they've spoken. Supposedly, the kid has quite the sordid past. Rumor has it, he got expelled from his last school for beating up a kid so badly he almost killed him. He also spent some time in juvie, too.

But Peters struggled last year and one of their other receivers has a torn ACL, so good old Riverside needs a replacement. Since Atlas's reputation on the field precedes him, Graham's father pulled some strings and got him a private tryout with the coach. Trouble or not, word has it he'll start.

"I don't know. I mean, it's my senior year. I want to win State, and he can get us there." He shrugs, but the motion is stiff, which is how I know he still has reservations. "Besides, it might be cool to reconnect. We used to be tight. I just hope he jives well with the guys and things go smoothly. So far he seems a little standoffish. And Peters only has himself to blame for having butter hands."

"Is Atlas really as bad as everyone's saying?" I ask, choosing my words carefully.

Graham arches a brow as he comes to a stoplight. "Let's just say, I'm giving him the benefit of the doubt for now."

I can tell he's holding back.

"But you don't trust him, do you?"

"The truth is, I don't know him like I used to."

We make small talk the rest of the way to school, and for that I'm grateful because by the time he parks and I get out of his car, my nerves have returned full force and I think I might be sick. "Come on," he says, and this time, he does reach out and take my hand.

We walk into the school together, Graham pulling me along as everyone greets us, and whatever nerves I had prior to coming here slowly disappear. Everyone acts as though my presence back in the halls of Riverside is no big deal. It's as if I never left in the first place, or the whole school hadn't held a prayer vigil in my name almost a year ago.

Or like I didn't have swelling in my .

Instead, I'm greeted with welcoming smiles, invitations for lunch, and after-school events. Slowly and miraculously, the knot in my chest loosens by the time Graham drops me off at my locker.

"You can go," I say to him as I pop the combination open. "I'm good."

"You sure?"

"Yes, promise. I'm just going to put my stuff inside and get things organized. Maybe talk to a couple of the girls," I say, scanning the hallway and focusing on Caroline and Tiff down the hall.

It's a lie, and a pang of guilt rumbles through my chest in its wake. But somehow, I sense the truth won't be well-received—that what I really want to do is search the halls for the boy I met at Crow's Creek.

At Graham's hesitation, I reach out and touch his arm. "If you want, meet me back here and we'll walk to first period together."

He nods and the tension in his expression dissipates. "Okay. I want to find Atlas anyway, see if he needs anything."

"Maybe you can introduce us?"

"Sure thing." He raps his knuckles against the door beside mine, then flashes me a smile and turns to leave me staring into the depths of my locker.

I place my school supplies on the top shelf, then dig in my book bag for the little magnetic mirror I brought with me and adhere it to the inside of the door. From this vantage point, my wide eyes stare back at me along with a furrowed brow, so I exhale and relax my tense features before I slip a tube of lipstick out of my bag and smooth a thin layer of Flame Red onto my full lips. Angling my face to the side, I eye my features—the perfect application of my makeup this morning, the smooth, brown waves spilling over my shoulders—and smile with approval.

This is going to be a good year. A perfect year. I'm going to show the cheer team they made the right decision by allowing me back on the squad, no questions asked. I'm going to ace all my classes. Go to every single dance and rekindle all my friendships. Make up for lost time and figure out what I want to do with my life come spring.

Maybe even fall in love.

My heart kick-starts at the thought.

I smile as movement catches my eye a few lockers down, and I glance over to see Peters hiding in the corner with Henderson. Money exchanges hands and the next thing I know Henderson slides him a baggie of something I can't make out from here, but knowing his reputation, it can only be one thing: weed. Everyone at Riverside knows Jimmy Henderson is the one you go to if you want to be hooked up.

I quickly glance away before they see me staring when a low rumble spreads through the hallway. My gaze catches the commotion behind me in the mirror. Turning my head, I peek over my shoulder to see what the buzz is about—still half expecting it to be me.

But it's not.

Apparently, there are more interesting things to talk about than the girl who almost died, and I'd have to agree with them, because my eyes are currently soaking in the boy across from me. *Him*—the guy from Friday night.

He leans against a locker talking to someone beside him, cigarette tucked behind his ear like the night of our encounter, looking dangerously alluring in black pants, a gray T-shirt, and combat boots.

A teacher hurries by and clears her throat, motioning to his ear. Confidence oozes from his pores as he removes the cigarette and continues his conversation with the petite blonde I now recognize as Jenna Payne, Riverside's cheerleading captain—my replacement.

I want to pull my eyes away, but I can't. Despite all the reasons I should keep my distance, I'm drawn to him for reasons beyond my understanding. Ones I fear will get me into trouble.

As if he senses me watching, his dark eyes meet mine. He winks, and my stomach clenches in response at the same time my cheeks catch fire.

Jerking my head back around to my locker, I zip my book bag shut and take a deep breath for courage, wondering if I've gone insane. I probably have, because I know what I need to do. It's all I've thought about all weekend.

I slam the door shut with a clang and spin around before I can change my mind, noting how he leans in and whispers something in Jenna's ear. A peel of laughter bursts from her throat, and I almost turn back and run down the hall to where I know Graham will be waiting—to safety and common sense.

Instead, I move determinedly in his direction until I'm standing right in front of him. Everyone is staring, and I get it; the boy is something to look at, that's for sure.

I clear my throat and as I wait for his attention, I swear all conversations around us cease. The hall falls eerily quiet, and I can sense everyone's waiting to see what will happen next. What could Mackenzie Hart possibly want with Riverside's new bad boy?

He's everything I'm not: reckless and rebellious. Everything I should steer clear of. Yet here I am.

When he pays me no attention, I clear my throat again, and after a moment, he finally glances my way while Jenna stares daggers at the side of my face. "What do you want, doll?"

Doll?

I frown at the new nickname, momentarily thrown.

"Wait. You two know each other?" Jenna asks, and I know what she's thinking. How on earth do I know him when I've practically been in hiding during the past year and he's essentially the new guy on campus?

"Yea—"

"No," he cuts me off.

My smile tightens, as I say, "We're recent acquaintances." Apparently, he's as sullen during the day as he is late at night.

"Right." Jenna eyes me a moment before glancing back at her prey. Her posture and gaze tell me she's already called dibs on him, and right now, she's sizing me up, trying to determine how much of a threat I am.

"Um. Can I have a moment with him?" I ask, keeping my eyes locked on his. "*Alone?*"

She inhales as if she might protest, but then he rolls his eyes and pushes off the locker, motioning for Jenna to leave us. I expect her to argue, but she does what she's told like a good little girl, and I wonder if he has that much control with all the girls he talks to.

"What do you want?" he asks, once she's gone.

"Good morning to you, too," I say with a saccharine smile.

"Cut the bullshit, Hart."

My eyes widen at his animosity, but I don't know why. It's not like he was entirely kind to me the night we met. But even when he was rude, I sensed a softness lurking underneath the surface, one I'm willing to bet he hides from the world.

"Can't I come and say hello without wanting something from you?"

He leans closer, until I can make out the musky scent of his skin and says, "Girls like you *always* want something."

My brows pinch. *Girls like me?* Sometimes even I'm not sure who I am anymore. Regardless, I don't like what he's insinuating. Then again, I do want something from him, so he's not entirely off base either.

He must read my thoughts through my expression because his lip curls in a bitter grin like he knows he's right.

With a sigh, I glance around us. Some of the gawkers have moved on, but several groups of people are still standing idly by, watching.

"Okay, fine," I say, making eye contact with him again. "Maybe I do want something."

He shakes his head and his smile falls. It makes me wonder if he hoped he was wrong. "Whatever it is," he says, turning his back to me and popping open his locker, "find someone else to be your bitch."

"You haven't even heard what I want yet."

"Don't need to. Whatever it is, can't be good, because girls like you don't ask guys like me for a favor."

There he goes again with his assumptions. "And what exactly does that mean? Who do you think I am?"

He spins back around, a black bag slung over his shoulder. "Little Miss Perfect, the chief's daughter. I bet you've never broken a rule in your life."

"That's not true." I say, trying to keep the indignance from my voice and failing.

He arches a brow. "I bet you've never even skipped a day of school."

I have. Once. The day of the accident. It's the first and last time I ever will.

But I don't say that. Instead, my gaze falls to the floor. "I snuck out the other night, didn't I?"

"Yeah, and look how well that turned out for you. You're a real party animal."

He brushes past me and heads down the hall with me trailing after him, nipping at his heels. "Wait," I protest, but he ignores me. "Can you just stop?" I ask, and this time, I catch up enough to push him against a nearby locker.

His dark eyes heat at my touch, and he spins me around so fast my breath snags in my throat. My back braces against the cool, hard metal as his arms cage me in. A dark gleam I'm sure is meant to intimidate me enters his eye, but I won't back down. Not now. Not ever. Because I've never needed anything more than I need this.

My chest heaves as I fight for breath. "I thought a lot about what you said, about how I need to get over what happened and face my fears. So, I want you to help me remember the day my mother died, the afternoon I crashed my car. It's all I think about. Some nights, it consumes me, and I know I'll never fully move on until I know what happened."

He laughs. *Laughs!*

Embarrassment roils in my veins, making me hate him all that much more.

"Why me? Why not Riverside's golden boy?"

I frown, unsure of who's referring to until I remember how he spoke about the guys on Friday night, and I take a guess. "Graham?"

"Wouldn't that be easier? After all, he actually *likes* you. He'll want to help." He drops his arms, backing off the tiniest bit, giving me room to breathe. I hate it.

"I can't ask Graham," I admit.

"Oh? And why's that?"

"Because of the very reasons you just mentioned. He won't push me. He'll be too understanding and gentle and kind. I need someone like you. Someone who . . . who . . ." I trail off, frustrated he's being so obstinate about this. Frustrated I can't come up with the words to convince him.

Maybe he's right. Maybe I am used to everyone doing my bidding; I'm certainly used to them coddling me.

"Someone who what?" he snaps.

"Someone who hates me. Someone who isn't concerned about breaking me."

"And what if that's exactly what I do, doll." He leans down again, until I can feel his breath on the side of my face, practically taste his minty toothpaste on my tongue. "What if I break you entirely?" he whispers.

"You won't." I swallow.

"You sure about that?"

I nod, even though I'm not sure at all. "You drove me home the other night when you could've easily let me walk."

His jaw tightens, the muscle flickering in his cheek as he turns his gaze away from me. "I just didn't want to be responsible for letting you get creamed on a country road. Or worse. With my luck, your father would find out I let you go and charge me with something."

It's a bullshit excuse, but I don't call him on it.

Instead, I say, "*Please.* I need your help. I can't do what I need to alone. I need transportation, and besides, I've tried to spur my memory, but I fail every time. I always retreat because I'm too scared. You said so yourself; I need to learn to drive again. Move on. I can't do that until I know what happened."

"And what's in it for me?" His dark gaze trails over my body. Heat scorches my limbs and licks over my skin as though his eyes are made of torch flame. Grinning, he licks his lips, and I shudder in response. "I can be bribed."

A choking sound comes from the back of my throat because I know exactly what kind of bribe he's referring to. "Go to hell."

"I'm already there." He chuckles, then shrugs and steps back just as the comforting warmth of a familiar body tugs me into their side.

I glance up, into the tranquil, green pools of Graham's eyes. "Kenzie?" His forehead scrunches as he glances between us. "You've met Atlas already?"

CHAPTER 8

GRAHAM

I NARROW MY EYES, glancing between my best friend and my cousin as I pull Kenzie closer. Any closer and she'll be another appendage.

Blinking up at me, Kenzie's eyes widen to saucers, and I wonder if it's because I caught them in an unexpected moment, or because she's surprised by the revelation that the boy she's with is Atlas, my cousin. I'm too busy trying to decipher what I saw on my way back to her locker to make sense of anything—Atlas, leaning toward her like he wanted to take a bite out of her. Their body language suggests he's known her for a whole lot more than five minutes. Yet my brain won't compute because that's impossible, given the few minutes I've been gone.

"Um, yeah, actually—"

"I gave her a ride home Friday night," Atlas interrupts her. "Isn't that right, sweetheart?" He winks at her, then turns his gaze on me. "She was abandoned, and it was late."

Suddenly, Atlas asking me if I have something going with Kenzie makes a whole lot more sense. And, of course, I put up a front and said no. Clearly, I'm an idiot.

I try to relax. After all, I don't know whether he has any kind of intentions. Besides, I should be grateful that he made sure she got home safely. Shouldn't I?

Then why do I feel like I want to smash something with my fist, Atlas's smug face in particular?

"Talk about being in the right place at the right time," I choke out.

He shrugs, and I can't tell if he's being a smartass or if this arrogant air about him is the norm. "Something like that."

"Well, thanks for taking care of her for me," I say, squeezing her a little more.

"It was my pleasure." Atlas's grin spreads across his face as he glances at her. "But I'm happy to hand back the reins." Then he backs away and heads down the hall.

When I glance down at Kenzie, her cheeks bloom a bright shade of red.

"Atlas was the one that drove you home on Friday night? Why didn't you just say so?" I ask, unsure of how I feel about it.

"I told you," she says, tucking a lock of hair behind her ear as she starts walking toward her next class, as if she's trying to distract me from her answer. But that's ridiculous, right? "I never got his name. How was I supposed to know he was your cousin? Trust me, I'm every bit as surprised it was him I spoke to as you are."

I let this digest for a moment. She has a point. "He wasn't harassing you just now, was he?"

Her head jerks toward me. "No. What makes you think that?"

"It's just . . . the way he was standing, with you between his arms, it looked . . ." *Intimate,* I think. "Threatening."

"Oh." She peers down the hall, and I wonder if she's looking for him. "No. It was nothing," she says. There's a hint of disappointment in her voice..

I should be relieved, but my stomach clenches. "So, what do you think of him?"

"Um. He's . . ." She bites her lip. "Hard to read, I guess. I'm not sure what I think other than I'm not so sure he likes me very much."

"I wouldn't say that." In fact, from where I was standing it looked like he liked her a bit *too* much. But no way am I telling her that.

"Just be careful. Like I said earlier. I really don't know that much about him anymore."

"You have nothing to worry about," she says, pausing in front of her first period class. Then, leaning in, she gives me a quick hug. "See you at lunch?"

I smile and watch her go with a sinking feeling in the pit of my stomach, like I've lost a game I haven't even played yet.

ATLAS

A locker room can either be a place of togetherness or great division depending on the day and time. Regardless, there are certain things you come to expect—the squeak of rubber soles on the linoleum, the stale scent of sweat mingling with deodorant and body products, frequent cussing and guy-speak.

I stand in my boxer briefs in Riverside's locker room, getting dressed in my gear as I glance around me. I'm so used to the peeling paint and cinderblock walls of my old high school locker room that I feel out of place surrounded by the crisp white sheetrock with the large, vinyl Rebel logo painted on it. It's been less than a week since I first set foot on Riverside's field and yet I'm still not used to it. Maybe I never will be.

I pull on my pads and jersey while the cacophonous sound of the guys chattering and laughing fills the air. My new teammates. I know this, and yet I don't feel any more loyalty toward them than a bunch of kids off the street. Then again, my only loyalty is to myself. Always has been, always will be.

Beside me, Jace Taggert, another wide receiver, jumps up on the bench and whips a towel at Graham. "Hear ye, hear ye, my brothers," he says in what I assume is meant to be a poor impersonation of an old-world English accent. "I call this meeting to discuss how abso—*fucking*—lutely hot Mackenzie Hart looked today." He tips his head back and howls like a dog, and I roll my eyes while the other fuckers around me laugh.

"Shut up, dude," Graham shoves him off the bench while Jace crows, which is how I know he said it to get a rise out of him. After seeing the possessive way

Graham held onto her this morning, I don't need any more convincing that he wants her. He can say they're just friends all he wants, he's clearly into her.

Not that Mackenzie didn't look good. She looked so damn good in that little blue dress, I wanted to eat her up like cotton candy, and my guess is she tastes every bit as sweet.

"Oh, come on, man." Jace yanks his practice jersey over his head as he talks. "I mean, that pale blue dress." He bites his knuckles and contorts his face like he's in pain. "Those legs. That fine booty. Her rack—"

"I *said*"—Graham's arm shoots out, and he fists the front of Jace's shirt in his hand—"shut up."

But Jace just laughs, which also tells me this ribbing about Mackenzie is normal for them.

Jace puts his hands up good naturedly and takes a step back at the same time Graham releases him. "Just sayin'. But let a man know if you're not gonna get on that? Because I might have to—"

I slam my locker door shut with a thunderous crack, cutting him off because I've heard enough. Teeth clenched, I spin back around to find everyone's eyes on me. Ignoring them, I crouch over the bench and tie my cleats in swift, sharp movements as my thoughts resentfully drift once more to Mackenzie.

I thought about her all weekend.

And now she's freaking everywhere.

Every time I turned around today at school, she'd been there, walking in the halls or hanging at her locker or headed to class. And when she wasn't, she was constantly in my thoughts, serving me a reminder of her presence. I couldn't get her out of my head.

Ice blue eyes.

Pouty lips.

That perfect body and her sharp mouth.

When she came to me this morning and asked for my help, I was thrown. I figured once I dropped her off safely at her door that night, or rather, her window, she'd forget about me. As she should.

But the second her eyes met mine this morning, I knew I was in trouble. Because Mackenzie Hart hadn't forgotten about me, and she wasn't going away. Which is inconvenient for the both of us. For her, because Daddy won't want her associating with the likes of me. And for me, because the last thing I need right now is a distraction.

And Mackenzie is just that. One giant distraction.

I inhale through my nose, remembering the look on her face when I told her I wouldn't help her. Worse yet, when I insulted her. But then I remind myself who I am.

Atlas Scott.

The boy from the wrong side of the tracks.

Trailer trash.

Loner.

Player.

Best damn high school wide receiver in the state of Ohio.

There are dozens of labels for me, and none of them include the kind of man who's selfless, who will just help a girl they hardly know for the sake of being kind.

All that matters is football. Getting a scholarship and a ticket out of here to somewhere far away. Somewhere better. Somewhere with a future. *That* is my sole focus. And no girl is going to help me with that, no matter how hot or how special she thinks she is.

A shadow falls over me, breaking through my train of thought, and I glance up to find Graham hovering over me, his green eyes warily taking me in. I say nothing as I straighten, grabbing my helmet off the bench and tucking it under my arm. While it's true to say Graham and I used to be close, it's also accurate to say we've barely spoken since middle school. It was before seventh grade to be exact, around the same time my father asked my Uncle Cal for his fiftieth loan and Cal cut him off.

Not that I blame him.

But it's also about that time Dad and I started living out of our van. Try being a preteen whose whole life fits in the backseat of an old Chrysler Town and Country. I guess Graham didn't want to be seen with a poor kid.

Shortly after, Dad moved us to the slums of Cincinnati, and I started stealing food from the local Stop and Go just to get by. Puberty is tough on any kid, but it's a hell of a lot tougher when your dad's too busy finding his next fix to worry about things like dinner for his twelve-year-old son. But as I got older, I got smarter. I learned how to apply for assistance and started stealing cash from the old man's wallet when he was too strung out to squirrel away for necessities. It might not have been enough to get us a decent place, but it was enough for food.

Fast forward to the present and I no longer rely on him for anything. I work a couple of gigs doing repair work for thirsty single housewives whose worthless husbands don't know the end of a wrench from a hole in the ground. And if the ladies just so happen to enjoy the show while I work shirtless underneath their kitchen sink or the hood of a car, so be it. Let 'em watch. Their husbands are too damn busy at work to pay any attention to them, and are probably banging their secretaries, anyway. Besides, the tips are great and it beats begging for food and money or stealing.

I try to move past Graham toward the door, but he shifts his body, standing in my way. We're the same height—almost eye to eye—and I stare him down, wondering if this is going to be some kind of bro chat or a confrontation about Mackenzie.

I wish he wasn't so predictable.

"Can I help you?" I ask, trying to keep my tone casual.

"So you drove Kenz home, huh?" He narrows his eyes, jaw clenched like he's looking for a fight.

I rake a hand through my hair. He's just getting started, yet I'm already frustrated with his line of questioning. "Yeah. I was there, so was she, and it was clear she had no way home. We've already been over this."

When he says nothing, I add, "You know, you seem kind of protective for a *friend*."

Some kind of emotion tightens his features, maybe anger, or embarrassment. I can't be sure. I don't know him well enough anymore to tell.

"It's just . . . I don't know how much you've heard, but she's been through a lot."

"Okay?" I shrug.

"I don't want to see her get hurt."

"If you think I have any interest in Mackenzie Hart, you can relax. She's not my type. Besides, I don't do relationships."

Relief flickers in his eyes, and I fight the urge to roll mine. I'm grateful for the opportunity to play ball for one of the most competitive schools in the state, but Graham's making it real hard for me not to hate him for being a predictable douche bag.

"That's fair. I just thought—"

"I know what you thought," I snap. Clearly, he's heard the rumors about me and believes all of them. "But you've got it backward," I say, unable to help myself. "Why don't you ask your BFF what *she* wants from *me*?"

I watch as this piece of information sinks in and confusion settles on his features, then I head for the door and push my way outside. I jog out of the tunnel and onto the field, past a gaggle of cheerleaders. One of them is a familiar brunette with killer legs and eyes as cool and striking as an iceberg.

I turn my gaze away from her and catch Graham watching us from the entrance of the tunnel.

Well, this should be interesting.

Chapter 9

ATLAS

Practice is winding down when Coach calls my name, waving his clipboard for me to come over.

Dread settles in the pit of my stomach as I rip my helmet off and jog toward him. My mind is reeling with what he could possibly want to talk about, and my gut tells me it's nothing good.

"What's up, Coach?" I say, taking a moment to catch my breath.

"Let's have a word." He turns for the tunnel and motions for me to follow. "My office."

I head inside and sit opposite him, white-knuckling the arms of the chair as I stare at Coach's impassive expression. He rests his elbows on his desk and steeples his hands in front of him, his baseball cap casting shadows over his eyes. "I wanted to chat with you for a minute, get a feel for how you're settling in with the new team."

"Uh, pretty good, sir."

"You getting along with the guys?"

I frown wondering if someone's said something to the contrary.

"I mean, yeah. To be honest, I haven't had much of a chance to socialize with most of them outside of school, but as you know, Graham and I are cousins."

He nods. "I am well aware, as I'm sure you're also aware that Mr. Scott, your uncle, is one of the reasons you're here."

"Yes, sir." I swallow, anxious for him to get to the point.

"Look," he says, leaning across his desk, and I hold my breath because I know this is it, the part where he gets to the point. "With Drake injured, we brought you here with the intention of playing first string receiver."

I straighten in my chair, disliking where this is headed.

"To be blunt, Peters struggled last year without Drake by his side. He would've been starting alongside Jace, but then you showed up and things changed. Our intention is for you to still be a starter. But with so much riding on having a winning season, and you having just gotten settled a week ago, I think we're going to start Peters on Friday night." He spreads his hands out. "Just as insurance since you're so fresh and just learning the place, building camaraderie, and so on. I thought you should know."

Iced water chinks through my veins. It just so happens Riverside is set to play their rival on Friday. It'll be a big game, and word is scouts are coming. It's my chance to start the season off with a bang, but from the sounds of it, I'll be starting it with a dismal flop from the bench instead.

"Sir, with all due respect, I've been studying the plays, and I'll work my butt off to learn them before then. As for the guys, we're cool. I may not have history with them, but I don't have any beef with them either. I'm confident I can play alongside anyone."

"I'm sure you can, son, and trust me, I didn't make this decision lightly, but my whole team needs to be at the top of their game. And if that means playing with guys they have a rapport with, well . . ." He shrugs.

My thoughts flash to Graham and his crappy throws this afternoon and anger boils in my guts. I'm getting blamed for his poor performance at practice? Un-freaking-believable.

Because he sucks up the field, I'm riding the bench.

I clench my jaw as Coach rambles on about being a team player and how this is only temporary or something like that. I don't know, and I don't care. Because all that matters is time on that field. Time I won't have now.

I listen dully as he dismisses me, then make my way out of his office on leaden legs, straight into the locker room. Practice will be over by now and I'd prefer to change and get the hell out of here while I can.

The guys start pouring in just as I'm lifting my bag to my shoulder. "You outta here already, Scott?" Jace asks as he passes me.

"Yep. Got somewhere to be," I lie. The only thing I have to go home to is my father, who's probably passed out in our single-wide with beer cans littered all around him.

"You're not salty that I outperformed you today, are you?"

I purse my lips, my grip tightening on my bag. Jace is a clown, I know that. But his words still bite, considering the conversation I just had with Coach, which makes them a little hard to laugh off.

Still, I force a chuckle past my lips as I slap him on the back good naturedly and push my way out the door, knowing they'll probably talk shit about me after I leave. No doubt everyone is wondering what Coach wanted. Peters is probably pissing his pants right now at the prospect of starting in Friday night's game.

I squint into the sunlight as I step outside only to see Doll and Golden Boy standing right in my line of vision, looking like a picture-perfect couple. For some reason this irritates me even more.

Pushing past them, I note Mackenzie's defensive posture and how Graham is holding his helmet so tight his knuckles turn white. It's then I recognize the flicker of irritation in his eyes and realize they must be having some kind of a disagreement. For some reason, this revelation brings me more joy than it should.

I take the sidewalk at the same time I hear the slapping of someone's shoes behind me and grind my teeth. The last person I want to talk to is Graham. I know we used to be close, and I have no idea if he was behind Coach's decision not to play me on Friday, but right now is not the time to rekindle our friendship.

"Hey, wait up, will you?" a sharp soprano calls out.

Worse than Graham. Mackenzie.

"What do you want, Hart?" I call over my shoulder.

"I want to talk to you."

I shake my head. "No dice. We did enough talking this morning."

I close in on my bike, ready to ride off and forget the last thirty minutes, when Mackenzie's lithe little body springs in front of me like a panther, blocking my ride.

She crosses her arms in front of her chest, her mouth pressed into a thin line. The short little spandex shorts she wore in cheer practice, along with the tight tank she has on, showcase her curves but they're not enough to make me want to stand here and converse with her. Not when I'm trying so hard to stay away. Not when I'm pissed at her pseudo boyfriend or whatever the hell he is.

"I'm not moving until you talk to me."

I snort and step forward. Reaching out, I wrap my hands around her tiny waist, lift her up, and place her a few feet to the side while she squeals in protest. "Good thing you're bite-size," I say.

"Wait. I have a deal for you," she calls out.

"I already heard what you're offering and I'm not interested." I swing one leg over the side of the bike before I grab my helmet off the back.

"You haven't heard this."

"Still not interested." I throttle the engine.

"I know you're not playing Friday night," she blurts.

I slowly lift my head and scowl. "How would you know anything about that?"

She lifts one delicate shoulder. "I saw Coach call you out and overheard your conversation on my way to the bathroom."

I shake my head ready to tell her it changes nothing when she says, "I can help you."

I pause and soak her in, wondering how she can possibly help me with my situation. I should leave, but if she's for real, I can't afford to pass this up. "How?"

"I can get Peters suspended."

My brows rise to my hairline. Out of all the things I expected to come out her mouth, that was not it. "Suspended?" I ask.

A suspension would certainly mean I'd play in Friday's game. And every game after, for that matter, until his suspension was over.

She nods. "I saw him in the hall this morning, buying weed. All I have to do is mention it to my dad. Say something about how it makes me uncomfortable and he'll make a call, have drug dogs here tomorrow morning for a locker search."

I rub my jaw, fighting off a grin as stubble scratches my hand. "You really think he'll do that?"

"I know he'll do that. He's so worried about how my year will go and making sure I'm comfortable. Besides, he's anything if not predictable. All you have to do in exchange is give me a ride when I need it so I can try and stoke my memory of the crash."

"What if you never remember? What if it's impossible?" I challenge.

"It's not. I know it's not," she says, closing her eyes so that her long, dark lashes fan over her rosy cheeks. "There are times when I can feel the memories, like they're right there, shimmering under the surface, waiting for me to dig them up. I just need someone who will help me ruthlessly pursue the details of that day."

Laughter rumbles inside my chest. "I gotta hand it to you, Hart. I did not expect this."

She shrugs. "When I want something, I don't stop until I get it."

"I don't doubt that you do," I say, though I believe she gets everything she wants regardless of how hard she has to work for it.

"So, will you do it?" She clasps her hands out in front of her, bouncing on her toes, and I can't help but wonder what I'm getting myself into.

"If the K9s come tomorrow and Peters gets busted, I'll help you."

"Thank you." She grins, and I can tell she's holding back phone in my hand, saying, "I'll need your number so we can coordinate."

"Fine." I take it, typing my number into her contacts before I hand it back. "But we do it on my terms, how I want."

"Of course. I'll make it as painless as possible. You won't regret this," she says, then heads back toward the locker rooms while I watch her go, wondering if she's going to meet Graham, and why the hell I care.

Chapter 10

GRAHAM

By the time I leave the locker room, Kenzie's waiting for me by the car, and the sight of her is like a hit of Valium to my system. I can breathe a little easier. The knots in my chest loosen, and the cobwebs in my head vanish, allowing me to think clearly.

When she grabbed me after practice to let me know she needed to talk to Atlas before she left, my heart leapt into my throat. I'm not naive enough to believe she's any less affected by him than the other girls at school seem to be. I see the way they gawk at him and whisper in the halls. All day, they kept asking me about him. They assumed that just because I'm his cousin, I should know his relationship status, or anything else about him for that matter. Even before school started, I heard the rumors about his time in juvie and his violent tendencies circulating. Now that classes have begun, they're getting out of hand. Most of them are ridiculous, like the one where he robbed the local mini mart at gunpoint and that's why he went to juvie. Or the one where he had an intimate relationship with a teacher twice his age. Though there's a grain of truth to some of them, I can't help but wonder if it's his bad-boy reputation they're drawn to. It certainly can't be his bedside manner, considering the only interactions I've witnessed give me the impression he's a complete dick to girls.

Surely Kenzie's not interested in him, is she?

I pause in front of my car, standing directly in front of Kenzie now, taking her in—her long, sleek ponytail, rosy cheeks, pouty mouth, and tight spandex from cheer practice. God, she's beautiful. Just looking at her makes my heart hurt.

"Still mad at me?" she asks, staring up at me with eyes as cool as a long drink of water.

I roll my eyes, playing it off like it's no big deal, but don't look at her as I say, "I was never mad."

"Liar," she teases. Stepping forward, she reaches up and places the palms of her hands on either side of my face, forcing me to meet her gaze as the warmth of her touch sinks into my bones. "Tell me the real reason you don't want me talking to him?"

This is it. The moment of truth. I can come clean about my feelings for her right now and make her understand I'm nothing more than a jealous asshole.

I search her earnest expression and open my mouth, ready to tell her, when I imagine what it might be like if she rejects me, if it changes how she sees me and affects our friendship, and I snap my mouth shut.

Instead, I close my eyes and lean into her touch like a purring kitten while my heart races. Does she know how badly I want her? Would it scare her if she did?

There's a stirring in my gut I recognize, but I shove it aside because I have zero reason to be jealous. It's not like Kenzie owes me anything. She can talk to whomever she wants whenever she wants. Besides, just because she wanted to talk to him earlier doesn't mean she's interested. It could've been about anything—thanking him for the ride home the other night, asking him a question about class. She owes me no explanations, yet I find myself wanting one, just to be sure.

She drops her hands, but I snag one before it falls to her side, holding it between us and rubbing my thumb against the delicate bones. "I just . . . want you to be careful, that's all. I know a lot of the girls are excited about a new prospect, but it's been a few years and I don't know that much about him. What I do know doesn't exactly make him out to be an angel."

"First of all, I'm not interested in him." Her cheeks pinken, and I can't help but wonder if it's a lie. "The other girls might be, but he's not exactly Prince Charming."

I frown, unable to help myself as I ask, "Then what did you want with him?"

She chews the inside of her cheek for a moment and gives me a tiny shrug. "It was nothing, really. Just a tiny favor that has to do with the other night when he brought me home."

"Just watch yourself around him. That's all I ask."

"Is he really *that* bad?" She laughs.

"All I know is his father's an addict, and his mom left when he was little, so his childhood was rough. Atlas got caught shoplifting a couple of times when he was fourteen. Suspended a few times from school. And those rumors about nearly beating a kid to death, there's some truth to them. He did a small stint at juvie for it. Then, supposedly, someone noticed his raw talent and got him into football. To my knowledge, he hasn't gotten into trouble since, but that doesn't mean I trust him. Look," I say, tipping her chin with my finger and forcing her gaze back to mine, "all I'm saying is, he might be completely harmless. Maybe he's turned a new leaf. I don't know. But I'm not taking chances. At least not with you."

She circles her hand around my wrist and a soft smile touches her lips. "You worry too much. Nothing's going to happen to me, Graham. I'm right here, and I'm fine. I'm good." She stretches to her toes and kisses me on the end of my nose. The gesture is friendlier than I'd like.

I swallow and give her a small nod.

"Besides," she says, reaching out and wrapping her arms around me, "that's why I have you to protect me."

MACKENZIE

It's a nice night. The sky is clear, and a soft breeze ruffles the leaves on the trees, whisking away the heat. Dad and I take dinner out to the patio—takeout from the little Italian place down the street—where I settle in the seat across from him, Goliath sprawled at my feet. Though I'm itching for a run, I sit with my father first because I know he's dying to see me after my first day, to make sure I'm okay and hear about how it went. Besides, I have my own business to attend to that can't wait.

I open the plastic clamshell container to a bed of steaming pasta atop eggplant parmesan and inhale the savory scent of the tomato sauce, wondering how to play my cards when Dad gets the ball rolling.

"So, how was school?" he asks after taking a bite of his pasta.

I twirl spaghetti around my fork while I answer honestly. "It was really good. My classes seem okay, and it was nice to be back."

"Everyone treat you well?"

"Of course." *Everyone except Atlas, maybe.* "I thought it might be weird or awkward. That some of the kids I hadn't seen last year after the accident might ask me questions or make a thing of it, but no one did."

It was almost like it never happened.

My gaze moves to the empty seat beside me, the one Mom always used to sit in. And just like that, I'm reminded it *did* happen, and I feel her loss, knowing no matter how normal things become, life will never be the same without her.

"Good." Dad nods and flashes me a tight smile, making me wonder if he wishes it had gone poorly. Because the truth is he likes having me home, safe and sound.

As quickly as the thought enters my mind, I push it away. It's unfair to make assumptions.

I shift on my chair, fiddling with my fork as I decide how to launch into what I need to say. "There was really only one bad thing that happened. I mean, it wasn't *that* bad," I murmur, almost as if talking to myself, "but I guess it did make me kind of uncomfortable. It definitely surprised me, especially seeing as it was only the first day . . ."

I glance at him under the tips of my lashes, watching as he pauses, fork midway to his mouth, eyes narrowed.

"What was it?"

"Well, it's just"—I shake my head and glance down at my food—"it's probably nothing, but I saw Jamie Peters buy drugs right out in the open." I drop my fork with a dramatic flair, hoping I'm not overdoing it. "I mean, it was in the middle of the hallway, for crying out loud."

"What kind of drugs?" Dad practically barks. If there's one thing he hates, it's substance abuse. I've never seen him drink a drop of alcohol in my life. My father is a picture of willpower and self-control in all things.

"Not sure. It was a baggie of something, though, and from where I was standing, it didn't look like weed." I push down the pang of guilt at the half-truth. I *did* see him accept a baggie of something, but it *was* most definitely marijuana.

"And you're sure it was drugs?"

I nod enthusiastically. "He got it from this kid, Henderson. Everyone at Riverside knows he's the kid you go to if you want the hook up. Besides, I saw Peters pay him, too."

Dad straightens in his seat, his food forgotten. "Maybe it's worth bringing in a K9. I know they don't usually do it this early in the year, but it might be good to shake things up, catch these kids off guard and nip things in the bud."

"No. Dad, you can't." I widen my eyes and shake my head. "What if he knows it was me?"

"He'll have no idea."

"Is it really that big a deal?"

"It's a very big deal. You know how I feel about drug use. And in school?" He blinks a few times, then pushes his seat back from the table. "What if he uses, then gets in the car and drives? Heck, the primary school is one campus over. Listen, don't worry about it, okay? It'll be fine. I'll take care of it." He smiles in a way I know is meant to put me at ease, then reaches across the table to pat the top of my hand as he stands.

"Wait. Where are you going?" My gaze tracks him as he rounds the table.

"I just need to make a quick phone call and then I'll be right back," he says over his shoulder as he heads for the door.

"But if he gets into trouble at school, won't he be suspended from the football team?" I call after him.

Dad stops for a moment, hand braced on the doorknob, before he glances at me over his shoulder. "Probably. But we can't bend the rules for athletes, and Riverside has strict policies about such things. We hold our kids to a higher standard. Sometimes there are more important things than football."

I fight the smile threatening to curl the corners of my lips. I deserve a freaking Academy Award for perfect execution.

"Yeah. I guess you're right," I murmur.

Dad says something else about the dangers of drugs affecting more than just the people who use them, but I'm not listening because all I can think about is how Peters will get busted, Atlas will play in Friday's game, and he'll owe me.

Chapter 11

ATLAS

After practice, I get a text from one of my clients. I've been summoned to take a look at her car; it's making a strange noise when she starts it. So, I head over to her place and fix a bad ignition switch, then rotate the tires and change the oil while I'm there for some extra cash before I head home.

I pull up to the yellow double-wide. Mildew coats the white window frames. A sagging makeshift porch hangs off the front of the mobile home beneath an ugly brown door. If I had any inclination or my father wasn't trashed half the time, I would fix the place up and make it nice for the times I'll be here—hell for the time *he'll* be here after I'm gone—but there's no point. Dad's rarely coherent to notice, and I plan on getting out of here come summer. With any luck, I'll finish my year at Riverside, then leave for greener pastures. And by greener pastures, I mean one of the Big Ten and a nice, fat scholarship. Then I'll get my degree, and even if no one in the NFL wants me, at least I'll have something to fall back on.

And if I don't get a scholarship...

I hate to think of where I'll be in five years. Fixing busted sinks and changing oil for cougars the rest of my life? It might be a decent way to get by now, but if I have to cater to these wealthy, bored housewives for the rest of my life, you might as well shoot me now.

But the system doesn't exactly help guys like me. Financial aid isn't an option, considering no institution would ever risk giving me a loan.

Which is why playing on Friday night is so important. And every night after that, for that matter. Not only do I need to play, but we need to make it to State. We need to be the best team in the whole damned conference. In that respect, Coach is right. All his players need to be on their A game, so whatever the hell had gotten into Graham today, better get fixed really quick. Like it or not, we depend on each other when we're out on that field.

It's just another reason to stay away from Mackenzie. Because truth be told, I know exactly what got to Graham, or should I say *who*.

From the first moment I heard Mackenzie's name come out of his mouth, I could tell he considers her as his. Even the way the other guys talk about her and poke fun at his expense tell me he has a thing for her. The dumbass is smitten, and the brunette bombshell has zero clue about it. Either that or she just isn't interested, which is an interesting theory. One I'd greedily explore if I wasn't so hellbent on keeping my distance.

Only keeping my distance is about to become a whole lot harder if she follows through on her promise. And as much as I loathe spending time with her, I need her to make good on her word, which means finding a way to help her without pissing Graham off so much it affects the team.

I push through the front door of our new digs and my chest tightens. A putrid smell greets me, strong enough to leave me cupping a hand over my nose. Dad lies sprawled out on the couch, eyes shut and mouth gaping open. A bottle of pills sits cockeyed on the scarred coffee table in front of him. Behind him, beer cans line the kitchen counter, along with remnants of his last meal. Trash spills from the tipped garbage can onto the floor—the source of the smell.

I have a half a mind to turn right back around and find someplace—anyplace—else to be.

Maybe I could lose myself in one of those housewives. Today, Mrs. Winslow raked her long red fingernails playfully over my forearm as she told me how much I'd filled out since she last saw me. Never mind that I'm a minor and seventeen for a few more months. She's so starved for attention from her husband, I know it wouldn't take much. A word. A look. It's all I'd need to start something I know I'd come to regret.

But I'm not that guy. Even if sometimes I want to be.

Disgusted, I slam the door closed behind me with a kick of my foot. Dad doesn't even flinch.

My stomach rumbles as I step further into the living room, though I have no idea how I manage it with the place being such a mess. Heading into the kitchen, I open the fridge to see if we have anything I can throw together for some semblance of a supper, but all I see are a dozen eggs, a piece of rotting fruit, and half a gallon of milk.

I slam the door closed and turn to the sink before I grab a clean dishrag from a drawer, then begin to do the dishes. Next, I sweep the floor and take out the trash before I wipe off the counters, and by the time I finish and the place looks at least somewhat acceptable, I dig back inside the icebox to forage for food. Finding a small block of cheese, I whisk some eggs and milk together, then fry myself up a huge omelet. Once cooked, I sit down at the tiny two-person table in the corner to eat as I watch Monday night football while Dad sleeps off his bender.

My gaze wanders to where he lies. His dark hair is greasy and falls in his face, concealing the dark circles underneath his eyes like gray crescent moons. The old T-shirt he wears is stained and ratty. His entire presence is a reminder of everything I have to lose if I can't make a scout notice me.

Dad played football once, too. Uncle Cal told me about it. Apparently, he'd been slated to play for Green Bay, he was that good. Better than Cal. But then he got Mom pregnant halfway through their junior year in college and things fell apart. Dad started drinking. He got so drunk one night, he fell down a flight of stairs and messed up his knee. The rest is history. You can't play pro football with a bum knee. So, while Uncle Cal went on to play for Pittsburgh, Dad prepared to be a new father. Only he missed the memo which explained that staying sober was sort of essential. After a while, Mom got tired of his shit and left. Can't say I blame her. The only reason I hate her is because she didn't take me with her.

The thoughts tire me, and when I stand, I'm so exhausted my bones ache. I drop my plate in the sink at the same time my phone buzzes in my pocket. I slide it out and check the screen, seeing a text from an unfamiliar number.

Unknown: *It's done. Get ready to pay your debt.*

Mackenzie.

My jaw tightens as I grip the phone in my hand at the same time Dad groans. He blinks his eyes open, glancing around him like he has no clue where the fuck he is, and all I can think is, she better be right.

Because I can't end up like him. I won't.

MACKENZIE

I slog through the morning on pins and needles, waiting to see if Peters gets busted, hoping I made the right decision. Then again, it was my only option, the only thing I have to offer Atlas other than my body. Which he isn't getting.

When I overheard Atlas talking to Coach in his office yesterday, it was like a gift. I never meant to eavesdrop—okay, maybe I was a little bit curious when I heard the sound of their voices drift toward me out in the hall—and I couldn't help but wonder if Graham's poor performance was part of the reason Coach wigged out and decided to bench Atlas.

I've seen Graham play hundreds of times but never so poorly. Could Atlas be affecting his game? Or is it his father? Maybe both. I know how much pressure Cal puts on his son to be the best, and I worry about him cracking with someone else like Atlas at Riverside who might potentially steal the spotlight.

I can only hope my meddling doesn't add to the problem.

The bell rings and I gather my things, leaving English to head toward lunch, when I see Jenna walking beside Atlas in the hall. Every so often, she reaches out and touches his arm, staring up at him with doe eyes, despite the fact Atlas looks bored as sin. Yesterday, she spent the first fifteen minutes of cheer talking about how she had every intention of earning his jersey by the end of the season. At Riverside, wearing a player's jersey on game day was like carving his name on your chest, and apparently Jenna was letting us know she's called dibs.

I wonder what Atlas thinks about that. Something tells me he doesn't care, not one bit.

I'm still staring at them as they stop by the water fountain, and I nearly ram into someone's back.

I glance up to see a massive cluster of students forming around the lockers, staring at something up ahead, but I can't for the life of me see what it is.

The murmur of voices grows as I skirt around the throng of people, then freeze. Three uniformed officers flank the lockers at the end of the hallway while two K9s sit on their haunches beside them. Peters hovers opposite them, hair falling over his downcast eyes.

All around me, students whisper, and I strain to hear. "Peters got caught with weed," someone standing near me says. Others are speculating whether he'll get suspended when Principal Weaver joins the melee.

She exchanges a few words with the officers, then nods her head, her expression grim as she turns her knife-like gaze on Peters, who hangs his head in despair and follows her to her office.

Part of me feels guilty. It sits inside my stomach, hard and unyielding like a stone I can't pass. I hope him getting in trouble doesn't mess with his future for the sake of preserving mine.

Maybe Atlas was right. Maybe I'm so used to getting what I want I now step on the backs of others to get there.

I feel the burn of something on the side of my face and track the source of the heat until I find Atlas, several yards in front of me to my right, his dark eyes penetrating, hot enough to melt flesh from bone.

With a flick of the hand, he dismisses Jenna, and she leaves him with a pout before he crosses toward me.

All I can do is stare right back. The muscles in his chest and arms strain against the soft fabric of his shirt, matching the tension in his jaw. He towers over me, forcing me to tip my head up so I can look him in the eyes.

"Today. Meet me after practice," he says.

No gratitude. No pretenses. All business.

"So soon?"

"Scared?" His mouth curls into a twisted grin. Something tells me he wants me scared.

"No," I say, because it's the truth.

Though I should be, and not just because of Graham's warnings to be careful. But because everything about him screams trouble, and my father would rather lock me up in my room than see me spend time with someone like Atlas Scott.

Yet I still don't regret the deal I made.

"Good." He leans down and whispers, "Because the sooner you remember, the sooner my debt is paid."

Chapter 12

MACKENZIE

I join Atlas by the bleachers after practice, having purposefully taken my time to change back into my street clothes in the hope of avoiding Graham as he leaves to go home. My plan works, and by the time I show my face again, the parking lot is empty. Atlas, however, looks annoyed at having to wait.

"What the hell took you so long?" He scowls at me as he pushes off the bleachers and towers over me.

"Sorry. I got caught up with something," I say, my tone defensive.

Atlas stares at me for a moment and it's as if he can see right through me. "Does Graham know you're with me?"

When I say nothing, a smirk curls the corners of his lips. "What, am I your dirty little secret, Hart? Should I be flattered?" He places one of his big hands over his chest in a mock swoon, and I give him a light shove.

"Shut up."

He chuckles and follows after me as I take off for the parking lot. "You ride with him to and from school, right?"

"Yeah." I shrug.

"So, what's the reason you gave him for not needing a ride home?"

"Why's it matter?"

"Call me curious."

I glance over at him, eyes sharp on his face. No way am I admitting the reason I gave to Graham; my father was picking me up to take me to dinner. I can imagine how much fun he'd have with that. "Look, can we just go?"

"Eager to get started, huh? Where are we headed, anyway?"

I wait until I reach his bike before I turn around and answer, "To the crash site."

"The crash site," he says like he's disappointed. "That's your grand plan to trigger your memory? Visiting the crash site? If you've already been there before, I don't see how—"

"I haven't." I interrupt him quickly.

"Come again?" He cocks his head like he hasn't heard me.

"I haven't been to the crash site since . . ." I swallow. "Since the accident."

"How is that even possible?" He glances around him, arms spread out as if someone else nearby might corroborate how stupid a notion this is. "Riverside isn't that big. How have you not just come across it?"

I sigh and rake my hands through my hair, not wanting to get into this with him. Then again, I'm the one asking for his help. Clueing him in is kind of essential.

"First off, it's just outside of town. And my dad, he's . . ." I pause, searching for the right word. Overprotective doesn't quite fit. "He almost lost me, so he worries a lot about me now. After the accident, when I woke up and found out what happened to my mother, I freaked out and sort of spiraled. I was blaming myself a lot. It took weeks for me to come out of it, then months to break through the depression that followed. It took more than four months just to get me in a moving vehicle again without curling into a ball on the floorboards."

"Shit." He rubs the back of his neck. "That bad, huh? You were a real head-case."

I don't take offense to his comment, because he's right. I was.

"I tried therapy. They had me go into this sort of meditative state and recall the day's events and everything leading up to the crash that I could remember, but it didn't help. I freaked and quit going."

"Still . . ."

"I'm sure it seems weird to you, but Dad was worried I'd break down or lose it if I went back to therapy again, and honestly, a part of me was worried about that, too. More so, I think I was afraid of what I *would* remember." I glance down at my hands. "But I'm not letting that stop me anymore."

Even though I want to know what happened, there's this teeny tiny piece of me that's petrified. I already think the accident was my fault, but as long as I can't recall what or how it happened, there's always the chance that it wasn't. That it was just a freak occurrence like everyone says, a poor stroke of fate. But if I remember and it was something I did wrong, then . . .

My throat bobs with emotion. "Let's just say if I remember and it really is my fault she died, I'm not sure I'll ever fully recover from that. I mean, how do you get past killing your own mom?"

Atlas whistles slowly. "Wow, Hart. And you think I can help with this? I got news for you," he says, lowering his face so it hovers just above mine, "I can't. But I'll give you a ride because we had a deal. Just don't expect much."

"Noted."

"I still can't understand why you don't just have Graham take you."

"If I get upset, Graham will take me straight home or coddle me. And besides, Graham and my father don't get it. All they want is for me to move forward and stop living in the past, but what they don't understand is I've been treading water this whole time when what I really need is to accept the past and everything in it before I can swim. But I can't do that if I don't know what really happened. Something tells me you know a little bit about that." My shoulders sag, and it takes everything in me not to cave under the weight of defeat as I take him in, hoping to hit a chord.

"Are you comparing us, doll? Because you and I"—he points between us—"are nothing alike."

"Maybe. But something tells me you know a little about accepting the past, no matter how unfortunate your circumstances."

His lip curls, and he shakes his head. "You know nothing about my past."

I think about my conversation with Graham. I know Atlas didn't have an easy childhood, and he went through a rebellious phase only football seemed to save him from.

"But I *could* know. If you'd let me."

He scoffs as he reaches to the back of the bike and grabs the shiny black helmet I wore the other night, shoving it into my arms. "Put this on," he barks, then swings one leg over the bike and starts it, throttling the engine while I hover beside him, beating back the nerves ballooning inside my chest.

I rode with him once before and I was fine, I remind myself. But it was easier then because I had no choice. I do now, even if it doesn't feel like it.

Still, I force myself to move, put one foot in front of the other until I'm straddling the motorcycle and wrapping my arms around the hard planes of his torso while I tell him where to go, and then we're off, the wind whipping my arms, exposed by my tank top.

Atlas leans into the curves, taking the bends in the road like a pro. Even though I can feel my heart beating in my chest like a drum, I begin to relax, confident in his ability to maneuver the powerful machine beneath us and bend it to his will. Part of me wonders if he exerts this much control in all areas of his life, but then I guess not. Because everything I've been told about Atlas confirms that he's reckless, maybe even a little bit dangerous. But as I sink into the warmth of his muscled back as he drives, he doesn't seem so bad.

After fifteen minutes, I start counting the miles, watching the landmarks, and when my skin prickles with awareness, I know we're close. Far too soon, he slows the bike and begins to pull over in the parking lot of a convenience store on the corner. When the engine dies, my heart leaps into my throat, beating there until I think I might choke on it.

I sit there, my body curved around his like a parenthesis, focusing on the breath going in and out of my lungs when he looks at me over his shoulder.

"You getting off anytime soon, or do you just plan on jogging your memory by staring at my back?" There's zero humor in his voice.

I bark out a laugh, oddly grateful he's so rude.

Slowly, I swing down from the bike on numb legs. Pins and needles prick my feet as I stand, unable to reply with my own sarcasm because I'm too nervous, my stomach a bed of snakes.

I remove my helmet and sit it on the back of the bike before I take several steps to the edge of the parking lot and look out into the street. Only a few yards away is the intersection. It's a four-way stop but not a particularly busy one. We're all alone as I soak it in, staring at the stoplights, then the lines on the road followed by the berm. I'm half expecting there still to be wreckage, some proof this is where it happened. But there's nothing—just green grass and a small guardrail hugging the side of the road.

I glance around me, noting the empty streets. To my left, there's a bar called the Green Clover, and to my right, a small shopping center with eclectic shops. From everything I've been told, my car spun out of control, went off the road, and crashed into the telephone pole, hitting the front right of the car—the passenger side, where my mom was seated.

I head to the pole up ahead, staring at it as if it might tell me its secrets, as if it might be able to reveal exactly what happened that day. I feel Atlas behind me, quietly following and watching my every move, probably thinking how crazy I am. But I don't care what he thinks of me. I'm too wrapped up in my thoughts about that day and the fact that, for the first time since it happened, I'm standing on the piece of ground where my mother took her last breath.

I reach out and touch the wooden exterior of the telephone pole like it's a direct connection to my mom, grateful for Atlas's silence behind me. For as insensitive as he is, at least he knows when to shut up and allow me my thoughts. The pole is rough, slightly warm to the touch from the sun. I hold my hand there, fingers grazing its surface as if expecting to feel my mother's energy. Her last exhale. But I feel . . . nothing, which disappoints me. Ridiculous, I know.

Turning, I face the intersection, and a car passes by me as I go to the spot on the road where we would've been traveling had I been coming from home. I plant my feet, spinning around and taking in everything around me like it might trigger a memory, a feeling, *something*. I spread my arms out and tip my head back, closing my eyes, the sun warm on my skin. My thoughts drift back to that day, mentally retracing my steps like the therapist had me do after the accident. I remember being irritated about something, or at least I think I was, because I recall being short with my mother at breakfast, and barely looking at my father when he said goodbye and headed to work. I think that's one of the things that kills me the most. I couldn't even be nice to her. Then again, I had no idea what would happen.

I left the house, got in my car and drove myself to school because this was *before.* Before everything. Before my mother died. Before all the fear and the pain. Before Dad worried about me relentlessly and treated me with kid gloves.

Before I needed to be chauffeured around like a child.

I remember the ride to school, blasting my music and clutching the steering wheel. The image is burned in my mind, so much so that throughout the year I've questioned whether it was really from that fateful morning or if it was a different memory disassociated from the crash.

After that, I remember nothing. I only know I skipped school because the accident occurred around noon and there was no note on file, no phone call from my parents asking for me to be released early.

So how did Mom get in my car? Had she found me at home? And if so, where were we headed? The spot where I currently stand is in the opposite direction of Riverside High.

I have so many questions and zero answers because the only other person there that day is dead.

I squeeze my eyes harder, until red dots burst beneath my eyelids, willing my mother to somehow speak to me, communicate the answers I need so I can move on with my life. Let the guilt go, along with the fear.

A soft blaring noise fills my subconscious, but I'm focused so hard on remembering something, I ignore it. Like a movie reel, a memory flickers to life. Someone lifting a wine glass to their lips, the scent of food permeating the air. The chink of silverware and the soft buzz of voices.

And then something rams into my side, knocking the air from my lungs as I collide with the solid ground beneath me.

Oof.

My eyes fly open, and a car zooms past, horn blaring. But all I can do is blink up into eyes as dark as motor oil.

Atlas.

His legs are tangled with mine, his chest pressing against my own, rising and falling in rapid succession as I struggle to draw an aching breath into my lungs.

"What the hell, Hart?" He jumps off me like I'm on fire. "Are you trying to get yourself killed? Didn't do the job the first time, so you thought you'd try again?"

His words should bite, but I'm still reeling from the heat of his body and the feel of all that hard muscle.

Slowly, I roll to my side, body throbbing like a toothache as I turn onto all fours, then get to my feet as I stand to face him, dusting the dirt off me with a wince.

"I'm sorry, I—" My words cut off as my gaze catches on something behind him. A restaurant called Manja, Manja at the end of the shopping center. I don't even finish my sentence or pause to tell Atlas what I'm thinking. Instead, I start heading back across the intersection, drawn to it with a magnetism I can't explain.

My feet move swiftly over the pavement, until I reach the parking lot of the shopping center and pause in front of the restaurant, staring at the large glass windows that reveal a dimly lit and intimate atmosphere inside.

The same memory from before flickers again, only this time, I see a pair of hands intertwined between the wine glasses on the table.

"Do you remember something?" Atlas appears beside me, and I glance over at him, pulled from the image.

"This restaurant. I remember it like I've been here, but I don't think I have."

Did Mom and I go to lunch? Maybe she found me at home, playing hooky, and instead of lecturing me, she took me out. But something about the theory feels off.

"Of all things, why am I remembering this?" I murmur to myself. "I'm going in," I say before I hurry off, swiftly walking toward the entrance.

"Are we taking a pit stop to have dinner?" Atlas follows behind me. "I don't see how this is gonna help," he says as he keeps pace, his long stride making it look easy.

"I can't explain it, but I got a glimpse of something. I think it's a memory." I shake my head, unsure. "I don't know. But I just feel like this place has some kind of significance."

I burst inside the restaurant with Atlas fast on my heels and head straight for the hostess, opening my mouth to say something. Before anything comes tumbling out, I pause, drawing a blank on what to say because I hadn't thought that far ahead before I barreled in here like a bat out of hell.

"Um, are you okay, Miss?" the hostess, an older lady, asks.

"Um, no. Yes." I shake my head and wave off the concern flickering in her eyes while Atlas snickers behind me. "I just . . . I was in the area. It's been a while since I've been in here, and I thought I saw someone I know. Sorry." My cheeks heat as I back away from her and she stares at me like I have a third head.

Glancing around me, I try to feel another spark, but there's nothing.

Deflating, I turn toward Atlas. He arches a brow and I sigh, raking a hand through my hair. "That was your grand plan?" he asks.

"Shut up. I just . . ." I shrug. "I thought maybe they'd have record of me and my mother eating here that day or something, but then I realized that's stupid. Even if she had given them our name, it was nearly nine months ago. They don't keep stuff like that on file." I cross my arms over my chest. I should've expected this outcome, yet I still find myself frustrated.

I watch the patrons eating their meals—smiling, happy. Someone waits to be seated, but for the most part, they're not particularly busy. A waiter appears from behind a set of double doors, and my gaze flickers to a man dressed in black slacks, a dress shirt, and tie as he speaks to a couple at a nearby table. His hair is dark, with a closely trimmed beard, and when he smiles, a sense of familiarity hits me square in the chest, along with an odd sense of déjà vu.

I know this man. But how . . . ? Who . . . ?

Did he wait on us the day of the crash?

I turn to the hostess once more, ignoring her overtly sympathetic expression when I ask, "Do you know who that is?" I point.

"Anthony?" She stares at him, and I nod. "That's Mr. Mancetti, the owner. Why? Is that the person you know?"

I swallow and turn to Atlas, ignoring her question. "I think we came here the day of the accident. Everything's familiar."

He shrugs. "But that still gives you zero clues as to how the actual crash went down."

I bite my lip because he's right. Even if Mom and I did come here together, it has nothing to do with the accident itself. "I know," I say, trying not to sound as dejected as I feel. "But at least I'm remembering. Or sort of remembering. It's better than nothing."

"So, what now?" Atlas asks, but I ignore him.

"I need to speak to him." Turning back around, my gaze drifts back to the spot where the man just stood, but he's gone.

I exhale, then turn my attention toward the hostess, waiting as she takes someone's name and party down, then step forward again. "Excuse me, but I need to speak to him. Anthony," I add.

"Okay. Just a moment," she says, then picks a cordless phone up off the podium she's standing behind and dials a number. When they pick up, I hear a female voice on the other line. "Yeah, can I have Anthony out here? I have someone asking for him." She pauses for a moment and listens before she says, "Oh, I see. Thanks," and hangs up. "I'm sorry, but you missed him. He just left," she tells me as she glances back at me.

I deflate at the news and thank her before I push through the doors back into the warm evening air, a wave of exhaustion suddenly hitting me.

"Well, *that* wasn't the revelation I was hoping for," Atlas announces, and I turn on him, poking a finger in his chest.

"Wasn't the revelation *you* were hoping for? Seriously?"

He smiles, and his dark eyes gleam as the sharp angles of his face soften. He's so gorgeous, it makes my head spin. Too bad he's heartless.

"Sorry to disappoint," I spit, swallowing over the lump in the back of my throat, because there's no way I'm going to get emotional in front of him. "Let's call it a night," I say, staring back out into the empty intersection. "I'm not going to remember anything else today."

With a sigh, he reaches out and grabs me by the elbow, tugging me across the parking lot and to a bench in front of one the boutique shops. "You're a pain in my rear, doll."

Once we sit, he stretches out his long legs and crosses his arms over his chest, like he's planning to stay a while and is just getting comfortable.

"What are we doing?" I ask, confused. One minute, he's acting like I'm a total inconvenience and the next, he's settling in for a chat.

Everything about this boy confounds me.

It's several long minutes before he speaks, and when he does his raspy baritone makes my stomach do a backflip. "Is there a chance you'll never find out?" he asks.

"It's called dissociative amnesia. Most people do remember eventually, but there is a chance I won't."

"And if you don't?"

I glance at him to find him already staring at me. "Then I guess I have to live with that."

He swallows. "Do you miss her?"

"All the time." I tuck a lock of hair behind my ear, mesmerized by those endless dark eyes. I couldn't look away if I tried. "She had a reddish hue to her hair, dark blue eyes, and a wide smile. Every Sunday, she'd make brunch. Everything from scratch. I'd come down the stairs after sleeping in and help her. By the time we finished, we'd used every bowl and plate in the cupboard, then we'd leave the dishes for later and play cards or watch a movie or go for a walk. She never missed a school play or a class party when I was younger. Once I was older, she went to all the football games to watch me cheer. And she had this laugh . . . it was so loud and boisterous, just full of life. I swear it had the power to light up an entire room." I grow quiet, thinking of her as the familiar ache of my loss blooms inside of me. "She was my best friend. My confidant. Some days I can hardly believe she's gone."

The pinky of Atlas's finger brushes mine, and I have no idea if it's on purpose or by accident, but I like to think it's a show of support, however small.

"Have you ever lost someone?" I ask.

Atlas freezes, and his mouth twists. In pain? Regret? I'm not sure. I don't know him well enough to recognize his tells.

"My mother," he murmurs. "I didn't lose her like you, though," he quickly adds. "She left us, but I lost her all the same. She may as well be dead to me."

I swallow because I can't imagine a mother leaving her child voluntarily. "When did she leave?"

"I was four at the time. My dad's drinking was already out of control, but my guess is when he started on the pills she'd had enough. She left and never looked back."

"Wow. That's . . ."

"Fucked up?"

I nod.

"The funny thing is I don't even blame her for leaving him. But why the hell didn't she take me with her? That's the question I used to ask myself over and over. I was just a kid. What kind of mother abandons her child?" he asks, his tone gruff as he pulls his gaze from mine and stares off into the distance. "Now *that* I can blame her for, because no one should ever leave their kid behind, at least not with an addict."

I shift, staring off into the distance. As much as I miss my mother, at least I had her in my life for nearly seventeen years. "And how's your dad now?"

"Still a piss-poor father. He's a drunk and a junkie. I've been fighting just to survive for so long, I barely remember what anything else feels like."

"So, all the rumors about you, are those true?"

Atlas barks out a laugh, and the corners of his eyes crinkle when he glances over at me, his smile stretched wide, striking in its perfection below his shock of dark hair and onyx eyes. It's the most genuine smile I've seen since I met him. And it's breathtaking.

"You mean rumors like the one that I nearly killed a dude simply because he gave me lip at a party?" he scoffs.

"That's one, yeah."

"No. I mean, I did beat the kid's ass, but not because of his mouth, and I didn't nearly kill him either." His jaw hardens. "Although maybe I should've, because when you're at a party and you walk in on one of your friends' girl getting assaulted, you make damn sure the guy doesn't walk out of there."

My stomach roils at the picture in my head. "You helped her, so why would you get sent to juvie?"

"Why else? Because I dislocated Pretty Boy's jaw and his daddy has deep pockets."

"That's terrible."

"The one thing I've learned is that justice is nothing more than a murky shade of gray—when there's any at all, that is."

"Still, they shouldn't get away with that," I tell him.

He meets my eyes. "No, they should not."

"And the shoplifting?" I ask, needing to know. Suddenly, I want to know everything about this boy. What's real, what's not. How he feels. Thinks. Dreams.

What the heck is wrong with me?

"A kids gotta eat," he says with a shrug.

My lips part, but I stay quiet, because what do I say? The truth is, Atlas Scott is an anomaly I can't wrap my head around. There are a million layers of him to unwrap.

"Don't look at me like that, doll," he says, his tone fierce. "I don't take well to pity."

"I don't pity you," I say, revolted by the thought. Though it's only partially true, because my heart aches for him. "Believe it or not, I respect what you've gone through." Also true.

He lifts a shoulder. "I had some hard knocks, but I've come a long way from stealing cans of tuna and peanut butter." A smirk curls the corners of his mouth. "And now I'm playing football at one of the top schools in the state as a starting receiver. Things are looking up."

"Thanks in part to me."

He laughs. "Yeah. Thanks for that, by the way."

I grin back at him, thinking how much lighter he seems when we're talking like this. At the same time a car pulls to the curb in front of us, and when I glance at it, my stomach drops.

It's a Riverside PD cruiser.

And when the door opens and my father steps out, a rumble of fear skitters under the surface of my skin. Because it's no coincidence he's here.

Chapter 13

MACKENZIE

I suck in a breath as I stare at the cruiser and Atlas tenses beside me. My father's gaze flickers between us, knife-sharp before it settles on me. "Mackenzie, get in the car."

"What? No. Dad, we're just hanging out—talking."

His eyes widen, like he hadn't expected me to fight him on this. "And how exactly do you plan on getting home?"

"The same way she got here." Atlas's voice rumbles beside me, shooting like a firecracker straight to my gut. "With me."

The corners of Dad's eyes crease as he narrows his eyes. Tension thickens the air like a wet blanket, heavy and unyielding as he glances back to the restaurant, then to Atlas's bike, and back to the bench where we're sitting. "On that thing? I don't think so."

"Dad—"

"Now!" he barks out, and I jump.

Embarrassment heats my cheeks at the admonishment, and I don't dare risk a glance at Atlas to see his reaction. "I'll see you tomorrow," I murmur, pushing to my feet.

I hang my head and hurry toward my father's car, relieved to see he doesn't stay to speak to Atlas. Instead, he follows behind me and slides inside his cruiser next to me. I don't even offer Atlas a parting glance, although not even a minute goes by before he blasts past us on the highway and my father curses under his breath.

"What were you doing with that boy? I thought Graham was supposed to take you home?"

"He was," I say, my tone flat.

My father glances over at me; I can feel his gaze, heavy on the side of my face, but I refuse to acknowledge him. I'm too mad, too upset at being treated like a child when I did nothing wrong.

"If I can't trust you to be where you say you're going to be, then maybe we need to rethink—"

"Sending me to school?" My head jerks toward him. "You can't lock me in my room forever."

His jaw tightens. "I need to be able to trust you're safe."

"How did you know where I was, anyway?"

"You weren't at home."

"That doesn't answer the question," I snap.

"I don't want you hanging out with Atlas Scott."

My stomach clenches. Though his demand isn't a surprise, it's surprisingly painful. "Why?"

"Because he's dangerous, that's why." He glances over at me like I should know better, and I do. I knew my dad wouldn't want me out hanging out with Atlas, yet he was still the one I turned to.

"He has a record, Kenz. He's been suspended from school multiple times. The kid does whatever he wants. He lives in a trailer with his junkie father, for heaven's sake."

"So, what, we're too good for him?" I ask, my voice hitching.

"I don't think you understand. His father's an addict, complete trash."

And mine's a control freak, I want to spit back. But I don't. I have no idea why I'm so defensive of Atlas. Everything my father said is true, even if context makes it more palatable, and I have zero reason to be loyal to him. He's so much as told me he can't stand me, and yet I find my blood boiling at my father's judgment.

"I mean, you return to school after nine months and this is who you choose to spend your time with? I'm all for you having a social life. It's why I agreed for you to join the cheer team again and everything else, but this guy . . ." He shakes his head. "I don't want him anywhere near you."

"He's Graham's—"

"I don't care if he's the president's son, Kenz," he cuts me off. "He's bad news, a lost cause."

Moisture pricks the back of my eyes. Which is ridiculous; I barely know him, and I have no reason to care whether I see him again or not. Yet the urge to defend him rises inside of me like a tsunami. "What if he's not? What if you're wrong?"

"I'm not willing to risk my daughter to find out."

I turn toward the window, staring at the passing trees as we drive in silence the rest of the way, thinking about Atlas and his cynical worldview. He's had an uphill battle from the moment he was brought into this world. Yet he chose none of it. Not his addict father, or his absent mother, but did what he had to do to survive. Now he's trying to rise above his circumstances in the only way he knows how. But as long as you have people like my father, who make snap judgments, he'll always have an uphill battle. He can play it off like he's Mr. Tough Guy, but I see him. And I know the truth.

Once we're home, my father pulls into the driveway, and I get out before he's even killed the engine. I slam the door closed as he follows on my heels. "Don't you have to go back to work?" I shout over my shoulder.

"I took a couple hours of personal leave."

I huff out a laugh with a tiny shake of the head and mutter "unbelievable," before I stomp inside and grab Goliath's leash. All I have to do is whistle and he comes running.

"You're going out *now*?" my father asks from behind me.

When I turn to him, I note the fear in his eyes and deflate a little. It's driving his words and actions. I know this, but I also won't be a prisoner anymore, either. If I waited for him to be ready for me to take on the world again, I might be waiting forever. He shouldn't get to choose the people I have in my life. *I* should. And I've never given him a reason not to trust me.

"I need to run" I say, knowing he won't deny me this—the one thing that's brought peace and healing to my life following the accident.

He nods, his expression tight as Goliath makes his way down the hall toward me. I snap on his leash, and step back outside when Dad stops me with a hand on my arm. "Kenz..."

I glance up at him, waiting. I stare into his hazel eyes, wondering if maybe he'll have a change of heart. If he'll trust me enough to make my own decisions.

"If I catch you with the Scott boy again, I'll pull you from the cheer team. It'll be straight to school, and straight home. And if that's still not enough to deter you, there's always virtual school. Trust goes both ways."

My pulse thunders in my veins, and I'm so angry, my hands shake.

I want to scream and shout, because I've done nothing wrong.

But I don't, because I know it'll get me nowhere, so instead I start to run.

My feet carry me down the yard and to the sidewalk. The air is thick with the coming rain, clouds darkening above me as I make my way past our house with a heavy heart.

My thoughts come in waves, pounding along with my feet on the pavement. With every step, I leave my problems behind. My frustration with my father. The embarrassment I felt when he spoke to me like a child in front of Atlas. My mother and how I still haven't remembered anything of significance about that day. All I want to do is forget, so I push myself harder, faster. I sprint until the burning in my muscles fades as my body acclimates to my speed. Until my mind goes numb and the thoughts disappear into the fog. Until all I can think about is the strength in my legs and the burning in my lungs.

I push myself to the limit, Goliath keeping pace with me the whole time. We run together like that for several miles. Only the sound of our breath fills the silence between us, and before I realize it, I veer off course and head toward Graham's neighborhood.

I turn on his street where the houses change from upscale suburban neighborhoods to the elite of Riverside. I pass manicured lawns, impeccably landscaped. Three and four-car garages with Mercedes and BMWs dotting the driveways.

Sweat beads on my forehead as my feet move on autopilot, as if my subconscious willed me here. Because the run isn't enough to clear my head. I need to talk to someone. Someone who will understand. I can't talk to my father, and even if I could go to Atlas, he doesn't care enough about me to listen to me ramble about the past. But Graham is my rock; he's always there for me. He's the one person I can rely on, who will understand.

I think of all those days I laid in the hospital, and the ones after where I holed up in my room. He was there for me, making me laugh, and entertaining me with stories about our friends, binge-watching all our favorite shows. He forced me out of the house when I didn't even want to move. And though I lied to him today about where I was going after school, I know he'll forgive me. Because that's what we do. Forgive and forget. Graham and I are the real deal, friends to the end. There isn't much I wouldn't do for him, and if the past is any indicator, he feels the same.

I slow down as I approach his house, the large picture windows gleaming in the fading light. I make my way up the sidewalk and to the front door where I pause and catch my breath, taking a moment to scratch Goliath behind the ears.

His tongue lolls out of his mouth as he pants and stares up at me, gratitude for the adoration I give him shining in his deep brown eyes. I give him another quick pat, then turn and ring the doorbell.

The sound of footsteps echoes from within, and a moment later, Graham swings open the door, shirtless, with nothing but a pair of swim trunks riding low on his hips. My gaze wanders to his muscled abdomen, and a ball of fire ignites in my gut I try very hard to ignore. I tear my eyes away, heat licking at my cheeks, wondering why in the world I was just checking out my best friend. It's not like I've never seen him in the pool before.

"Kenz?" He frowns, concern flickering in his eyes.

"Hey," I say. "I just went for a run and thought I'd stop by. Did I interrupt something?" My gaze shifts involuntarily to his chest.

"I was just going for a quick swim."

"Want me to leave?" I say, getting ready to turn around, suddenly flustered for reasons foreign to me. Either that, or maybe it's just the smooth, golden planes of his chest making me want to flee.

"No." He grabs my wrist and stops me. "It looks like rain anyway. Hey," he says when I don't meet his eyes, "everything okay?" He ducks his head to meet my gaze.

I nod, my smile tightening as he tugs me forward. "I have Goliath," I say, glancing behind me, but he just nods.

"Goliath can come too. Wanna go out back?" His gaze flickers toward the huge glass windows that show off the massive pool in his backyard.

"Yeah, that would be nice."

He changes direction and pads across the gleaming marble floor of the foyer, toward the massive set of French doors and we step back outside into the cooling night air with Goliath happily following on our heels.

I settle in on a massive outdoor sectional while Graham heads to the mini bar behind the pool where he shrugs on a T-shirt, much to my dismay, then grabs a dish, fills it with water, and places it in front of Goliath. "Here ya go, buddy."

I offer him a smile. "Thanks," I say at the same time the French doors open behind him, and his father appears in the entryway.

Instinctively, I straighten as Graham stiffens.

"Mackenzie? I thought I heard you." Mr. Scott's greeting smile widens as he steps outside, and I force myself to respond in kind.

Graham's father is a huge man. He played five years as a quarterback for Pittsburgh, and it still shows. Even pushing fifty, he's an imposing man with broad shoulders and a muscled physique. Though he's always been kind toward me, I don't particularly like him. Mostly, because I hate the way he talks to Graham and the pressure he puts on him to follow in his footsteps.

He comes to a stop beside the sectional and crosses his arms over his chest, his tanned forearms on display. "You know, I told Graham he should be reviewing plays, not basking in the sun, but"—he shrugs—"what do I know? I only played five years of professional ball." He reaches out and nudges Graham's shoulder. "Isn't that right, Graham?"

"I had practice after school, then reviewed tape for an hour. This is my first break," Graham snaps.

I clear my throat, hoping to defuse the tension. "From what I hear Coach Clancy is working them pretty hard this year, and Graham looks great."

"Like he should. But you can never be too prepared. Unless you like to lose." Mr. Scott barks out a laugh.

"I'll get back to it in a bit." Graham pinches the bridge of his nose, and I can hear the frustration in his voice. "Is there anything else you need, other than to chastise me and remind me how inferior I am?"

"Your generation is so easily offended." He laughs and claps his son on the shoulder, and for a minute, I think Graham might rip his hand off. "Then again, nothing's the same. I remember back in my day, the work never stopped, you know? I'd go to school, practice, do homework if I had any, squeezing it in when and where I could. Then the minute I got home, I ate and reviewed plays until my parents forced me to bed. Now that's dedication. But the work ethic nowadays just isn't what it used to be."

My plastic smile wavers, and it takes everything in me to keep it in place.

"Yeah, I hear about it all the time, Dad," Graham mutters.

"We play South Central on Friday, so it's a huge game. Tons of scouts will be there."

"Graham told me," I say, my tone flat.

"It's going to be a game changer for the boys who shine. Well, anyway, I'll leave you to it. I just wanted to say hi. Tell your dad I send my best, will you?"

"Of course."

He lifts a hand in a wave, which I return, waiting until he disappears inside before I allow my smile to slip and turn back to Graham, who runs a hand over his face. "Like I'm not under enough pressure as it is."

I touch his arm; my heart goes out to him. "I know. I'm sorry."

"Why does he have to be like that all the time? I mean, shit." He fists a hand in his hair, then lets it fall to his side. "He's been reminding me for weeks about how important this game is, telling me how many scouts will be there and talking about how if I don't impress them with my arm on Friday, I might as well kiss any chance of an offer goodbye. Like I don't know already."

"It's a lot of pressure."

Graham sighs, then sinks back into the cushions of the sectional and appraises me a moment before he says, "You didn't come here to talk about football. How was your run?"

"I can talk about whatever you want to talk about. Even football."

He raises a brow and tips his chin. "How was your run?" he asks again, a little slower this time.

I press my lips together because he knows me too well.

Sighing, I stare out at the crystal blue waters of the pool and blurt, "I went back to the site of the crash today."

Graham sucks in a breath. "With your dad?"

I shake my head.

"Does he know you went?"

"He does now," I say with a bitter laugh.

Graham's lips twist. "I take it that didn't go well?"

"Uh, no."

He falls silent, and I can tell he's contemplating this new information, absorbing it before he says anything else. It's one of the things I love about him. Graham doesn't just speak for the sake of hearing himself talk. Every word *means* something. And I know what he's going to ask next before he even opens his mouth.

"So, if your dad didn't take you, who did?"

I bite my lip and hang my head, dreading the truth because I've already dealt with my share of disappointment for the day, and Graham's disapproval might push me over the edge. Still, we don't make it a habit to lie to each other, and the guilt I've felt since striking my deal with Atlas has been eating me alive.

"Atlas." I risk a glance back up at him from underneath my lashes just as the jolt of shock registers over his handsome face.

"What?" His forehead creases like he doesn't understand, and he runs a hand over the back of his neck. "You asked Atlas to take you?"

I hear the hurt in his voice, and I hate myself for it.

"All you had to do was say something, Kenz. Just say the word and I would've been there, done anything."

"I know," I say, "and I'm sorry."

"I thought you decided it was best not to dwell on the past anymore, to move forward and push past the holes in your memory."

"No. My father decided that for me," I say a little too harshly. "I just got tired of spinning my wheels and getting nowhere. Dad wanted me to stop putting pressure on myself to remember because it was eating me up inside, so I gave in like I always do. But just because I stopped talking about it, doesn't mean it just went away. It doesn't mean that I don't wake up every morning and think about what happened, wondering if maybe it was a freak accident and not me who killed my mother. Maybe there was no possible way I could've prevented it. But as it is, I live every single day with the crushing weight of that guilt. Do you even know what that's like?"

Graham blows out a long breath, leaning forward, resting his elbows on his knees. "So let me help you then. You don't even know Atlas."

"Exactly. He doesn't care if I fall apart at what I learn, whereas you want to protect me. Which I love," I say quickly, "but I need someone impartial who's not going to take me home because I'm freaking out."

His eyes darken as he stares at me like he doesn't even recognize me anymore. But I give him time, because he's doing what he usually does; working through something in his head.

"Do you have a thing for him?" he asks, his voice cracking over the words.

"What?" I flinch. "No."

It's not a lie, not really. Even if I thought Atlas might be interested in me, we'd never go anywhere. My father forbade me from even hanging out with him.

"You sure about that? Because every other girl with a pulse at our school sure seems to. He comes along, and it's like, suddenly, every chick in all of Riverside has a thing for bad boys who ride bikes and act like their shit don't stink, when I know better. And it just blows my mind that after everything you've been through, you'd hop on the back of that thing and trust him with something so important."

I frown at his assessment. "I'm nothing like those girls. I'm not falling at his feet like Jenna Barnes is. It was just a ride, Graham."

"That's two rides now."

I scoff. "You're keeping count?"

He raises one shoulder in a half-shrug. "Maybe."

My lips part. I barely know what to say; I've never seen him act like this. "Well, then you might recall that one of those times was *your* fault."

He glances away from me, but not before I see the punch of guilt register in his eyes. "All I know is, you've known the guy for all of two seconds before you're taking rides with him on his motorcycle to the place where your mother died. All of this *after* I told you what I know about him and asked you to be careful."

Unbelievable. He sounds just like my father. I expected Dad to be this angry, but not him. Not my best friend. I mean, yeah, I knew Graham would be hurt because I asked Atlas to help me instead of him. But I hadn't expected *this*. Whatever this is.

Frustration fills the void in my chest until it feels like it might burst.

"You know what?" I shake my head. "I don't need this. I came here because I needed a friend. Because I thought you'd make me feel better about today and the fact I remembered absolutely nothing about the accident. Because as ridiculous as it was, like a fool, I thought I'd have some big breakthrough where everything came tumbling back!" I yell, gesturing with my hands. "I hoped I'd remember it wasn't my negligence that caused us to smash into that pole. Because then maybe I could finally move on. And, yeah, I knew you'd be a little upset about me hanging out with Atlas, but I didn't think it would be your main concern."

I huff out a breath because it hurts. "If I wanted another lecture, I would've stayed at home because, trust me, I got an earful from him, too." I shoot to my feet and turn to leave, snapping my fingers for Goliath to follow when Graham reaches out and grabs my wrist, standing up as he does so.

"Kenz..."

I pause, breathing hard as my tear-filled gaze settles on the stone beneath my feet.

"I'm sorry," he says, his voice dropping. "I'm being an ass. Please don't go."

I exhale and slowly turn to face him again, blinking my eyes in a bid to hold back the tears. "That's the first true thing you've said."

He barks out a single laugh, then shakes his head. "I think I just... Maybe the truth is I don't like sharing."

I suck in a breath as he stares down at me, his emerald eyes fierce as my chest tightens. Reaching out, I take his other hand in mine, amazed at how well they fit together. But that's how Graham and I have always been—a perfect pair, right from the start. "I'm not going anywhere. I'm still your best friend, and I always will be. You know that, right?"

A flicker of emotion I don't recognize darkens his gaze, and he opens his mouth as if to say something else before he snaps it back shut and nods. "Right." He smiles but drops my hands and sits back down. "So, you didn't remember anything at all?" he asks, his tone soft.

I shake my head and the despair from earlier returns as I take the seat next to him. "Nothing. I mean, there was a moment where I felt like maybe I was having a flashback, a memory from that day. It involved a nearby restaurant, that little Italian place on the corner, Manja, Manja. I remembered two people drinking wine, and then I saw this man, and his face was so familiar, I was sure it had to be from memory."

"Well, did you talk to him?" Graham frowned.

I shook my head. "The hostess told me it was the manager, but when I inquired after him, he'd already gone."

"And you really think you remember him from that day?"

"I don't know." I shrug. "Who knows? Maybe Mom and I went to lunch, and he simply passed by our table or spoke to us about our meal, but for some reason, he feels significant somehow."

"So maybe it wasn't a waste of time. Maybe it did trigger a memory, and you should keep going back there. Maybe next time, you'll remember some more."

"I thought the same thing, but my dad caught me there with Atlas. Needless to say, he wasn't happy. I'll be lucky if he lets me leave the house again." I swallow at the memory of Dad's lecture. "I may have screwed myself."

"He's not gonna tighten the reins just because you were out with someone he doesn't trust."

"You sure about that?"

"He won't," Graham says, nudging my knee with his. "I'll make sure of it. I mean, I need someone cheering for me on Friday night," he says with a wink.

"I see how it is. You only want me around so I can cheer for you?"

"Well, that, and you look pretty damn good in that cheer skirt." His smile widens and his dimples pop, and I'm reminded just how gorgeous my best friend is.

"So let me get this straight, you're only keeping me around for my ability to wave a pom pom and the way I look in my cheer uniform?"

Graham purses his lips. "Pretty much, yeah."

I laugh and fake punch him in the arm because, of course, I know he's joking, but he's faster than me. Reaching out, he grabs my fist, pulling me onto his lap and attacking my ribs with his fingers. I yelp as he tickles me, laughing hysterically as I try to get away. And it's not until tears run down my face that he finally lets up.

Breathing heavily, I wrap my arms around his neck as I stare into the emerald eyes of my best friend and my heart squeezes. "Thank you."

"For what?"

"For always knowing just the thing to make me laugh."

Chapter 14

MACKENZIE

Friday comes and I somehow manage to avoid Atlas in the halls. Not that I think he might actually want to see me. After all, he never would've even spent time with me had I not made that bet. Still, I secretly hope he'll seek me out, that he might actually care how I'm doing and if I got in too much trouble with my father.

Newsflash: he doesn't.

But his silence is for the best. I'm playing with fire by associating with him, and I've known it from the moment I met him. I've worked too hard to recover from the accident and enter the real world again. The last thing I want is to get punished and have my freedom stripped away all on account of some misguided attraction for a boy who doesn't care about me in the first place. Not to mention it seems to be causing problems with Graham. Whether it's Atlas's reputation he's worried about or some kind of jealousy on his part, I have no idea, but I'm not going to find out. Graham is the best friend I could ever ask for, the yin to my yang, and I won't risk that for anything.

Who knows? Maybe if I stay out of the picture, Atlas and Graham will grow close again. After all, they both have a lot more in common than they think. Their love of football for one, and their issues with their fathers as another. The biggest difference they share is that one grew up with a silver spoon in his mouth, while the other grew up with nothing.

Despite Atlas's absence, the day passes quickly. The girls and I are getting ready for the opening game after spending the last couple of hours making banners for the boys and painting inspirational messages on their parking spaces in the student lot. My red cheer skirt hits me mid-thigh, showcasing my lean, tan legs, while the long sleeve crop top shows a sliver of my midriff, and I can't help but wonder what my father will think, seeing as how he's more strict than ever following the accident. A hint of a grin touches my lips at the thought. Considering he's a big fan of modesty, I can't imagine he'll like it, which gives me just the tiniest bit of satisfaction.

Exhaling, I check my lip gloss in the mirror and smooth a hand over my dark locks, which are curled into beach waves and pulled back with a huge bow. A giant glittery, red number eleven graces my left cheek—Graham's number.

I take a deep breath, staring at my reflection one last time. This is it, I think. The first big game of the year where I'll cheer in front of a raving crowd of Rebel fans. My senior year. One last year to have fun with my friends and make memories before graduation. So why don't I feel more excited?

"Earth to Mackenzie . . ." Jenna pulls me from my thoughts, and my vision focuses to see her staring back at me, her smile wide as she puts the finishing touches on her makeup. She looks gorgeous, of course. Her thick blonde hair is pin straight, with the front pulled back by her bow. She paints her lips a glossy red, which makes the red number pop on her cheek against her milky complexion. Number fifty-two. I have no idea whose number it is, but I can guess, and I wonder if he'll be happy she's claimed it. I push the thought away as quickly as it appeared because it's none of my business.

"Sorry," I say to her with a little laugh. "Just lost in thought."

"I saw Graham a while ago, and, dang, girl, he looks *hot*. I mean, Graham's always been built but those biceps? Sheesh. Girl, you better lock that down because he's not going to stay single forever."

My stomach churns at the thought of Graham with another girl, and even though he hasn't seriously dated anyone since the summer before our sophomore year, I know Jenna's right. Friend or not, Graham's smoking, and it won't be long before someone swoops in and steals his heart. And shouldn't I want that for him? We don't talk about dating much, probably because it hasn't been big on my priority list this past year, but I know him well enough to know he wants to find someone. Graham is just that way—sweet and kind and thoughtful. He'd make the perfect boyfriend.

My cheeks heat as I wave her away. "Graham and I are just friends."

"You sure about that?" Adriane drawls as she appears beside me, brush in hand. "I've had guy friends and they don't look at me the way Graham looks at you."

"And how does he look at me?" I ask curiously.

"Like you're a snack, and he's *starved*," she purrs, then she and Jenna laugh.

A riot of butterflies take flight in my stomach, and my traitorous thoughts drift back to the other night and the sight of Graham in nothing but swim trunks, and my skin heats.

"Maybe something to think about?" Jenna murmurs, as if she can read my thoughts.

She chuckles at whatever expression plays out on my face, then pivots on her heel and heads for the door. "Anyhoo, it's almost game time. I'll see you ladies out there."

"Where are you headed?" Adriane asks.

"Oh, you know." Jenna's grin turns serpentine. "I just have a little *business* to attend to before game time." She wiggles her brows, then trills, "Don't be late!"

"She's totally going to hunt Atlas down." Adriane smirks, while I try to hide my frown.

My gaze drifts to the door as she disappears behind it and icy fingers grip my chest. "You think?" I ask, trying to keep my tone even. I tell myself it doesn't matter. He's hers to claim. I talked to the boy all of two or three times. I have no stake in the game. No interest in him at all.

But it feels like a lie.

"I don't just think. I *know*. She's playing that fiddle hard, honey, and there's no way she's going to pass up the opportunity to show him she's painted his number on her face, maybe give him a little kiss for good luck."

My stomach clenches. "It's not like painting his number on her face means anything," I mumble.

"Doesn't it?" Adriane arches a brow, her gaze drifting to the number on mine.

I swallow, wanting to tell her that's different. Graham's my best friend. My ride or die. My day one. I'll always be his biggest fan. But I say nothing. Somehow the words don't quite fit even though they're true, because there is no real way to define what Graham and I have. It's greater than friendship but less than something *more*.

All I know is I can't stop thinking about Jenna flirting with Atlas as I get to my feet and murmur, "Excuse me," then head for the door, telling myself I'm not hoping to see Atlas. I'm only going to wish Graham good luck.

GRAHAM

I grip the shoulder pads underneath my jersey as I kiss my mother on the cheek, then watch as she climbs the stands beside my father. They sit in the lower portion of the stands where there are actual plastic stadium seats instead of the metal bleachers, and are right above the row reserved for staff and on-field help. It's like they're fucking VIP or something.

I turn away from my father's probing gaze and take a step toward the locker room, knowing it's probably time to rally the team before the game when I freeze at the sight of Kenz walking toward me. My gaze tracks her movement, drifting down her body in slow perusal, and I swallow. I've seen Kenz in a million different states of dress over the years, some a lot skimpier than this, but nothing compares to the sight of her in an itty-bitty cheer uniform.

Her long legs eat the ground as she walks and the urge to touch the inch of tan skin below the hem of her cropped top is so strong, my fingers twitch.

She shifts her gaze from where she's scanning the sidelines and sees she has my attention and smiles, offering me a little wave, oblivious to the fact that I've been practically undressing her with my eyes for the past sixty seconds.

She comes to a stop in front of me and the smell of apples drifts toward me. After six years of friendship, I'm close enough to know it's the lotion she uses, but it still makes me want to drink her in all the same, see if she tastes as good as she smells.

My gaze drops to her glossy pink lips, and I'm willing to bet she does.

"You ready?" she asks.

It takes a Herculean effort to raise my eyes to hers. "As ready as I'll ever be, I guess. You just barely missed my father's motivating speech on how if I screw up tonight, I'll destroy any chance I have of a future in football. Oh, and if I were him, I'd play a passing game all night long because if a quarterback doesn't have a good arm, what good is he?"

Her lips quirk. "Dang. I'm sorry I missed it. Sounds super uplifting."

"No worries." I nudge her in the arm and my skin heats at the touch. "I'm sure you'll get a replay next week."

"Well, don't let him get to you. You're going to be amazing."

"Yeah, easier said than done." I exhale a long breath and glance around us. The stands are already packed and it's not even game time. I try to spot the scouts in the throng of people hanging by the fence, but it's too crowded, and I can't make them out. "There's so much riding on tonight's game."

"Maybe there is, but you've got this. You guys had a winning season last year, and you'll have a winning season this year, too."

"Yeah, but we've lost a couple guys, and this is it. One last year to make it all the way."

"Maybe. But you've also gained some."

Atlas.

"He's never played with us before, not in a game, anyway," I tell her.

"No. But he's good, right? Like, really good."

I nod. I hate she knows this and is singing his praises, which is ridiculous. I need to worry about myself, not Atlas. "Yeah, you're right. Peters was second string, anyway. I'm sure we'll crush it with Atlas playing." I reach out and take her hand. "Now, enough about me. Look at you in that cheerleading getup." I raise her arm above her head, giving her a little spin, then whistle. "Damn girl."

She laughs and her cheeks pinken. "Stop."

"How's my girl?" I ask, a smile in my voice.

"Good. A little nervous, I guess. It's been a while. Not that cheerleading is all that hard, but I'm a little paranoid everyone will be staring at me. What if they see my scars?" She runs her hands down her tiny skirt self-consciously, as if doing so will erase the scars altogether.

My gaze instinctively shifts to her left leg where I know there are several jagged scars on the outside of her thigh as a result of the paramedics pulling her from the car. You can't even see them unless she's in a swimsuit.

"Or what if I screw up on one of the tosses and fall?" she continues. "I'm being paranoid, right?"

Kenzie's a flier, and I know that's one of the things she's been nervous about. She's worried it might trigger something in her, and she'll freak out.

I reach out and grip her arms, dipping my head to meet her gaze. "No one's going to be staring. And most of the people in town have seen you at one point or another over the summer. As for your scars, you can't see them, and even if you could, they're fucking beautiful," I say, watching as her eyes soften. "Do you hear me, Kenzie Hart?"

She bites her lower lip, and I can see she's fighting off a smile. "Loud and clear."

"Good," I say, pulling her into a bear hug. "Because I hate to disappoint you, but you're not nearly the freak show you think you are."

"I am excited to see you play. So maybe I'll just focus on that," she tells me, her voice muffled against my chest.

"Now that's a plan I can get behind." I pull back and brush a finger just below the number painted on her cheek and my stomach fucking tumbles. I want so badly for her to be mine. "I see you're sporting the quarterback's number. So, you're rooting for him, huh? I hear he's pretty damn good."

"Is that so?" She grins.

"I mean, so I've been told," I say, unable to hide my smile as I drape an arm over her shoulder, then drop a kiss to the top of her head before I ask, "Your dad here?"

"Not yet. He's working midnights this week, but he said he'd stop by and see me cheer."

I nod and release her just as Atlas walks by me and puts his hand out for me to shake. We slap palms, and my heart beats like a racehorse as I wait for Kenzie to notice him, but her gaze barely shifts his way before she focuses back on me again, that gorgeous smile eating up her face.

To say I'm relieved is an understatement, and I relax a little. Maybe I was being ridiculous the other night. Of course, there was nothing going on between them. He'd given her a ride or two, that was it. And could I blame her for asking him to take her to the crash site? The girl has a point, her dad might be a helicopter parent but sometimes I'm not much better. I worry about her endlessly, and I'd shelter her from the whole world if I could, especially if it meant protecting her and keeping her both safe and happy.

"Hey, bro!" Jace calls, breaking through my train of thought.

I glance up and see him a few paces off, a shit-eating grin on his face. "Kiss your girlfriend goodbye, will ya. It's go-time motherfucker."

I roll my eyes at him and flip him the bird as a blush creeps up Kenzie's neck. "Duty calls. I better go. See you after the game?"

She nods, and I fight the urge to lean down and claim her lips before I take one final lingering look, spin around, and jog off toward the locker rooms.

ATLAS

We're in the bottom of the fourth quarter and South Central is winning by seven. It's been a hell of a game. I've scored three touchdowns myself, two of them by the skin of my teeth considering they weren't the best throws and I had men crawling all over me. It's a miracle they haven't gotten more than two interceptions already. We've been fighting for our lives, but I'll be damned if we're gonna just give them the game.

Graham calls the play. We're fifty yards from the endzone, and he's going to fake to me, then pass to Jace. My chest rises and falls as I try to catch my breath and squint through the sweat dripping in my eyes. "Are you sure you want another pass play?" I ask.

Graham drills me with a look. "Are you the QB, or am I?"

I shrug and roll with it, though the dude hasn't done a running play since the first quarter. I have no idea what the hell he's trying to prove or why he won't move the ball while we're on our feet but it's his funeral. I wouldn't care except he's taking us all under with him.

We break and line up. The offensive lineman hikes the ball and I'm off. There are a couple of guys on my tail, and I don't go very far before I turn around and start looking for Graham to fake it to me. He does but hesitates before throwing the ball to Jace, and when I look across the field, I can see why. He's not in position, and there are men all over him. By this time, three guys cover me, and Graham is two seconds away from being taken down, so I pivot and spin, running as fast as my ass can carry me, getting out of their stronghold. Thank God Graham makes the pass just before a lineman plows into him.

The ball spirals through the air and hits my fingertips. I grapple with it before securing it in my grasp and tuck it into my chest as I run the remaining five yards into the endzone and spike the ball.

Tied game, baby.

By the time we get possession again, there's only a few minutes left on the clock. We need to score or we'll go into overtime, and none of us want extra time at this point. Graham calls the play—he's going to pass it off to me and I'm supposed to lob it to Jace. But the second the ball enters Graham's hands, everything goes wrong.

They come straight for him, and just when he thinks he's going to get sacked, he chucks me the ball. It's a lousy throw, and South Central intercepts, then takes off for the endzone before I lunge at the target with everything I've got.

My fingers latch onto his thighs, and the weight of my body is enough to take him down. The ball slips from his grip, bouncing on the turf, and I leap forward, picking it up. I pivot on my feet and fly, spinning when a man comes at me, leaving him with nothing. I dodge one more opponent on my way down the field, and then I'm free, feet flying across the turf, heart pounding, the crowd screaming in the background until I race across those lines to score the winning touchdown.

Jace flies at me, lifting me off my feet before planting me back on the ground. Teagan and Knox smack my helmet and several others congratulate me as I make my way down the field toward the spot where Graham still stands, his helmet now wedged beneath his arm. He lifts his chin and I come to a stop, taking a moment to catch my breath as he says, "Good game, man. I was worried about how you'd mesh with us, but you certainly proved yourself tonight."

He slaps me on the back, and I grin as I slide off my helmet. "I appreciate it."

"I'll meet ya in there," he says, then he turns and I see him stop on the sidelines where his father waits. I watch as he leans in, allowing his dad to speak in his ear while longing wrenches through my chest. What I wouldn't give to have my own father here, watching me, cheering me on and lending me advice.

Hell, I'd give just about anything to have him act like a grown-up for once in his life instead of the child.

I swallow and push the thought away, because there's no point in wishing for something that'll never happen when my eyes lock on Kenzie's. Her pom poms hang by her side, and she wears a smile so bright it rivals the stadium lights above. Her dark, wavy hair is in a ponytail which falls down her back, and she's wearing one of those ridiculous bows the girls wear. When her gaze catches mine, I boldly stare back, allowing my gaze to linger a little more.

In a Riverside cheer uniform, she's all long, lean legs, tan skin, and curves in the right places. I promised myself I wouldn't look at her, not like this, but I'm high on our win, and though our victory is only for tonight, it somehow feels like a pass. So, I take my fill until she bites her lip and tears her gaze away, and I make my way off the field.

An hour later, I'm showered, dressed in fresh clothes, and on my way to Crow's Creek at Jace and Teagan's insistence. Even Graham told me I should come, so I caved. It'll be good for the team, I told myself. It has nothing to do with the fact I'm 99 percent sure Mackenzie will be there.

Nothing at all.

I park my bike at the bottom of the hill like last time. Only tonight as I make my way up the bluff, it's different. Several cars are parked by the pull-off, and I can feel a charge in the air, hear the laughter from above, and see the flicker of firelight.

Everyone cheers when they see me. A large group of my teammates together with a handful of girls sit around a fire on a circle of large stones, while several other groups of people mingle about the field, lost in their own conversations, only pausing to see what the commotion is about.

Jace whistles, and lifts his beer in the air, light flickering over his face as he says, "It's the man of the hour. Atlas, get your fine ass up here."

I step out of the shadows and into the firelight and accept a beer from Knox, though I have zero intention of drinking it.

"What's up fellas?" I say, making my rounds, offering each of them a fist bump or a slap to the back. From the looks of it, a few of them are already half lit, which is impressive considering the game hasn't been over for more than forty-five minutes.

Jenna Barnes appears out of nowhere, and I offer her a smile, even though I'm not interested, and she slips an arm around my waist. She leans toward me to whisper in my ear, and it's not lost on me the way she's pressing her chest into my side, before she purrs as she congratulates me on a good game.

The guys around me all snicker and laugh. Teagan and Jace start talking about one of the tight ends on the other team while Jenna continues to cling to me like a leech, and I scan the faces around me. I recognize most of them, but there's only one I care to see.

I feel Mackenzie before I see her. It's like an electric current creeping over the surface of my skin—both pleasure and pain. When I turn toward the sensation, I find her perched beside Graham, who currently has one arm wrapped around her like he owns her.

The inexplicable urge to rip that arm off catches me off guard, and I scold myself for it. As our quarterback, we kind of need him to be able to throw a ball.

I arch a brow as Mackenzie's eyes meet mine, staring pointedly at Graham's arm, and even from here, I can see her blush.

A smile snakes its way onto my lips, and I know I'm in trouble, because the red blooming in her cheeks might be my favorite fucking color in the world. So, I make up my mind and silence the voice inside of me telling me I have no time for women. Because before this night is through, I'll get Doll alone.

Tonight, we won, and I'm all about celebrating.

Tonight, I get a pass.

Chapter 15

MACKENZIE

I slowly sip my beer and listen in on the conversations behind me, while absorbing Graham's presence beside me. He's just like my favorite cashmere sweater; warm and comforting. More kids have arrived since we first got here, and there are now about sixty of us scattered in varying groups throughout the field. With so many people here, I shouldn't feel Atlas's eyes on me, but I do. Every once in a while, I allow myself a glance in his direction and our gazes lock, my skin catches fire, and I glance away again because looking into Atlas's eyes is like staring into the sun—both beautiful and dangerous—and I'm not sure I'm strong enough to risk it.

"Wanna go for a walk?" Graham's voice startles me from my thoughts.

When I glance up at him, I see he's watching me with those bright green eyes, and I wonder for how long. I nod, needing to get out of here, away from Atlas's burning gaze and the way it makes me feel—like there's a livewire underneath the surface of my skin.

Like talking to him is a good idea when I know it's not.

I push myself up while Graham grips my hand, helping me. I've only had half a beer, so I'm level-headed and steady on my feet for now, though I'm not used to drinking so I know if I have more than one, I'll have a killer buzz.

He guides me away from the group among the catcalls of his teammates, to which he offers an obscene gesture, and they laugh even harder. I'm tempted to glance back, to see if Atlas is one of them.

To see if he's watching, or if he cares I'm leaving with Graham.

But I don't. It doesn't matter. Atlas Scott is off-limits. And even if he weren't, he's not interested in me. The mere fact that he and Jenna have been all over each other all night is proof enough of that.

Graham slides his hand down to mine and steers me toward a little path that borders the woods and the hay field. "It's a perfect night," he says, and he's right. Winning the game, being here with our friends. Being away from my dad's overprotective gaze. It *is* a perfect night.

I follow suit and glance up to the sky where the stars shine like diamonds.

"How are you doing?" he asks when I say nothing. "It's not too much is it? You've been quiet."

He glances down at me, his forehead creased in concern, and I wave him off. "Just lost in my thoughts, I guess." I offer him a smile. "I'm good, I swear."

"You sure? 'Cause I can take you home if you want. We could hang out, watch a movie."

"I'm sure," I say at the same time he pulls us around a corner, underneath the branches of a large willow tree, and I gasp. At least a dozen flickering candles surround a blanket with pillows and cushions. It's beautiful and . . . romantic.

I peer up at him as Jace and Teagen's teasing lingers in the back of my mind, along with a flicker of doubt. Does Graham . . . He's not . . . Of course Graham doesn't have feelings for me. Does he?

I want to ask, but I'm too afraid of the answer.

I glance back at the spread where a large lantern sits beside a blanket, along with a red polka dotted box I'd recognize anywhere, and I forget all about how romantic the setup is as I point to it. "Are those . . . ?"

"Better Berries chocolate covered strawberries? Yes, ma'am."

I let out a little squeal and hurry to the giant cushy pillow beside the box of berries as Graham's laughter echoes behind me. I waste no time, sliding off first the bow, then the lid. Twelve plump strawberries encased in milk chocolate and mini chips stare back at me.

"Best. Friend. Ever." I grin up at Graham as he makes his way toward me, still chuckling at my enthusiasm, and takes a seat beside me. "What's the occasion?" I ask.

"It was your first week back at school, first game cheering, and you took it all like a champ. Plus, I kind of felt bad about acting like I did the other day at my house."

"Well, I'm glad to be back, and this is the best peace offering ever. Although, an unnecessary one." I scoot closer to him and shift to sit on my knees. "If anything, we should celebrate the fact my father is working the late shift tonight. Otherwise, I wouldn't have been able to come."

"That's definitely worth celebrating."

I smile and shake my head, wondering how I got so lucky when I got Graham. "Well, you sure know how to make a girl feel special." I lift one from the box and hold it out for him, laughing as I wave it in front of his lips, and wait for him to take a bite.

Once he does, I polish it off, enjoying every morsel before I lick my fingers and say, "You played a good game."

Graham groans and ruffles a hand through his hair. "My father would beg to differ."

"Did he say something to you?"

"He basically told me Atlas saved my ass tonight. And, you know, he's not wrong. I let him get in my head about making sure I had a good passing game, and it made me rigid. I made some crappy throws and even crappier calls. I think even Coach was a little pissed. I'm just lucky we won, or he would've given me hell. I guess I have Atlas to thank for that, 'cause I sure as hell can't claim this win."

I frown. "I think you're being hard on yourself."

"Maybe." Graham sighs and stares down at me, and I can tell there's something else, so I ask, "What is it?"

"What do you think about going to homecoming together?"

The change in subject takes me off guard, and the question about Graham's feelings toward me returns, though I'm probably being ridiculous. We went to homecoming together last year and had a blast. It was only a month before the accident and everything changed. What they say about friends making the best dates is true. But we haven't even discussed it before now, and because it's our senior year, I guess I assumed he'd want to go with someone special; someone he's interested in as more than friends.

Unless that someone is me.

"Are you sure you don't want to go with someone you like instead?" I say, testing the waters. "Don't get me wrong, going with a friend is amazing, but since this is our last homecoming, I just thought you might have someone you want to pursue."

"What if I want both?" I frown as he reaches a hand out, raking it through the back of my hair as he stares into my eyes, and my heart starts to race. His lips part and he leans closer, until I can see the pulse jumping in his neck. "Kenz, I—"

"Dude!" Teagan tears through the trees, and I jump, a startled yelp escaping my lips. "Oh, crap, man. Sorry," he says as he takes in the scene before him.

"Can I help you?" Graham grinds out.

"Yeah, I hate to interrupt, but you better help us, bro. Knox is trying to get his keys and he's had way too many and is sloppy as shit. Jace said he can sleep it off at the cabin, but we need help getting his sorry ass down there. Everyone else is either female or had too much to drink to be of any use."

Graham pinches the bridge of his nose, muttering a curse under his breath, before he glares over at Teagan again. "Seriously, dude? Now?"

"Er. I mean, I can come back in a minute. Is that enough time to . . ." He motions between us, and based on Graham's expression, I think he might kill him.

"You're an idiot," he says, resignation laced through his voice.

"Noted." Teagan grins.

With a sigh, Graham turns toward me. "I'll be right back, 'kay?"

I nod, heart pounding as he steps back and disappears with Teagan through the woods. My thoughts race with what might have happened had Teagan not shown up. Was Graham going to kiss me? Because I am 99 percent sure he was.

Did I want him to?

I press a hand to my stomach as I replay the last five minutes, the moment when his eyes locked on mine and the whole world stopped spinning. Kissing Graham would be like everything else between us. Easy. Effortless. Most definitely worth it.

But do I really want that when it might be at the expense of our friendship?

I'm not sure.

Shaking my head, I laugh at myself. Maybe that half a beer was too much after all. Because as close as Graham and I are, and as much as I know he cares for me, we're only friends. Best friends. And nothing would ever change that, nor would I want it to because I love him. I *need* him. A life without Graham would be a much darker place, and I want no part of that kind of world, which means protecting what we have at all costs.

Time passes, and it feels like I've been waiting forever. The distant sounds of the party trickle through the trees, and I contemplate heading back when leaves crunch behind me and I turn, my gaze darting along the tree line, wondering if it's Graham.

A shadow steps out from the trees, and I instantly know it's not him. I recognize the silhouette, the sharp lines, and slow, confidant stride, like a lion stalking its prey.

He moves closer, into the light of the moon and I take in his dark hair and equally dark eyes as his gaze flickers over the candles and pillows. He lets out a low whistle and says, "Wow. That's some setup you got there."

I swallow, glancing around as my cheeks heat.

"Did Golden Boy leave you already?" he asks when I say nothing.

I roll my eyes, trying my best to hide how much his presence affects me. "He had to go help Knox. Have you been hanging around, waiting for the first moment I'm alone? Because that's creepy."

He tips his head back and laughs, which annoys me. "And what if I have?" he asks, shoving his hands in his pockets, watching me as his answer registers.

I swallow. "If you wanted to talk to me so badly, you had all day at school. In fact, you've pretty much ignored me since Tuesday."

"Aw, did you miss me, doll? Don't get attached. I'm not that guy."

"Really? What a shock." I say, resisting the urge to roll my eyes.

So, this is how he's going to play it. Back to cynical Atlas. The boy I sat with on a bench outside a shopping center, the one who shared things about himself, is gone.

"Is that what you tell Jenna?" I ask, because I can't seem to help myself.

Atlas draws closer and takes a seat beside me on one of the cushions while I pick at a loose thread like it's the most fascinating thing in the world. "You think I want Jenna?"

"Don't you?" My gaze slides over him, to his T-shirt and jeans and the tattoos covering his arm. "She's captain of the cheerleading team, gorgeous, and all over you. Most guys want that."

"Not me." He shakes his head.

"So, what is it you want?"

A secret smile curls the corners of his mouth, but he says nothing, so I change the subject. "You played good tonight."

"I did, didn't I?"

I roll my eyes. "So modest."

My gaze drops to the unopened can of beer by his feet. He'd carried it with him. "I'm surprised you're not drinking like everyone else."

"And why's that?"

I shrug, feeling restless and needing some way to expel my energy. "To celebrate, I guess? Most of the guys like to party after the games because they worked hard all week."

"Not me." He reaches into his pocket and pulls out a pack of cigarettes, then shakes one out. Lifting it to his nose, he inhales before he slides it behind his ear.

"What's the deal with that?" I ask, motioning toward it.

"What?"

I huff out a breath. "The cigarettes? Any time we're not in class, I see you with one, but never actually see you smoke it."

"Does that bother you?"

"It's weird, right?"

"I don't know. Is it?"

I growl at the non-answer, which only makes him laugh.

"If you're just going to talk in short, clipped answers, you might as well leave."

"Oh, it's like that, is it?" His smile widens. "Does every conversation we have need to be deep?"

"Of course not."

But maybe I kind of liked getting to know him the other night. And, yeah, I want more, even if I shouldn't.

He bends one knee and casually drapes his arm over it as he snatches the cigarette from behind his ear and stares at it a moment. "You don't ever see me smoking one, because I don't smoke."

"But—"

"It's a reminder."

"A reminder?"

He nods. "Of the kind of man I don't want to be. Booze. Cigarettes. Weed. Pills. Doesn't matter. They're all vices, and I refuse to partake. Hell, even women can be a vice," he says, and the way he looks at me makes my cheeks heat.

"Because of your dad?"

His mouth flattens into a thin line before he says, "I refuse to be like him. But at the end of the day, I'm his son. We share blood."

I want to tell him he's not. That in just the short amount of time I've spoken to him, I know without a doubt, he's nothing like his father. He's amazing, maybe one of the strongest people I've ever met.

"Shit." He runs a hand over the back of his neck and laughter rumbles from his chest. "I don't know why I'm telling you all of this. I don't talk about this stuff with anyone."

I swallow, because I like being the person he talks to. More than I should.

"I don't mind," I tell him.

"Well, you should."

My forehead creases. "Why?"

"Because this"—he motions between us—"you and I can't happen."

"My father—"

"Your father isn't the only reason, doll. I don't do relationships."

I hang my head, hating the disappointment settling in the pit of my stomach. "Why do you call me that?"

"Doll?" he asks.

"First it was princess, but now it's doll. Why?"

He's quiet a moment before he says, "From everything I know about you—being the chief's daughter, living in this big gorgeous house, cheerleader, best friends with Golden Boy, I assumed you were entitled and spoiled. Maybe even a little sheltered. Then I quickly realized that didn't quite fit. I'm not so sure you're any of those things anymore. But it's become abundantly clear that everyone around you treats you like porcelain, like at any moment you might break or fall apart. Hell, I even think they have you believing it."

My breath catches in my throat, and I gaze up at him. They're the truest words I've heard in a long time. And I hate them. I don't want to be fragile or scared. I want to be strong and unyielding. Unbreakable.

I glance away from him again and lean back on my arms, staring out into the field, wondering if that's how Graham sees me, too, before I realize he'll be mad to find Atlas here once he returns.

"Anyway," Atlas clears his throat, interrupting my thoughts, "part of the reason I wanted to talk to you was to tell you I'm sorry if I got you into trouble with your dad."

My brows rise, surprised by his apology. "It's not your fault. If you remember correctly, it was me who asked *you* to give me a ride, not the other way around."

He shrugs. "Still, he was obviously pissed for reasons I can and can't understand. I think he babies you, but the fact is, I probably wouldn't want my daughter hanging out with me, either."

I ignore the babying comment, focusing on the one regarding him instead. "My father worries, and out of that worry comes judgment. But that doesn't make it okay."

"Maybe not. But he's not wrong about me."

I take him in, my gaze trailing over the ink on his arm. There are so many tattoos I can't make one from the other, but I want to. Part of me wants to lean in and study them like a Picasso painting, trace the lines and curves of them like I'm reading braille. Like maybe I can understand this beautiful broken boy by the artwork etched into his skin.

He's wearing a black T-shirt and dark jeans, and when he leans back on his hands, completely at ease, his biceps flex from supporting his weight. A lock of hair falls over his eyes, and his gaze never wavers from mine, even during my obvious perusal of him.

This boy is so damn gorgeous it makes my head spin, and as much as he wants me to believe he's no good, I know the truth. I feel it in my soul. Sure, he has a past, but who doesn't? What I see is a genuine human being that's been stuck in survival mode for so long he's not sure how to break free from it. Someone who wants to be better and is doing his damndest to ensure he makes good on that promise to himself.

I'm not sure why he allows others to define him when he so clearly isn't the bad boy everyone makes him out to be. Maybe he finds comfort in the lies. I don't know.

My guess is he uses the bad-boy schtick as a wall he resurrects between himself and anything that can hurt him, because he's already been wounded enough by the people who should love him the most.

It makes me want to bust down those walls down. Break through his tough shell to the soft underbelly of the boy I see before me.

"I think he's wrong," I whisper.

Atlas swallows and averts his gaze, and the movement of his Adam's apple draws my eye. "Did you remember anything else?"

I accept his deflection and shake my head as a fresh wave of disappointment washes over me. "No. But the more I think about it, the more I believe that man I saw . . . he's linked somehow. There's a significance there I can't understand, but I'm certain it's a piece of the puzzle."

"Did you ask your dad about it?"

"No."

He meets my eyes again. "Why not?"

"He doesn't like talking about the accident," I admit.

"Too damn bad," he grinds out.

I flinch. "That's harsh, considering his wife died and he almost lost his daughter."

"I'll give him that, but people cope in different ways, and maybe your way is different. Maybe you need to talk about it."

He's right. Boy, is he right. And maybe I should blame my father for keeping so quiet, but I can't because I understand the pain of his loss all too well.

But I don't want to talk about my father. Or Graham. Or anything else. I want to talk about Atlas, and for all I know, hidden in the shadows of this willow tree might be the last chance I get for a while seeing as how I can't be seen with him in public, or risk my father's wrath.

A trill of laughter echoes in the distance. It sounds like Jenna, and I briefly wonder who she's talking to in his absence.

"If Jenna's not your type, who is?" I ask.

"Don't." His gaze shifts to my mouth, his tone a warning, as butterflies swarm my stomach.

"Don't what?"

His jaw tightens. "You know what you're doing, doll?"

"I haven't a clue what you're talking about. What am I doing?"

He leans into me, and the scent of cedar and pine assaults my senses. "Playing with fire," he whispers, then brushes his lips over mine.

His mouth is soft, a teasing caress as he takes his time, like he's testing the waters to see if I pull away.

I should.

Every fiber inside my body tells me to leave now and return to the party to wait for Graham. Because there's no way I'll want to stop at one kiss. We've barely gotten started, and I already want more.

Tiny firecrackers come alive in my chest, shooting sparks through my veins, my bones, my limbs as I reach up and grip the soft material of his shirt. His hands tangle in my hair, taking control and tilting my head just enough to gain better access to my mouth, while his tongue lightly brushes mine.

A soft moan rattles behind my ribs. A kiss from Atlas is everything I thought it would be and then some—equal parts rough and hot and soft at the same time, and all I want is *more, more, more.*

His stubble scrapes against my chin as he presses me back against the blanket while continuing his assault on my mouth. His biceps cage me in, and his chest pins me to the ground so I can feel the beat of his racing heart.

He growls as he nips my bottom lip, and my body comes alive. Parts of me I never knew existed awaken. My heart pounds in my ears. Fire licks in my veins. And just when I think I'm about to lose my mind, he pulls away, staring into my eyes as I try and catch my breath.

My head spins. My body aches for more, and I'm about to ask him why he stopped when a prickling awareness creeps up my spine. Someone is watching.

Reality sinks in, and I think of Graham.

Please don't let it be him.

My head jerks up, and I sigh in relief when I see Teagan and Jace hovering just behind us.

Though I'm not sure these two are much better.

"Please, by all means, don't let us interrupt," Jace says, motioning between us.

Chapter 16

ATLAS

After Teagan and Jace give me and Kenzie shit for making out, I say my goodbyes and leave. I can still recall the flicker of disappointment in her eyes. Though I know she wanted me to stay longer, I also know it would not have led anywhere good. Teagan and Jace already caught us making out, which means Graham will find out soon enough, and the last thing I want is for a girl to affect the team.

Besides, had I stayed, Mackenzie would've wanted to return to the party eventually, and she's not the type of girl who makes out with a guy and then pretends it didn't happen. She'd want to sit with me, maybe hold my hand, or expect me to sling an arm over her shoulders. Stake my claim after the hottest fucking kiss of my life. Hell, if I know. But the truth is it doesn't matter what she wants because I can't give it to her. I don't know how to be that guy even if I want to be.

I hadn't expected to go to the field party tonight and make out with her. After her father caught us outside the restaurant the other night, I thought she'd stay as far away from me as possible. Chief Hart hadn't exactly been happy to see us together, and I have no doubt she got quite the lecture on the way home about my reputation, my junkie father, and all the reasons she should stay away. People like Chief Hart are nothing if not predictable. They don't believe in second chances or redemption, not really. Which is just as well because I need to keep my distance.

My focus is football. Period.

But now I've gone and fucked it all up by kissing her. Threw caution to the wind along with my inhibitions. All because I had a good game. I picked up Graham's slack tonight, and my performance hadn't gone unnoticed. Coach pulled me aside after our victory to inform me a recruiter from the University of Southern California had approached him.

USC has one of the top football programs in the country. I'd be lucky to get an offer from them, and the fact they asked after me, well, it made everything seem possible. Like the years of hard work on the field have paid off. Like I might succeed and make something of myself.

I tear through the streets of Riverside, heading toward home, aware of the scent of apple blossom that clings to my skin—Mackenzie's scent—along with the sweet taste of her on my lips: chocolate and strawberries.

She'd surprised me tonight. Hell, she surprises me every time I talk to her, and each time I push her away, she draws me back in—challenges me. And, yeah, maybe jealousy reared its head as I watched Graham with his arm around her staking his claim. And maybe it drove me to seek her out. Graham might be my cousin and a stand-up dude, but he knows shit about what Mackenzie wants. What she needs. I've known her all of a week and even I can see that much. She'd been sheltered and put in a box on a shelf her whole life, especially since the accident. What she needs now is to be set free, and Graham is never going to do that for her because he'll never be able to do anything but see her as this fragile doll he needs to protect. The truth is, she's a hell of a lot stronger than anyone gives her credit for.

There was certainly nothing fragile about the kiss we shared or the way she pressed herself up against me like she'd die if I didn't touch her.

I round the bend, making the turn toward home when red and blue lights come into view, blinking and rotating on the street in front of our house. It's like looking into a kaleidoscope.

My stomach sinks. I know those lights. I've seen them before, and as I approach our place, my fears are confirmed. They're coming from our house.

All thoughts of Mackenzie vanish as I pass the cruisers and pull into the driveway behind my father's beater car—the old Ford Fiesta with the smashed back bumper Pops never got fixed, probably because he'd been drunk when he dented it.

I park and rip my helmet off at the same time two police officers escort my father out of the house in cuffs. Jumping to my feet, I hurry through the yard as I make my way toward him. "What happened?" I bark.

"Step back, son." One of the officer's stretches his hand out as if to keep me back, as if I'm a threat.

"What did you do?" I demand as I stare at my old man, but he just blinks over at me, his familiar gaze glazed and unfocused.

He's wasted. Big surprise.

My stomach twists as I turn to one of the officers. "Can somebody tell me what the hell is going on?"

"Hey, hey, hey." Another officer appears out of nowhere and comes to my side, grabbing my arm and guiding me away from where they're shoving my father in the back of a cruiser. "Calm down, son."

I glance down at his hold on my arm and yank it from his grip. My gaze slides to his chest where a dozen ribbons adorn the spot above his badge. I have no idea what they mean, but as my gaze shifts and focuses on his name, I freeze. Because it's him. Of course, it is. Chief Hart.

"I just want to know what's going on. That's all, man," I say through gritted teeth, waving toward the officers as they shut the door on the cop car, obscuring my father from view. "That's my pops. Don't you think I have a right to know where you're taking him and why?"

"We have a warrant to arrest your father for forged prescriptions. Once we book him and get him settled, he'll be able to call. You can come in and talk to him, discuss bond."

I rake a hand through my hair and stare at the back of my father's head through the window. Piece of shit. Obviously, I always knew he did shady stuff to get drugs, but I guess I hoped he wasn't dumb enough to get caught.

"How long will they keep him?"

"It's hard to say. But is there someone else we can call? Your mother, perhaps?" he asks, and I wonder if he already knows the answer.

"No." I shake my head.

He stares at me for a moment, and I can tell he recognizes me, but he's sure as shit acting like he doesn't. "How old are you, son?"

"Are we doing this now? Pretending like you have no clue who I am?"

"I'm not sure I know what you're talking about. Why don't you just answer the question?"

A bitter laugh bubbles from my lips. This is rich, considering he just caught me on a bench with his daughter a few nights ago.

But whatever. I'll play his game.

"Seventeen," I hiss. "I turn eighteen in a couple months."

He nods like he expected as much, which of course he did. The fucker probably knows everything there is to know about me. Probably did an in-depth background search the moment he saw me with his daughter.

"So, you're a minor?"

I scoff. Is this guy for real? "In two months, I'll be eighteen."

"Still. I can't leave you alone."

"You've got to be fucking kidding me."

He stares at me, his eyes cold and hard, bottomless pits like the sky above us. I can tell he hates my guts, loathes me even, though he doesn't even know me. I wonder what he'd think if I told him I had his little princess wrapped around me as I shoved my tongue down her throat. Maybe I'd give him a visual of how she moaned into my mouth just for kicks.

"Maybe you've never been taught this, but the way we speak and present ourselves to the world"—his gaze flickers down my body, seemingly unimpressed as he fixates on the ink over my arm—"reflects who we are as people. The kind of person we want to be. Now," he drawls, before he reaches into his front pocket and slides out a pen and a small notepad. "Tell me who I can call for you."

My lips twist into a sneer as I say the name of the only other person who even knows or cares that I'm alive. "Cal Scott."

Chief Hart stills and his eyes narrow. "You know Cal?"

"He's my uncle."

His brows arch, and I enjoy the surprise in his gaze. The idiot must not have put two-and-two together.

"Your uncle," he repeats, and I nod. I can practically see the wheels spinning as this new piece of information sinks in. "I know his place. I'll take you there."

"Is that really necessary?"

"As I said, you're a minor. I can't just leave you here. Why don't you go inside and pack a bag. Your dad won't be home tonight. Then I'll drop you off at the Scott place after."

My jaw tightens, and I rack my brain for a way to get out of this, but I can't find one. Chief Hart doesn't strike me as the kind of man that bends the rules, especially for the likes of me.

I turn and head toward the house, up the rickety wooden steps and inside. I pick my way through the living room, seeing it through fresh eyes. The shaggy, stained carpet. Beer cans scattered on the counter and beside the couch. Empty food cartons littering the stove. I cringe thinking of Hart getting an eyeful. I'm sure the thought of Mackenzie hanging out with me makes his blood boil. I'm both glad and ashamed at the same time.

I head to my bedroom and grab the worn duffle bag from my closet, then begin removing clothes from drawers and shoving them inside, along with my shaving kit. There's not much, so I finish quickly, then glance around me. I can't say I'll miss this place; we've only been here a month, but I don't exactly relish the thought of anyone having to take in my sorry ass out of obligation. It doesn't sit right with me, and I sure as shit assume it won't sit right with Graham if he has any idea what went down with his girl tonight. Regardless, I decide to talk to Uncle Cal about it, convince him I'll be fine on my own until Pops gets home. It's not like his presence here does me any good. Cal can drop me back off here in the morning with no one the wiser.

I take one last look around, and for reasons I can't explain, the memory of Mackenzie's lips and the feel of her hands on my skin, hits me like an anvil to the chest. I could easily sink under the weight of her if I let myself. Tonight, I saw what it would be like to get lost in her, to forget what I'm fighting for. But the image of my father in cuffs and the state of our home is a harsh reminder of the realities that lie ahead for someone like me if I don't make something of myself. Without a football scholarship, I don't go to college. Which is why I can't allow Kenzie to get a hold on me. Not if I want to go places. And I'll be damned if I turn into my father.

I close my bedroom door and head back outside where Chief Hart is waiting, hands on his hips as he glances around the place with a gaze that says exactly what he's thinking—that my father and I are trash and arresting him was just like taking out the garbage.

I sling my bag over my shoulder, noting the fact that the cruiser carrying my father has already left. It's just us now.

"You ready?" Hart asks, his tone gruff.

I nod, saying nothing as he directs me to take the back seat instead of the front, like I'm a fucking criminal.

"I called ahead." He eyes me in the rearview mirror as he speaks. "They're expecting us."

I want to ask about my uncle's reaction to finding out my father got arrested, but I don't. I wonder if Uncle Cal regrets finding us a place here and getting me a spot on the team, but the last thing I want to do is give Hart the pleasure of knowing I'm worried about being a burden. Besides, I learned a long time ago not to ask questions I might not want the answers to.

The cruiser pulls out of our driveway and Hart steers us down the winding country roads of Riverside until the stretches of farmland disappear and the neighborhoods grow bigger and more crowded. I recognize the street my aunt and uncle live on by the perfectly manicured lawns maintained by sprinkler systems, the stained concrete driveways, and four-car garages. Most of these houses, if not all, boast large fenced-in swimming pools in the back yards, a luxury for a locale that only sees three months of hot weather. Funny how we're only a little more than ten minutes from my place, yet we might as well be ten hours they're so different.

He comes to a stop in front of the brick monstrosity I know is Uncle Cal's place. I haven't been here since the night Pops and I moved into our new digs and he wanted to make sure I'd settled in, and had everything I needed. I didn't feel comfortable with the luxury of the place then, and I don't feel comfortable with it now as I follow Hart up the sidewalk and to the large double doors.

They swing open before we even knock, and my uncle is standing there in flannel pants and a T-shirt. Clearly, he'd woken up to take Hart's call, which makes me feel even worse.

His shrewd eyes observe me as he and Hart exchange a few words. "Thank you, Chief. I'll take it from here," he says before Hart leaves, and I'm standing there alone.

"Come on in." Uncle Cal places a hand on my shoulder and guides me inside before he takes my bag and pulls me into his arms for a brief hug. "You played a great game tonight, son." He leans back and meets my eyes. "I watched you with pride. I'm just sorry it had to be sullied with all this."

My stomach clenches. "Thank you, sir," I say, hating the threat of tears stinging the back of my eyes.

What in the actual hell?

"You know, I thought getting you guys a place and bringing you here might knock some sense into him, and maybe the change would do your father some good. Guess I was wrong, but it sure looks like it's going to serve you well."

I nod and straighten, pulling my shit together. "I appreciate the chance you've given me here, and I won't screw it up."

"I'm sure you won't." He smiles, and I wonder what it would be like to have him as my father. Someone who'd give me opportunities at every turn. Someone who'd support and encourage me instead of making life more difficult.

"Why don't I show you to your room?" He starts up the vast stairway, with me following behind. "Your Aunt Sheila's in bed, and Graham still hasn't gotten home yet. Off celebrating, I guess," he says as he guides me down the hall. "Not that he has much worth celebrating tonight," he mumbles under his breath. "Here you go." He pauses in front of the doorway to a spare bedroom and waves me inside.

My gaze makes quick work of the space. The walls are painted a grayish brown with big windows framed by dark curtains. A huge leather upholstered bed sits in the center of the room—twice the size of the one I'm used to. Rich mahogany furniture fills the rest of the space, and I can just barely make out what appears to be my own bathroom.

It's by far the nicest place I've ever stayed in.

"Make yourself comfortable. It's late, so we can talk in the morning. In the meantime, shower, get some rest, whatever you need, and I'll see you in the morning." He smiles before he closes the door, and I'm left alone, glancing at my surroundings and wondering how the hell I got here.

Oddly grateful he doesn't want to talk tonight, I carry my bag to the bed where I take a seat on the edge of it, the mattress dipping with my weight. It's soft, the comforter buttery under my fingertips; it's unlike anything I'm used to. Everything in here looks pristine and new. Part of me is afraid to touch anything for fear I'll sully it.

Kind of like Kenzie. Yet that didn't stop me.

I smooth a hand over the soft blanket beneath me. Maybe staying here won't be so bad, after all. Uncle Cal didn't seem too bent out of shape about it, and it might give me time to pick his brain. To see if he has any tips or advice on how I can improve my game.

A couple of days, I tell myself. Then if Pops isn't out, I'll convince him to let me go home.

Chapter 17

GRAHAM

Jace, Teagan, and I head back up to the field through the woods behind the house. It's the quickest way to Kenzie, and I don't want to leave her waiting any longer than necessary. I'm anxious to get back to her and I've been cursing the fact I had to leave. But the guys needed my help to usher Knox down to the cabin. More like carry him down. The stupid ass could barely walk and once we got him there, he kept messing around until we finally got him settled on the couch with a glass of water and some aspirin.

The bastard owes me big time.

The moonlight filters through the trees as we grow closer, and the sky brightens as we step out into the clearing. The candles and blankets are up ahead, only a few feet away. I can make out the flickering light from here and head toward it with a singular determination, my mind set on picking things back up with Kenzie when Jace and Teagan stop in their tracks in front of me.

Teagan covers his mouth with a fist and mutters, "Oh shit," while Jace hisses out a breath.

My head jerks up, and the bottom drops out from under me.

The world and everything in it spin.

Only yards away Atlas is pressing Kenzie back on the blanket, his mouth on hers.

"Gra—" Jace starts, but I don't wanna hear it.

I spin around before he can even get my name out and storm toward the bonfire. It's all I can do to keep my cool and fight the urge to stomp over to Kenzie like a caveman and throw her over my shoulder. Or punch Atlas in the face. Both sound pretty enticing at the moment.

"Hey," Jace grips my arm, whipping me around, and it takes a monumental effort not to glance back at the cozy couple again.

"What do you want?" I snap, even though this isn't his fault. Hell, he and Teagen spent an hour helping me lug all this shit out to the field in a bid to try and impress her.

"You all right?" There's so much concern in Teagan's eyes when he asks, I could drown in it.

"Yeah. I'm fine, bro," I say, my tone hard.

"We're here for you, man." Jace squeezes my shoulder, but I shrug him off.

"I said I'm good. It doesn't matter."

Jace nods, his expression tight, but Teagen doesn't look as convinced. "Is this gonna be a problem?" he asks. "Because the team . . ."

That's what he's worried about? The motherfucking team?

"The team will be fine. I'll handle it."

"No drama on the field," Jace says.

"No drama," I repeat because even through my anger, I know he's right. I struggled enough as it was tonight. The last thing I need is for this to affect my playing or I'll find myself in a nice warm seat on the bench.

I leave them standing there to gawk all they want while I head toward the bonfire where I sink down like a rock in front of the fire, letting it thaw all the numb places inside me as I try and wipe the image of Kenzie kissing Atlas from my head.

Forty minutes. That's all it took for Atlas to take up residence on *my* spot—the one I painstakingly set up for Kenzie. The one where I planned to finally kiss her, to tell her how I feel, like I was in some cheesy-ass teen romance flick. Instead, all my plans have been blown to shreds, and here I am sitting alone while another guy steals my girl.

Not five minutes pass before Teagan and Jace return to the fire with Kenzie following behind. I wish I could say I'm glad, but I'm not. I'm not ready to see her just yet.

My gaze travels the area behind her in search of Atlas, but I don't find him, and I wonder if they ran him off or if he left on his own accord like a coward. I have yet to spend some time reconnecting with my cousin outside of football, so I don't know what his intentions are. Whether he's a stand-up dude with a rough past, or a generally shitty human being like his reputation suggests. But what I do know is I'll be damned if I let him hurt her.

She glances over at me and smiles, and my heart wrenches at the sight of her swollen lips. I swallow and glance away again, focusing on the bonfire just as Jace passes by me with a beer.

"Hey, I'll take another," I say, and he tosses me one. I hardly drank anything earlier because I wanted to keep a level head for Kenz, but that ship has sailed. No reason for me to stay sober now and a whole hell of a lot of reasons for me to get wasted.

I crack the beer open, feeling Kenzie's gaze on the side of my face as I tip the can back and chug. I drain it in less than a minute, then rise to my feet and grab another.

"Hey, are you okay?" she asks, and I can hear the concern etched in her voice.

When her slender fingers reach out and wrap around my forearm, I grip the can tighter, thinking of how her hands were all over Atlas just minutes ago, and take another sip.

"I'm fine," I grind out.

"Don't you think you should take it easy?"

"It's a party," I snap.

She draws back at my sharp tone, and I meet her eyes for the first time. I want to drown in them, they're so blue.

Maybe it would put me out of my misery. Because wanting Kenz is both the best and worst parts of my life.

Instead, I drown my sorrows in cheap cans of beer and avoid eye contact with her, because talking to her now would only cause me to say something I'd no doubt regret.

A couple of hours later, Kenzie and Jace drag me up the stairs in my house.

"Shit, man. How much do you fucking weigh?" Jace mutters as he braces me with his shoulder.

I burst out laughing, and they shush me, which only makes me laugh harder. When we make it to the top, I slump against the wall and everything spins.

"Get up, fat ass!" Jace punches me in the ribs, but I barely feel it. "Since when am I the responsible one?" he mutters.

"I don't understand. Graham never drinks this much," Kenz says, and I can hear the concern laced in her voice. It should make me feel bad, but it doesn't because her face is so close to mine when she says it, all I can see are her plump lips drawn down like a bow, which only makes me think about how they were pressed to Atlas's only a few hours ago.

Jace glances over at her, then back down to me as his mouth flattens into a thin line, and I can tell what he's thinking. He knows exactly why I drank a little too much tonight.

My eyes shoot daggers at him. I might be blitzed out of my mind, but I'm cognizant enough that if he so much as mutters a word about it to her, I'll castrate him myself—once I'm sober, of course.

"Yeah," he says, dryly, getting the hint. "It's a mystery."

"What in the Sam hell is going on here?" My father's voice booms through the hallway, and our heads whip up to see him hovering over us. I can only imagine how I look. Piss drunk and sprawled out at the top of the stairs.

Kenzie's gaze flickers down to me and she licks her lips. "Uh, Mr. Scott, we were just—"

"I appreciate you trying to cover for my son, but I know exactly what you're all doing, and there's no point in hiding it. It's quite apparent he's in no shape to get to his room on his own. Thank you for bringing him home, but you can leave. I'll take it from here." I can hear the curt tone in my father's voice and instantly know my night's about to get worse.

"Yep. I'm out," Jace says as he jumps to his feet and starts down the stairs.

Traitor, I want to call after him.

Kenzie, though, she lingers. Because we always protect our number one. I can tell by her expression she doesn't want to leave me.

"Go," I say, my voice soft. "I wouldn't want you to miss curfew."

"Uh, it's a little late for that."

I shake my head and curse under my breath. If I get her in trouble, I'll hate myself for it. "Kenz—"

"It's fine. He's working the night shift, remember?"

"Still. Go. Before Jace leaves without you," I slur.

"Are you sure?" she asks, concern lacing her voice.

I nod.

She stands and turns to my father. "We left Graham's car at Crow's Creek. I would've driven it home for him, but . . ." She trails off, leaving us to fill in the blanks. My father is no stranger to her situation.

"We'll take care of it. Thank you."

She offers him a weak smile, then heads down the stairs. It's not until I hear the sound of the door open and close that my father addresses me directly. "Get your ass in bed. We have some family news to discuss, and we can't do it with you like this," he hisses. "I don't care how drunk you are, I expect you up early."

I struggle to my feet, yanking myself up by the stair railing, then bow, almost losing my balance as I do. "Yes, Your Majesty," I say, and then I lose it again, tipping my head back in laughter.

Dad rolls his eyes. "Try not to wake your mother, will you?" he says before he heads back toward his bedroom, where the door snicks shut.

Somehow, I manage to get myself to my room where I crash and sleep like the dead once the world stops spinning.

When I wake up the next morning, it feels like a freaking rhino is sitting on my head and my mouth is stuffed with cotton. The pounding on my door doesn't help matters, and I wince when my father shouts, "Graham, downstairs in five!"

I groan and roll over, wondering what the hell's so important that he has to speak with me at—I squint at the clock beside my bed—eight a.m. on a Saturday. Even my punishment for being drunk could wait until noon.

I lie there another minute, then muster the energy to throw my legs over the bed and stand. My stomach clenches at the sudden movement, and for a moment, I wonder if I'll be sick as I make my way into the shower and let the hot water beat down on my pounding head.

A few minutes later, I successfully throw on a pair of sweats and a T-shirt, then head downstairs. Our house boasts an open floor plan, so the moment I step onto the landing, I have a bird's eye view through the living room, the kitchen, and part of the dining room where I can just make out my father's back as he sits in his usual spot at the end of the massive table.

The scent of my mother cooking breakfast fills the air, and I'm surprised to find my stomach doesn't threaten to revolt at the thought of eating. Instead, I'm ravenous and my stomach growls in response.

I round the corner, prepared to take my usual seat along with a lecture from Dad when I freeze in place.

My spot is already taken.

By Atlas.

I stiffen as he offers me a nod of acknowledgement, then returns his attention to his plate, which is piled high with pancakes. My mom's blueberry pancakes, to be exact.

Seems Atlas has a thing for taking what's mine.

"Glad you finally decided to join us," my father barks.

My head swings toward him and I take in the scowl on his face.

I want to ask what the hell Atlas is doing here, scream it from the top of my lungs because everywhere I fucking look, he's there. But I don't. Considering the state my father found me in last night, I have no leg to stand on.

Instead, I make my way to the opposite end of the table and load my own plate with enough food to feed an army. I stab a pancake with my fork, cut into it, and take a huge bite as my father toys with the rim of his coffee cup, eyeing me. "The reason I wanted you to come to breakfast is because I have news."

I glance over at Atlas and point my fork. "So, why's he here then? Last I checked, he wasn't privy to family meetings."

"He's the news."

I pause my chewing as I stare at my father and swallow the lump of food in my mouth, unsure of what that means. Regardless, I don't like the sound of it.

"As it turns out," my father continues, "Atlas will be staying with us for a while."

"What?" I choke out. "You mean, like, living here?"

"That's exactly what I mean."

"For how long?"

"Until his situation at home is resolved."

I drop my fork on my plate with a clatter and lean back in my chair. One glance at Atlas and I know whatever's happened must been bad. I can see it in his eyes and the way he stiffens at my father's words. The muscles strain in his neck, but I'm not about to make this easier on him. I'm being an ass, and I know it, but I can't seem to help myself. Not when the image of him with his dirty paws on Kenzie keeps playing on repeat in my head.

"Look at the bright side, maybe this will benefit you," my father says.

I laugh. "And how's that?"

"Maybe he could help you stay disciplined and improve your game, instead of coming home smelling like a brewery. You can review plays and focus on what's important, especially since your game last night could've used some focus. Quite frankly, he saved you a loss. You should be thanking him."

"Gee, Dad, say I'm not good enough without saying I'm not good enough."

"Nothing good ever comes out of sugarcoating the truth."

"Right." As usual, there's no love lost with my father. "Is that all, then?"

"That's all."

"Then if you don't mind, I'm going to excuse myself. I've got a hangover to nurse," I say, mostly because I know it'll piss him off.

I return to my room and pace the floor as I contemplate my current situation. Not only is it bad enough that my cousin, whom I don't trust, is moving in on the love of my life, but now I have to live with the fucker.

There's a knock on the door, even though it's open, and as I turn around, Atlas peeks his head in. "Can I come in?"

I barely restrain myself from asking if I have a choice. Instead, I shrug. "Sure, why not?"

Atlas sinks his hands in his pockets and enters my room like he's entering a war zone. Smart guy.

"Clearly you're pissed about my being here, and I don't blame you, but just so you know, the reason I'm here is because my father was arrested last night. If there was any other way . . ." He trails off, as if waiting for me to say something. If he thinks he's going to get my sympathy, he's wrong.

"Whatever. It's fine," I say, my voice flat. All I want is for him to get out of my room. Out of my life.

"If you're pissed about what your dad said, it's not true."

I laugh and shake my head. "It's true. I know it and you know it. He wouldn't have said it if it weren't. I played subpar, and subpar isn't recruiting material, as my father so lovingly likes to remind me."

"Well, at least he cares, man. You have someone pushing you, trying to make you better, and giving you advice. Do you know what I'd give to have that? Hell, I'd give my left nut just to have my father acknowledge I even exist most days."

I shake my head at his audacity. Does he seriously have the nerve to give me a lecture on gratitude right now?

"So, I'm supposed to be grateful at the fact he so often reminds me I'm not good enough? Is that it?" I say, my voice flat.

He shrugs. "We just see it differently, I guess."

"Damn straight, we do."

"Whatever, man. What do you want from me? I tried to convince your father to let me stay at my place alone, but he wasn't having it."

I step forward, into his personal space. "Just stay the hell out of my way. And keep your distance from Kenzie while you're at it."

Atlas's eyes widen, and I curse myself for showing my hand.

"That's what this is about, isn't it? Last night." He waits a beat for me to respond, but he'll be waiting forever. "Because you and I didn't have a problem until now."

I avoid his gaze. I've already said too much. "You're not good enough for her."

"Never said I was."

"Then leave her for someone who is."

"You mean, someone like you?"

I say nothing, the question hanging in the air between us. After a minute, Atlas shakes his head and leaves.

MACKENZIE

By the time Graham picks me up Monday morning, my insides are twisted with worry. I called and texted him countless times over the weekend with no response, so I can only assume that his father came down on him pretty hard after he caught him coming in at one a.m., wasted.

When I slide inside his car and settle in the passenger seat, he says nothing. His mood is completely different to how it'd been last week, so I give him space and we ride in silence as I try and figure out a way to approach him. He's usually so even-tempered I'm not sure how to handle him when he's so sullen.

I clear my throat and glance at him out of the corner of my eye. "I see you got your car back."

He nods but says nothing. Whatever is eating at him, it's clear he's not going to make it easy on me.

"So, how did it go with your father?"

"You know, same as usual. I'm a screwup who's going to waste his future," he says, his tone bitter.

"Why didn't you return any of my calls? I was worried."

Graham glances over at me, his gaze cool. "Sorry. I guess I didn't think I had to check-in with you."

I flinch at the animosity directed my way, and see a flicker of remorse in his eyes, but he says nothing. Instead, he turns his attention back to the road, his jaw tight as he drives. I rack my brain for what I could have possibly done to upset him.

Something had to have happened at the bonfire. He went from being his normal self to binge drinking until he could barely walk. And it all happened after he went to help Knox. Had Knox done something? Said something? Or had he seen me with Atlas?

The latter thought hits me square in the chest, causing me to swallow nervously, but before I can ask, he breaks the silence. "As it turns out, Dad's just like everyone else and has a new pet project."

I frown. "What are you talking about?"

"Atlas," he bites out bitterly.

"I don't understand," I say, confused.

"Well, apparently, while I was getting blitzed off my ass, he was moving his shit into one of the guest rooms at my house."

My eyes widen. "He's staying there?"

Graham laughs, but there's no humor in the sound. "You should see my dad with him. It's like the prodigal son has returned home, and my dad's welcomed him with open arms. He's got Atlas wrapped around his finger. He hangs on his every word, and my old man treats him like he's some bereft football star who can go all the way if only given half the chance," Graham says in a mocking tone. "Then there's me . . ."

"Your dad loves you, Graham. He just doesn't know how to show it."

"Well, the latter part of that statement we can agree on. I think his exact words were, 'your game last night could've used some focus.' Then he proceeded to explain how Atlas's influence would be good for me and said I should thank him for saving me from a loss."

"So, what are you gonna do?"

"There's not a damn thing I can do, is there?" He comes to a red light, and turns toward me, his expression knowing. "It's not like he's the only one with a savior complex. It seems there's more than one person who wants to be the one to save the bad boy and change his ways."

I swallow, my thoughts scattering in a thousand directions. I think back to the conversation he started before he left to help Knox. If he does know Atlas and I hooked up at the party, is he angry because he'd told me to stay away from him, or is it something more?

"Maybe he's not so bad?" I say. "Have you ever thought he might not be the guy people say he is? That maybe all the rumors aren't true?"

Graham scoffs. "Are you telling me he didn't beat the shit out of that kid, then get sent to juvie? Because I know for a fact that happened."

Irritation spikes my veins. I expected this from my father, but not Graham. "I'm telling you there might be more to the story. Not everything's as it seems."

Graham laughs as he turns into the school parking lot. "There's always more to the story with guys like him, isn't there?"

"Maybe you don't know him like you think you do," I say, my tone defensive

"And you do?" He arches a brow.

"It wouldn't kill you to actually talk to him, you know. Instead of judging him, just ask him about it. Give him an actual chance."

The minute he parks, I get out of the car and slam my door. I'm equal parts angry and bereft he's upset with me. Why can't he just trust me to make my own decisions on who to spend my time with?

I half expect him to hurry and catch up with me on the sidewalk, but he doesn't. Maybe it's just as well, I tell myself. Graham and I never fight, and he's never mad at me. Whatever his beef is, he needs to get over it.

I make my way down the hall toward Atlas's locker, excited to see him after the field party. I have no idea how he's going to act around me, but it's my hope we can pick up where we left off. I'm relieved when I see him alone, since every other morning Jenna seems to be a permanent fixture at his locker.

Unsure of how to act, I come up beside him and clear my throat. "Hey," I murmur. At the same time he turns around, Graham passes by and punches the door of a locker several yards down.

"Sorry." I shake my head. "I don't know what's gotten into him."

"I think I have an idea." His dark gaze drops to mine, and my heart flutters in my chest.

"So, about Friday night . . ." I start.

"What about it?" His tone is cool as he starts to collect his things from his locker, jamming them into his book bag as my stomach sinks.

"Um, you know, about the kiss . . . ?"

He turns back to me, his dark eyes devoid of emotion as he shrugs. "It was just a kiss, right? Let's not make a thing of it."

Then he winks and walks away, leaving me to stare after him while my heart falls at my feet.

Chapter 18

ATLAS

The hurt in Mackenzie's eyes this morning is about the saddest fucking thing I've ever experienced, and that's saying something seeing as how my mom left me when I was a kid and my dad's an addict. But I did what I had to do. We're both better off staying the hell away from each other; Graham's little hissy fit this morning is proof of that. Besides, I would only mess things up for her. Daddy Hart would come down on her hard if he knew she was spending any amount of time with me outside of school, and it's only a matter of time before he puts her on lockdown and screws with my life.

Then there's Graham. Clearly the dude has it bad. Whether he wants to admit it or not, he's in love with her. Anyone with eyes can see that, which makes me a selfish prick for kissing her. It also explains why he's acting like a little bitch. Obviously, he saw us kissing. And now I have to live with the dude when I have zero desire for added drama. It's bad enough his dad likes to piss him off. Pursuing Kenzie in any form is sure to put him over the edge when all I want to do is play ball in peace.

And the biggest reason of all to stay away from her? She'll only derail me from my plans. Everything about Mackenzie is intoxicating. One kiss and it's easy to see what it might be like to get lost in her. Because Doll isn't the kind of girl you mess around with, then walk away from. Hell, she's too good for me. Graham's right about that.

But no matter how appealing she is, I have goals, and I'll be damned if anyone comes between me and what I want to accomplish. Friday night only served as a bitter reminder of everything I have to lose if my focus slips.

I can't become my father.

I won't.

Which means staying in my lane. And Mackenzie Hart is on a whole other interstate.

I leave practice, sore all over, in gray sweats and a T-shirt with my duffel slung across my chest. Coach gave us a beating at practice, and all I want to do is go home and shove some food in my face, then sink into an ice bath. And though it's weird I'll be doing it at Uncle Cal's house, I can't say I mind the thought of a hot meal waiting for me and the massive soaker tub in my bedroom. The only downside is walking on eggshells around Graham and having to put on pretenses. Which is exactly why I'd opt to take my supper to my room and stay there. So, I'm in no mood when I close in on my bike and see Mackenzie standing there, waiting for me.

Cursing under my breath, I run a hand through my hair, still damp from my shower, then glance around me. The last thing I need is for Graham to see us, and I'm relieved to see his car is already gone from the student lot.

Shoving my hands in my pockets, I come to a stop in front of her. "What are you doing here?" I snap. I'm being an ass, but it can't be helped. It seems pushing her away is going to take some effort.

She arches a brow and lifts her chin. "If you think being rude to me is going to get me to leave you alone, you're wrong."

"What I think is you got one little taste and now you think you own me. It's going to take a hell of a lot more than one hot make-out session to get there, baby."

I take another step closer, and my gaze tracks down her body. "Now, if you really wanna try and stake your claim . . ." I lick my lips as I leer at her.

"Nice try, but I'm not buying, Atlas Scott. You wanna act like a creep to try and push me away? Well, it's not gonna work. I know you better than that."

I stiffen and clench my teeth. "You *think* you know me and let me guess. You also think you can fix me. Heal the wounded, broken bad boy. Well, no thanks. I like my demons just fine."

She crosses her arms over her chest. "You can front all you want, but I'm not buying it."

"I don't want you, doll. You need to learn to take a hint."

Her nostrils flare. She says nothing for a moment, and my chest freaking aches at the thought of hurting her, but it's all I can do to get it through that pretty little skull of hers that I'm not her guy.

I make a move for my bike, and she steps aside while my heart knocks against my ribs. Turns out getting through to her doesn't feel nearly as good as I thought it would.

The scent of apple blossom drifts toward me and desire stirs in my guts. It reminds me of the other night. Of what it felt like to have that sweet mouth on mine.

I shift as I slide onto my bike, taking a moment to hide how much I want her.

"Fine. You win," she says, and I expect her to leave, but she doesn't. "If you want to pretend that kiss the other night didn't blow you away, I'm not going to sit here and try to convince you otherwise. I was there. I know. But I need your help."

I bark out a laugh. This girl has balls. Whoever thought she was weak or helpless hasn't been paying attention.

"You're gonna ask me for a favor?" I arch a brow.

"I need a ride."

"To where?"

"The police station."

My head falls back in laughter. "Now I know you're crazy."

"I'm serious."

"I'm sure you are." I slide my helmet on and crank my bike. "Listen, do yourself a favor and get your best bud to do it. Trust me when I say he'll be more than willing to lick your wounds."

Her forehead creases. "This isn't about Graham, and I don't want his help right now. All I need is for you to get me the police reports from the accident. If I do it, the guys will tell my dad, and I don't want him knowing I'm looking into this further. None of the guys at the precinct know you, so they won't tip him off."

A smirk spreads across my lips. "We've been acquainted, trust me. They know who I am."

"How—"

"It's not important," I say before she can ask, because I'm in no mood to recap my weekend. "Go home, doll."

Her cheeks redden and tiny fists curl at her side. "If you won't take me to get the report, I'll find someone who will."

"Good idea."

She turns with a huff and starts walking through the parking lot toward the street, while I watch with a growing scowl. "What the hell do you think you're doing?" I yell.

She spins around. "What does it look like? Walking to the precinct."

She crosses the busy street and heads in the direction of downtown Riverside. When she gets to the intersection by the Grab-N-Go convenience store, I see her pause and speak to a shady man wearing all black and a leather studded collar around his neck.

Fuck.

I mutter a string of obscenities as I throttle the gas and pull out of the parking lot onto the road, coming to a roaring stop beside her and the man who's now joined her trek to the station. "Get on," I say, eyeing the guy beside her with an expression so sharp it could cut glass.

"No. I'm good. I don't need your help anymore. I've got . . ." She turns to the random dude and he mumbles something incoherent. His pupils are so large, they eat up his entire face. The guy is high as a fucking kite.

"Kip, here, is going to help me out," she informs me.

"Hell, no," I say, ripping my helmet off.

"Hey, man . . ." Kip slings his arm around Mackenzie's shoulders, ready to protest before I pin him with my knife-like gaze. When I zero in on the offending appendage with murder in my eyes, he slowly removes it from around her.

"Get on. Now," I bite out through gritted teeth, but she just crosses her arms over her chest.

"Last I checked, you had no desire to help me. I wouldn't want to bother you with my crazy," she says, throwing my words back at me.

This girl is so frustrating, I'm half tempted to throw her over my shoulder, give her ass a good spank, then throw her on my bike. "If you think for one second I'm going to let you walk all the way to the station with this pedo douche, you're wrong. So, get on my bike, and let's go. You've proved your point."

"I was just doing what you said," she quips and shrugs so nonchalantly, my blood pressure skyrockets.

When she steps away from me and proceeds to walk down the street with Kip, I calmly dismount my bike, place my helmet on the back and head toward her. My long stride closes the distance easily, and before she even knows what's happening, I lift her up and throw her over my shoulder like it's nothing.

A yelp escapes her lips before she pounds my back with her fists. "Hey! What do you think you're doing? You can't just haul me up like Tarzan and—"

I drop her on my bike so hard, her words cut off, then I shove the helmet over her head. "You're a pain in my ass, Hart."

Turning, I give Kip a little wave while he flips me a parting middle finger, then I straddle my Harley in front of Kenz.

"I refuse to hold onto you," she pouts, and if she weren't so damn cute when she's defiant, I'd probably kick her back off.

"Suit yourself." I throttle the engine and pull out, smiling when she snakes her arms around my waist, and we head into traffic.

I mostly take the back roads into the center of town, knowing exactly where the station is. When you grow up running into trouble with the law, you kind of have a habit of making it a necessity to scope out the local law enforcement everywhere you go.

After a few minutes, I pull into the precinct lot, and curse myself for coming here. It's suicide to be in Hart's domain, and with his daughter no less.

I cut the engine and set the kickstand on my bike. "Now what?" I ask, turning to her.

She removes her arms from around me, and I instantly feel the loss, but I ignore it. Her hair is a mess from my helmet and the wind, and as she stares up at me with those cool blue eyes, all I want to do is lean into her and press my lips to hers.

"Go in and ask for the police report," she says as if it's not a big deal.

"Trust me when I say your father won't be happy to see me."

"Well, then you're in luck because it's his day off, which also means he'll be expecting me home, so you might want to make it snappy."

"For real? First you coerce me into giving you a ride and now you're barking out orders on how quickly I need to do your bidding?"

"Pretty much." She nods, her tone clipped as she swings her leg down to get off the bike.

She's mad at me.

Good.

"Listen, when you go in and ask for it, they're going to tell you to look online," she says. "There's a database for crash reports and other minor incident police reports. But you need to tell them that every time you go to look it up, you get an error message from the system."

"Okay. What other information do I need?" I ask, simultaneously regretting agreeing to this and wanting to help her out.

"The date of the crash, the county, and a couple other things. They're all on here," she says, handing me a small piece of paper.

I sigh and curl the paper in my fist, then head inside.

Fifteen minutes later, I return to where she stands by my bike, triumphant. With a flourish, I wave the papers they gave me in the air. "Mission accomplished," I say, slapping them into her waiting hands. "You're welcome."

Her forehead creases as she scans the documents, and I can tell she's not really listening. I wait with bated breath until she lifts her head and stares off into the distance while her mouth turns down in a frown.

"Find something?" I ask, unable to help myself.

She glances up at me with eyes as clear and blue as a cloudless sky. "There was a witness."

"Okay, so what does that mean? That doesn't change anything, right?"

"No, not necessarily, but the fact he claims there was a second vehicle involved in the crash does." She begins pacing, reading from the report as she walks.

"It says here that a witness by the name of Anthony Mancetti witnessed the entire thing. He was standing outside on the sidewalk in front of Manja, Manja. We were going southbound, away from him, when another person came up on our tail, passed us, and made a right-hand turn." She glances up at me with wide eyes. "What if this car did something to make us crash? What if it wasn't my fault? Maybe the witness has information leading up to the crash that could help. I mean, maybe he saw my mom and I together. I don't know . . ."

She waves the papers in the air, getting more and more animated. "He might have *something* to give me some insight."

"You were probably just going to lunch. And this guy witnessed it as you left." I shrug, playing devil's advocate.

"Maybe." She chews on her lip, contemplating this. "But I do remember leaving for school angry that morning, and there's no signs of me being signed out by myself or my mom, which means I skipped class. But why? I wouldn't do that if I had an appointment, or I was taking a leisurely lunch with my mom. None of it adds up."

"Okay . . ."

She stares back down at the report, and I can see the wheels in her head spinning. Her entire being radiates hope. And maybe it's because I haven't felt hopeful about anything for as long as I can remember—if ever—but I want this for her. Whatever she hopes to find by remembering what happened on the day of the accident, I pray she gets it. Because no matter how much shit I've given to Mackenzie in the past about being privileged and sheltered, she's good people. Pure and honest and kind. Which is why, before I can even think it through, I yank the papers from her hands.

"So, let's go talk to this witness," I say.

She glances up at me, lips parting in shock.

Welcome to the club, sweetheart. I'm just as surprised as you.

Spending time with her is the last thing I should do. The more I'm around her, the more I wish I can be the kind of man she needs. I should be at home, focusing on football, prepping for Friday's game and icing my aching muscles. Instead, I'm staring at this girl, praying she says yes to my offer, even though I know she shouldn't because she has just as much at stake if she gets caught with me as I do.

MACKENZIE

I want to go and talk to the witness from the police report so bad I can taste the desire on the tip of my tongue.

"But my dad's home. He's expecting me," I say. I can't just—"

"Make something up. Tell him you're at a friend's house. Who's the one person he trusts, that he won't question?"

"Graham."

His jaw clenches and several seconds pass before he says, "So tell him you're still at school with Graham, working on a project or something."

I chew on my lower lip, thinking about Atlas's suggestion. Graham's already mad at me. If I lie and tell my father I'm with him when I'm really with Atlas and he finds out, he'll be furious, even more angry than he already is. Spending time with Atlas is like consorting with the enemy. Not to mention the not-so-minor issue of my father. If he finds out I'm lying, Graham will be the least of my concerns. He already threatened to pull me from the squad if he catches me with Atlas again, and worse, enroll me in virtual school. The man is petrified something is going to happen to me, and with Atlas's reputation, he isn't taking any chances.

My choices suck.

Defy the two people I love the most in this world or sacrifice my own desire and need to remember the truth, alongside the one person they both seem to hate.

The one I secretly want but can't have.

"Come on. What have you got to lose?" Atlas asks, his dark eyes boring into mine.

"My freedom for one," I say thinking of my father. "My best friend for another. He's already mad at me. If he finds out . . ."

"So don't let him find out." Atlas shrugs like it's no big deal.

"I don't get it. Why do you suddenly want to help me, anyway? I had to practically force your hand before, but now you're all about it?"

He grows quiet for a long while, staring off into the distance over my shoulder as the muscle in his jaw twitches. "It's been a while since I've had anything to be hopeful about. And I want that for you." Turning, he climbs onto his bike and stretches his hand out for me. "So, what'll it be, doll? Go home or drive to Anthony Mancetti's house? The choice is yours."

I groan and bounce on my toes, my options waging a silent war inside my head as I'm reminded of that first day we met—in the dark, back at Crow's Creek. I knew then the decision I'd make before I even made it, consequences be damned. Just like I know now before I even say it. Because I need to remember, and despite all the reasons I shouldn't lie to my father and Graham, I can't say no to Atlas. And at this moment, I'm as happy as hell he can't say no to me, either.

I've already lied to them both once today. What's one more?

Chapter 19

MACKENZIE

The address on the report is in Wickland, thirty minutes outside Riverside. It's a cute suburban area with mid-sized homes, a massive shopping mall, and plenty of restaurants and entertainment to keep its residents happy, unlike the quieter Riverside which only consists of a drive-in theater in the summer, a few restaurants, and boutiques.

We pull up to a pretty gray house with a bright red door and a white fence around the yard. It's quaint and well taken care of; the perfect home to raise a family.

"This is it," Atlas says, as we both get off his bike.

A golden retriever appears from around the side of the house, greeting us as we make our way up the sidewalk. I scratch him behind the ears, somehow comforted by his presence because it reminds me of Goliath. But no matter how comfortable the sweet boy makes me, it's not enough to banish the nerves twisting inside me like a nylon rope.

For the first time since reading the report, it dawns on me Anthony Mancetti might not even be home, and this trip is all for naught. My stomach sinks at the thought, and I exhale a steady breath as Atlas motions toward the door.

"You got this," he says, and I stare at him a moment, wondering how he can be so cold and unyielding one minute and warm the next. It's enough to give me whiplash.

Pushing my shoulders back, I ring the doorbell and wait as a melodic chime rings out. Only a minute passes before footsteps echo from within, and the door swings open to a middle-aged man with hair the color of an oil slick, a neatly trimmed beard, and eyes a stunning hazel.

Recognition slices through me like a knife as I suck in a sharp breath. "You," I whisper, too stunned for words.

The man hangs his head, avoiding my eyes. "I'm sorry. You must have the wrong house."

I've barely even processed what's happening when he starts to shut the door in my face, but not before Atlas slaps a hand over the slab of wood, pushing it back open. "Actually, I don't think she was done yet."

"What do you want?" the man asks, his tone wary.

"Are you Anthony Mancetti?" Atlas asks.

"Maybe. Depends on who's asking . . ." His gaze flickers between us, and his throat bobs.

"I'm Mackenzie Hart." I place my hand on my chest, hoping it draws his eye. "I was in a car crash nine months ago. You were a witness, and I was hoping you could answer some questions."

When he lifts his eyes to mine, a memory of him flickers in my mind like a movie reel. In it, he's smiling and holding a wine glass, and I'm almost certain it's from Manja, Manja.

"Look, I told the officers everything I know about that day," he says, holding his hands up, palms out, like we have him at gunpoint.

"Please," I beg. "My mother died in that crash, and she was my best friend, an amazing woman. I was driving that day, and I've been reeling from her death ever since. All I want is to know what you saw. Nothing more."

He hesitates before nodding, and maybe it's my imagination, but his expression softens.

"You said there was another car . . ."

"I did."

"But the police never followed up."

A bitter laugh escapes his lips. "Not a surprise. He didn't want to hear anything I had to say. Barely asked me anything and just sort of glossed over the report."

I swallow. "Who did?"

His eyes harden to stone. "Chief Hart." He drops the name like a bomb, then steps aside and signals for us to follow him inside. "Come . . . I'll try and answer whatever questions you have."

"Thank you." Atlas and I exchange a look before he steps in front of me, partially shielding me with his body as if I need his protection.

We follow Mr. Mancetti through a small foyer into a modest kitchen where he takes a seat at a large farmhouse table and motions for us to do the same. I stare over at him, noticing the stiff set of his shoulders and the muscles straining in his neck. It feels as if he's ready to burst with whatever emotion he's holding onto; everything about him screams with tension.

"I don't remember anything about the crash," I say, feeling the need to clarify.

"Nothing?" he asks, eyebrows raised.

I notice the slight widening of his eyes and shake my head. "I remember going to school earlier that morning, but everything after that is blank. I obviously know I was driving the car when it crashed. That I killed my mother. And I guess . . ." I trail off, pausing as I stop to collect myself. Moisture pools in my eyes and my throat aches with unshed tears. "I guess I'm hoping that I can have more clarity on how we crashed. I need closure. I need to know if I did something stupid and killed her. Or if maybe . . ." I glance down at the table and swallow over the lump in my throat. "Maybe it was something I couldn't have prevented even if I tried."

His throat bobs. "I saw you get in your car and start the engine, then your mother jumped inside as you pulled out of the parking lot."

I frown. "Were we fighting?"

He nods. "But I couldn't hear what you said to each other."

His answer seems evasive, but it makes sense considering the circumstances. "Then what?"

"You continued onto the road when another car came up behind you. He was flying. The car was blue, an older make and model, though I can't be sure what kind. It all happened so fast. He drove back into your lane without enough room and hit the front of your car, causing you to careen straight into the pole."

"Wait." I close my eyes, trying to comprehend what he's telling me, but my heart is beating so hard I can barely think over the pounding in my ears. "He actually hit us? You're sure. Because the report said—"

"The report won't have all of those details because, as I said, Chief Hart didn't seem particularly interested in what I had to say. He wouldn't listen much at all, actually."

I fall back into my chair and my forehead knots as I try to process what Anthony is saying—that my father refused to listen to an eyewitness. Why?

If someone caused me to crash, wouldn't he want me to know? Why wouldn't he want to find the person responsible?

"I don't understand." I glance over at Atlas, confused. The only scenario where hiding the truth makes sense is if he's protecting me from something, but what?

Atlas narrows his eyes at Mancetti and lifts his chin. "And you really believe this car was responsible for pushing them into the telephone pole?"

"Oh, I know it did. No doubt about it. The man driving that car killed Laura."

I sit back in my chair, stunned as his words sink in and I try to make sense of it all. The thought that I wasn't responsible for my mother's death feels like a gift; it's too good to be true. This whole time, I've blamed myself when it might have been someone else's negligence that killed her instead of my own.

Relief spreads inside me like eagles' wings as we thank Mancetti for the information and say our goodbyes.

Five minutes later, Atlas and I stop at a coffee shop a few miles away and order two Americanos to take out. As we sit outside, I clutch my paper cup, letting it warm me through because the flutter of hope inside me has died and withered, turning into a dull ache. "It makes no sense why he would hide this from me," I say as I turn my gaze to him.

Atlas stretches his long legs out in front of him while I try to ignore the way his gray T-shirt stretches across his broad chest. "Beats me." He shrugs. "Maybe he thought Mancetti was full of shit. I mean, something about the guy seems off."

"Maybe." I chew my lips, contemplating. "But he wasn't trying to cover up any negligence on my part. Why not investigate the other car, even if Mancetti didn't seem like a viable witness? You can't just ignore someone's report of what happened. It's his job. And it was my mother. *Me*. I almost died."

"Maybe Mancetti's known to be a liar?" Atlas muses. "Maybe they looked into the guy and found he isn't credible. Or maybe *he* was drunk. Who knows? The truth is we only a have a small piece of the puzzle."

The image I had of Mancetti drinking a glass of wine, head tipped back in laughter, flashes through my head once more, and I frown. I so badly want the accident to be someone else's fault. Am I making something out of nothing? Atlas's suggestion jives with the image in my head. It makes sense. Plus, I know my father is good at his job. What other explanation is there?

I pick at the paper sleeve of my coffee cup while disappointment rattles my bones. "I suppose you're right. I mean, there has to be a valid reason he'd ignore it."

Because if there isn't, it means my father hid the truth—a truth that would have relieved me from the burden of guilt I've felt these past nine months. It would be cruel not to tell me.

"Is it wrong that I want it to be someone else's fault? I mean, she's gone regardless." My voice cracks on the words and I hang my head, ashamed about my desire to shift the burden of guilt.

"Not at all." His tone is so soft, a lump forms in the back of my throat. "Doll, look at me."

When I ignore him, he places his fingers beneath my chin, forcing me to meet his gaze. "You'd be crazy not to want that."

I swallow, struggling to hold back the dam of tears. I thought they'd dried up long ago. "He just seemed so sure, ya know? I guess I got my hopes up."

"Doesn't mean it's not possible," Atlas replies. "Maybe they didn't think Mancetti was believable, or maybe no one corroborated his story, so they dropped it. But that doesn't mean they couldn't be wrong."

"Yeah, I guess so," I say, though all the wind has already left my sails.

I take a sip of my coffee, ready to tell Atlas we should head back, when something Mancetti said hits me like a railroad tie.

No doubt about it. The man driving that car killed Laura.

A prickling awareness jogs up my spine, and I straighten in my chair, eyes wide. "Oh my God."

"What?"

"Mancetti. When we asked if he was sure about the other car. He said 'the man driving that car killed Laura.'"

Atlas frowns. "Laura's your mom, right? So?"

"How the hell does Mancetti know her by name?"

Atlas's mouth drops open. "Holy shit."

"I highly doubt my father would have given him her name, and even if he did, doesn't it seem odd that he'd refer to her that way so casually?"

"Unless he knew her."

"And knew her well." I frown.

"There's something he's not telling us."

"We need to go back there." I hop up from my seat as Atlas grabs our cups, throwing them in the trash, then reaching for my hand.

"Looks like we have more questions to ask."

ATLAS

We stand outside Mancetti's house and pound on the door, but no one answers.

"All the lights are out," I say, taking a step back and peering up at the darkened second story of the house.

"We were here only twenty minutes ago, and he's gone? Doesn't that seem weird to you?"

"It's certainly a coincidence," I murmur.

"My guess is he's home but avoiding us." Mackenzie rubs her arms, and I glance down to see goose bumps covering her skin. "There's more to the story, and he knows what it is."

And so does your father, I think, but I keep that to myself.

"Well, if you're right, he's not gonna talk." I motion for my bike and reach for her hand. "Come on. We better get you back before your father figures out you're not with Graham."

Twenty minutes later, I park at the gas station a little less than a mile from Mackenzie's house so I can walk her at least partway home without alerting her father.

We take the back roads and walk side by side in silence, both of us lost in our thoughts. Mine in particular keep circling back to the fact that no matter how hard I try, I can't seem to keep my distance from the girl beside me. I'm drawn to her in a way I can't begin to understand, and it makes me want to stop fighting it and give in and see where this leads.

"Now what?" I ask, needing to hear her voice, to think about something, *anything*, else.

She shrugs, staring off into the distance. "I don't know. Pray my memory returns? Talk to my dad? Try and confront Anthony Mancetti again? Go back to the restaurant?"

"Do you think you'll do that, ask your dad about it?"

"I don't know. I need to process everything first, but I can't help but feel he has answers he's not giving me."

I nod like I understand, but I don't. If it were me, I'd be so far up his ass demanding the truth, I'd come out the other side.

My phone rings, and I glance at the screen, though I know who it will be even before I take in the local number. My dad's been trying to call me from the prison all day. I know this from the voice mail he left this morning. Just like I know I'm not answering.

"Do you need to get that?" Mackenzie asks when it rings again.

I glance down at her to see she's staring.

I shake my head. "It's nothing important."

"Seems important."

I rub a hand over the back of my neck and pause on the sidewalk as I turn to face her. The last thing I want is for her to know just how fucked up I am, but Graham's her best friend. If I don't tell her, I have no doubt he will. I'm sure he'd love nothing more than to rub my father's dirty laundry in my face.

"It's my dad," I tell her.

"Did you two have a fight or something?"

I snort. "We don't fight, doll. Hell, I'm lucky he even acknowledges me half the time. In fact, I'm actually shocked he even knows how to reach me." I shove my phone back in my pocket and shrug. "He's in jail," I say, pushing the words out as if they mean nothing.

Mackenzie doesn't flinch; she doesn't even blink. Either she has one hell of a poker face, or Graham beat me to it.

"Arrested? For what?" she asks.

"Forging prescriptions."

"Won't he get out on bail?"

I smirk. "No chance of that when he hasn't a dime to his name, and I'm sure as shit not about to bail him out."

Maybe he'll get sober.

I shake off the thought as quickly as it enters my mind because there's no point in hoping for the impossible.

"When did this happen?"

"Friday night. When I got home from the party, a cruiser was parked outside our house." I shake my head. "Fun times. Just when you think life throws you a bone, it takes it away and kicks you while you're down."

"Is that why you tried to push me away?"

I suck in a breath because she's too observant for her own damn good.

"No, doll. Not just that. There are far more reasons for you and I to stay away from each other than there are for us to be together, and seeing as how your father was the one to escort me to my new digs while my old man is locked up, I can't imagine he'll be welcoming me into your life anytime soon."

"Maybe I don't care what my father thinks."

Her nonchalant tone bothers me.

"You should," I snap. "Because this won't end well," I say, gesturing between us. "That ultimately makes him right. All I can focus on right now is football. That's it. I don't have room for anything else."

"Graham mentioned you're staying with him," she says, ignoring what I just said.

So, he *has* snitched. "Yeah, and Golden Boy is *not* happy about it," I say.

She falls silent and starts to walk again. "I'm sorry," she says after a moment.

My jaw hardens as I return to her side. "Not your fault."

"Maybe you should talk to your father. Give him a chance and see what he has to say."

I shake my head. "I've got nothing to say to him right now. I'll talk to him when I'm ready. Hell, he might even be sober by then. That'll be a first."

Mackenzie reaches out and places a hand on my arm. Her fingers are soft and warm, her touch electric. "Listen, I know what you said, and you can push me away all you want, but I'm not going anywhere."

Her words hit the walls I've resurrected around myself like bullets, punching tiny holes in the plaster. "I wish you would."

"Why?"

"Because you don't want me, doll." I tuck a stray lock of hair behind her ear. "I'm damaged goods, not to mention all wrong for you. I'm not cut out to be a relationship guy. My black heart doesn't even know what that looks like."

"Why don't you let me decide what I want?"

Her words are a revelation, giving me pause. Everyone in Mackenzie's life likes to tell her what's good for her, and I've more or less done the same thing. The last thing I want is to be that guy. It makes me wonder if maybe it's not really her I'm protecting. Maybe it's me.

I brush the thought aside. "You need someone steady. Someone you can rely on. Someone safe, like Graham."

"Graham and I are just friends," she says a little too quickly.

"You sure about that?"

Her forehead creases, and I fight the urge to reach out and smooth the furrow in her brow with my fingertips.

"You can put on this hard front all you want, Atlas Scott, but I know who you are. You're a good man, and nothing like your father. Inside that tough outer shell is a heart of gold."

I glance away from her, unable to look into her eyes because she makes me feel things I shouldn't. "It's not smart to have so much faith in me," I say, my voice gruff with emotion.

She steps closer, placing both her hands on either side of my face as her warm breath flutters over my cheek, and before I can stop her, she guides my face down to hers.

"That's where you're wrong," she whispers, and then her mouth finds mine.

Chapter 20

GRAHAM

I'm sitting on Jace's sofa, tossing a football in the air while we watch Perry High defeat South Central. A notebook sits in my lap so I can take notes, and half a dozen empty pizza boxes litter the coffee table in front of me. There's a handful of my teammates lounging around the room while we comment on the footage.

"Well look who the cat dragged in," Jace croons.

My head whips in his direction, thinking it's Atlas finally joining us when I spot Kenzie hovering outside the door to Jace's den.

I quickly turn back as guilt settles like a stone inside my chest. I've barely spoken a word to her all week. I've been unusually quiet in the mornings on the way into school as I try to work through a range of emotions that run the gamut from jealousy to disappointment and self-pity. Not that she seems to notice. I'm pretty sure she's been running around with Atlas all week, doing Lord knows what. Or at least, that's what I heard from a couple of the guys. Atlas for his part, is smart enough to stay out of my way.

"Mackenzie Hart, aren't you a fresh breath of sunshine in athletic wear," Jace teases, and I can't help myself. I glance at her from the corner of my eye, allowing my gaze to travel from her black leggings to the cropped top she wears, and I swallow.

She must've been running. Which means she's working through something. Welcome to the club.

Still, I hate the way Jace is looking at her, arms crossed over his chest, leering at her like she's a piece of meat.

"Kenz, what are you doing here?" I ask, even though I have a pretty good idea. It's Thursday. And on Thursday, we watch game tapes. It's usually a group of us at my house, Mackenzie included. But Atlas is there, and even though he's a part of the team, I can't stand to sit with him for hours right now in my own home and act like we're cool.

"Can I talk to you for a sec?" Her pouty mouth curves into a frown, and the urge to kiss it away hits me like a throat punch.

"We're kind of in the middle of something," I say, hating the way I always want her, even when I shouldn't.

"Uh oh, lovers quarrel." Jace glances between us and I want to punch him.

I roll my eyes, then get to my feet and head her way before Jace can be any more of a jackass. "What's up?" I ask, stepping into the hallway and away from prying eyes.

Her mouth parts and she stares at me for a moment, like she's shocked I even have to ask. "You really don't know?"

I shrug.

"*I* usually watch film with you."

"Well, tonight I'm watching it here with just the guys."

She stills, digesting my words before she bites her lip and stares at the wall. "Did I do something . . . ?"

My stomach clenches, and I shake my head.

"Is this about the party Friday night?"

"I barely remember the party," I say, but it's only partially true. The sight of her kissing Atlas is seared into my memory. Everything after that, though . . . it's a little foggy.

"Then is this about Atlas?"

"Listen, I just have some stuff going on you don't know about, and it's hard to concentrate, so I came here to focus. Don't take it personally."

She flinches at my words like they're daggers and she's my target. "Since when do we keep things from each other?"

Since you chose him, I want to say. But that's not fair because she doesn't even realize there's a choice to make in the first place.

I bow my head, ashamed of myself for being such a coward.

"Look," I hook a thumb in the direction of the door, "I better get back. But I'll see you tomorrow?"

She nods, silently spinning on her heal, while the hurt in her eyes stays with me for the rest of the night.

ATLAS

I slide my phone in my pocket and step out into the hallway, eyeing Graham's closed door as I pass. Every morning this week has been the same routine. I enter the kitchen on pins and needles, only to find him grabbing a protein shake before he leaves without so much as a glance in my direction.

The fact he's going to pick up Mackenzie is not lost on me. And though I try not to let it bother me, I can't say it doesn't sting at least a little bit. Despite my warnings about not being good for her, ever since Monday when we went to see Mancetti, we've been talking nonstop and catching small bits of time together when we can. Each time I'm with her, I'm reminded that I'll never be the kind of guy her father approves of. One who can pick her up for school in the mornings or drop her off and kiss her goodnight. But Graham is. Which is why I'm relieved to see he's already gone when I step inside the massive open-concept kitchen.

Avoiding the inevitable truth that I'll never be good enough for Mackenzie is a lot easier than facing it.

I don't know what I feel for her. Even though we're casual friends, I find myself thinking about her when I shouldn't—in class, at practice—hell, she's even infiltrated my dreams. All I know is when I'm with her, she makes everything seem possible. Like maybe I'm not just some boy with a rough past and a questionable future. She makes me feel like maybe I'm worthy of something other than my skills on the field.

She makes me question things, which is dangerous because more and more I find myself wanting things I know I don't deserve. Things I have no right wanting. Like her.

Which is why I need to be careful.

I tell myself I can handle it—I can spend time with Mackenzie and keep her at bay—while shoving down the voice of doubt.

With these thoughts heavy on my mind, I find Uncle Cal hovering by the stainless steel espresso machine, sipping from a large white mug. "Just the man I'm looking for. Atlas, why don't you take a seat."

When he motions to one of the leather stools behind the massive marble-topped island, I do as he says, noting Aunt Sheila's absence. Most days they have breakfast together; an elaborate spread of ham, eggs, fresh fruit, and pastries. Certainly not the generic Cheerios I was used to have before moving in. Some days it's still hard to get used to the lavishness of this place. And most days, I feel like a mooch. But I learned early on that declining my uncle's generosity doesn't go over well.

I sit, my spine stiff with suspicion that the conversation we're about to have is about my father, and curse myself when the prospect of his release and going home squeezes my stomach like a vice.

Newsflash, Atlas, you don't live here.

Uncle Cal's dark eyes soften as he comes around the island and tucks his hands in his pockets. "I wanted to talk to you about your father."

So, this is about him . . .

Just the mention of him wrenches inside my chest.

"Has he tried to call you?" His eyes search mine, and I swallow.

"Yes, but I haven't taken any of his calls."

"You're mad, upset. I understand that."

I say nothing in response, because what can I say? Hell yes, I'm mad. I'm fucking pissed. Over the years, I've put up with the drinking and the pills because he was all I had. Despite the fact he was a shitty father, at least he stuck around. I can give him credit for that much. But now he's left me too, and that might be the one thing I can't forgive.

"Is he getting out?" I ask.

"Well, that's the thing. This isn't his first brush with the law, so they've set bail for him, and I've given this a lot of thought before coming to a decision. I'm willing to post bond—"

"I'll find a way to pay you back," I quickly interrupt. I don't want him to think I'm happy to freeload off him any more than I already have.

Uncle Cal raises a hand. "This isn't about that. What happens with your father affects you. Which is why I want your input. I ran it by him, so I imagine it's the same reason he's been trying to get a hold of you."

"Okay." The bundle of nerves perching in my gut squeezes. "What is it?"

"I'll post his bail, but only if he goes to rehab. I found a nice facility that'll take him with no notice. It's a residential place, so he'll have to live on site for ninety days, but they have an amazing reputation. He'll be allowed out for court dates, but that's it."

"What's the catch?" If there's one thing I've learned in life, it's that most people have an angle. The problem with Uncle Cal is I can't figure out what his is.

"If I do this, it means you have to continue staying here for three more months. You're a grown man, Atlas, even if the law doesn't say so. Hell, my guess is you've been taking care of yourself for quite some time. So, if you'd rather me just bail him out and let them release him so you can go home, I will. Just say the word. But you and I both know he'll go back to his old ways. He always does."

I fight back the prickle of emotion, the sting in my eyes. No one has ever cared enough to give me a choice when it comes to my father. I've always been alone, completely on my own. And the thought that my pops would be given a chance to clean up his act—a real chance I can't give him—fills me with a kind of gratitude I've never known. Angle or not, I can't pass this up.

"Uh," I clear my throat, my voice cracking over the words, "I'm okay with him going to rehab."

"Now I don't know if it'll stick. Addiction is a hard road, son. We have several generations of addicts in our blood. I broke the cycle. Sadly, your dad didn't, but I've seen firsthand what kind of fight we're up against."

The soft flutter of hope emerges from the shadows of my heart, but I smother it—starve it of oxygen before it can grow wings because I know how this goes.

"I know. I understand. And I'm grateful for everything," I say, meaning it. "Thank you."

"Don't thank me, son. I should've done something a hell of a lot sooner, but, well, I guess I didn't know just how bad things had gotten. And that's on me. Just play a kick-ass game tonight and we'll call it even, okay?" He winks at me, and I grin.

"That I can do." I get to my feet, sensing the conversation is over, when he snaps his fingers, and I pause.

"One more thing. The housekeeper has yet to go grocery shopping, so Sheila and I are going to breakfast with friends this morning, but get yourself something to eat on the way into school." He reaches into his back pocket, pulls out a gold money clip filled with cash, and throws a twenty-dollar bill down on the island as I shake my head.

"No. I'm fine. I can get myself—"

"Take it." He shoves it closer and taps his fingers over the bill. "My house. My rules. We pay for everything around here while you're living under this roof."

"But—"

His sharp gaze cuts through my excuses. "Your job is to focus on your grades and that pigskin in your hands tonight. Got it?"

When I hesitate, he arches a brow, so I reach out and take the money.

"Sheila wants us to have dinner here tonight," he continues. "We'll celebrate your big win, and you being the new man in the house. Feel free to bring someone with you, if you'd like. Our home is your home, Atlas, and I want you to feel comfortable."

"I appreciate that, sir. Uh, will Graham be there?" I ask, wondering how this news went down with him.

"Both of you are expected to be here, so as soon as you wrap up, head home."

"Yes of course." I turn and head out of the kitchen, mulling this over.

Ever since Chief Hart dropped me off here, forcing my uncle to take me in, I've been torn between feeling like a charity case and waiting to see if there's some kind of angle he's playing. But ever since, he's been nothing but welcoming. Which is more than I can say for Graham. And if I'm being honest, there are other perks of being here as well, such as unlimited advice on my game. He actually pays attention, like, really pays attention to how I play and the areas in which I need to be pushed. The feedback he gives is better than anything Coach or anyone else has given me. Not to mention the connections he has, the doors he can open. Seeing as how I need every single advantage I can get, I'm not about to pass any of that up on account of my pride or skepticism.

Maybe he doesn't give a shit about me, I don't know. I'm not saying I blindly trust the man. Hell, I don't blindly trust anyone. And I'm no fool. There were a lot of years when I was young when I could've used help and he was nowhere to be found. But having support is something I'm not used to, which is probably why it's so damn hard for me to accept it now. But when it comes to football, I'll take anything I can get, considering it's my only ticket out of small-town Ohio to a bigger, brighter future. So, if that means attending awkward-ass family dinners, so be it. I suppose I should count myself lucky this is the first one considering I've been here a week now. Usually, by the time we get home from football my aunt and uncle have already eaten, and have left plates for Graham and me warming in the oven.

Honestly, having someone remember me startled me so much at first, I didn't even mind the nights Graham and I arrived at the same time and he took one to his room, leaving me to eat alone. I'm used to solitude. But the prospect of me sitting down at a catered dinner with them all together twists my stomach in knots. I don't remember a time when I've ever eaten as a family, so I have no idea what it entails, but my guess is when Uncle Cal told Graham about it, he wasn't too happy, which is why he hightailed it out of here.

I sling my backpack over my shoulder and head for my bike, pausing before I climb on to shoot Mackenzie a text.

Me: *Meet me at my locker. I need to talk to you about something.*

I shove my phone in my bag, mount my bike, and head to school while the desire to see Mackenzie fills me up like a hunger I can't quench. I know I'm playing with fire by asking her to come to dinner tonight. It's stupid and reckless continuing this thing between us, especially when it's pissing Graham off, but I'm trying to find a reason to care enough to stop.

One of us is bound to get burned. But I just can't seem to help myself.

MACKENZIE

I push my cereal around with my spoon as I wait for Graham to pick me up for school, wondering if he'll be as sullen today as he's been all week, when my father enters the kitchen in his uniform, eyeing me as he heads to the coffee pot. I set my spoon down, afraid to tip him off with my dubious mood.

"Working early today?" I ask, forcing a cheerful tone.

He fills his travel mug as he says, "I'll be done in time for the game. Will you be coming home straight after?"

Considering Graham's not speaking to me, and I'm unsure of what's going on between him and Atlas, I doubt I'll be going to the field party.

"Probably. Unless Tiff and Anastasia want to hang out. I thought about seeing if they want to catch a movie."

My father's eyes light up at the prospect of me hanging with the girls instead of Graham, which only makes me resent the idea.

"Sure thing. Let me know if you need some cash." His gaze shifts to my bowl and he nods toward my uneaten cereal and frowns. "Not hungry?"

"Just preoccupied. Big test today in Spanish," I lie.

"I'm sure you'll do just fine. Everything else at school going well?"

"Of course," I answer a little too quickly.

"What about this Atlas kid? Is he keeping his distance?"

"Dad, he's not who you think he—"

"I asked you to stay away from him"—his dark gaze slices through me, along with his sharp tone—"and I expect you to follow my rules."

I stare at him for a moment, wondering why he can't trust me enough to make my own judgments. But I don't say anything. Instead, I smile and mutter, "I'm following them. No worries. As I said, I have no plans tonight."

He stares at me a beat longer before his expression softens. "For the record, I think hanging with the girls is a great idea."

I'm sure you do, I want to say, but I bite the snide comment back because it'll get me nowhere. "I'll let you know." The second the words leave my mouth, the telltale sound of an engine pulling up in our driveway cuts the tension. "That's Graham," I say and jump up from my seat, then hurry outside, grateful to be saved from further inquisition.

For the first time all week, Graham actually talks to me on the drive to school. I'm not sure what's responsible for the sudden good mood, but I'm not about to jinx it, so after we arrive, I talk to him a few minutes longer until he leaves me to get his things, and I sneak off to meet Atlas.

Frankly, I have no idea what's going on between us. Ever since Monday, we've talked daily, sneaking time together when we can, both at school and before practice. Every time I'm around him, he surprises me. He's so much more than his reputation insinuates. It's people like my father who can't see past the rough exterior and his roots to the person within. But I know the truth, even if he tries to deny it. Atlas Scott might be slightly prickly on the outside, but he's soft as butter at the core.

When I spot him leaning against his locker, hands shoved in his pockets, I smile. I like the idea he's waiting for me. More and more, I'm starting to discover how much his presence disarms me, how it makes me hope for things I can't have.

He tracks my movements as I close in on him, and I can feel the heat of his gaze everywhere—on my bare legs, the exposed sliver of torso above my cheer skirt, my arms, lips, and finally, my eyes.

Goose bumps tease my skin at the attention as I stop in front of him and tuck a lock of hair behind my ear. "Hey," I say, fiddling with the strap of my book bag for fear I might melt over the attention. "You ready for tonight's game?"

"I'm always ready." The rumble of his voice sends chills up my spine, and I can't help but compare his easy confidence to how stressed Graham gets on game days. Sometimes I wonder if Graham even enjoys the sport anymore, or if he's gotten so caught up in being what's expected of him that he forgets why he started playing in the first place.

Atlas reaches for my hand and threads his fingers through mine. The gesture is intimate, and I try not to decipher its meaning. "I have a question for you . . ."

He licks his lips, and I think he might be nervous.

"Sure. What is it?" I ask.

"Uncle Cal is having this family dinner tonight after the game. It's supposed to be a welcome dinner since I'll be staying there a while longer, and a way to celebrate our preemptive win, but he said I could bring someone. And I'd like to take you."

Crap.

My thoughts drift first to my father then to Graham, and I swallow. I want to say yes, of course, I do. But things are already tense between Graham and I and I'm not sure showing up as Atlas's date will help matters. Not to mention my father's warning is fresh on my mind, and a dinner at the Scotts is risky. He and Uncle Cal are more than acquainted. The risk of him finding out is too high.

"Um, tonight?" I stall. My forehead creases and I bite my lip, giving the impression I'm trying to think of what I have going on. I hate lying, and I've done so much of it lately, I'm not sure I have the energy to try. Nor do I want to.

He drops my hand in the silence and takes a step back, putting distance between us as if I've already rejected him. "If you're busy, don't worry about it. I mean, it's just a stupid dinner. No biggie."

"Atlas." I reach out and grab his arm when he tries to turn toward his locker, forcing him to meet my gaze. I'm about to tell him I'm not sure it's a good idea when my stomach clenches at the hope in his eyes, and I say, "Of course, I'll go."

"Are you sure? Because it's not that big a deal if you can't."

My heart pounds as I think of what I'll tell my father. Lucky for me, I already mentioned hanging out with the girls.

"No. I want to. Really. I was just hesitating because I'll need to figure out what to tell my dad, but I've got it covered. No worries." I smile, even though I feel like crap about it. I have no idea what Graham's reaction to my being there will be, but it'll make one of them happy, even if I have to hurt the other.

"Great." Atlas nods and flashes me a brilliant smile, which lights up his entire face. "I mean, I'm kinda nervous because I don't think Graham particularly wants me there and taking me in was a big ask. Uncle Cal's been really good to me, though, so I don't want to screw things up, you know? But I have no idea what I'm doing. I mean, shoot, I've never sat down to a family dinner in my life, and I have a feeling it's going to be a big deal." He runs a hand through his hair, clearly on edge at the idea of a formal dinner.

It tugs on my heartstrings.

"You'll do great," I say, giving his arm a squeeze.

"Yeah, because I'll have you there," he murmurs. Then he leans in and presses his lips to mine. "I'll see you tonight, then," he whispers against my lips. And then he's gone.

Chapter 21

GRAHAM

The moment I get home from the game, I head to my room where I plan to get ready for dinner. There's a bounce to my step as I choose a dress shirt, tie, and slacks from the massive walk-in closet in my room. I played a solid game tonight, much improved than last week. It's something I could be proud of, and the number on the scoreboard proved it. Riverside brought Perry High to their knees in a landslide victory. Which is lucky for me, because my performance will undoubtedly be a topic of conversation with my father tonight. And the better I play, the less criticism I receive.

There's a knock on my door, and when I turn and answer it, I'm startled to see Atlas on the other side. Ever since he moved in and I warned him off Kenzie, he's barely spoken to me outside practice, which is fine by me. We played well tonight, so our issues haven't spread to the field. And, okay, maybe I feel a little better about Kenzie. The time and distance this week gave me the opportunity for reflection, and I realized I had no reason to get jealous and worked up over a single kiss with Atlas when she has no idea how I feel about her. Because if she has a choice, she'll choose me. I have to believe this. Which is why I'm going to tell her as soon as I have the chance.

I stare at him standing in my doorway and arch a brow in question.

"Hey, man, are we supposed to wear anything special to dinner?" he asks.

No doubt Atlas has never been to a formal dinner at home. Hell, I wonder if he's ever been to a family dinner at all where it didn't come out of a box with a side of Miller Light. His father was a real piece of work.

I grin over at him, extending an olive branch. "What, you don't think the great Calvin Scott would appreciate joggers and a hoodie?"

Atlas chuckles at my joke, and I'm momentarily proud of myself for being civil.

"Yeah, somehow I'm thinking whatever dress code is required isn't in my wardrobe."

I nod. "I got you covered. Hang on."

I'm guessing Atlas and I are about the same size, so it's easy to find something to fit him. I yank out a blue dress shirt and one of my black suits, together with a printed tie, then hand them to him. He exhales and the tension in his shoulders relaxes. "Thanks, man."

He hesitates a moment longer, and I wonder if he might say something else, possibly apologize for barging into my life, stealing my girl, and crashing my home, but instead, he offers me a nod and leaves. Which is fine by me. I'm not one for talking out my problems. I'd rather handle them on the field. Hell, it's how I've been handling my feelings for Kenzie, along with any accompanying sexual frustration, for years.

I shower and change, taking my time. No need to rush into a dinner with my parents and my burgeoning enemy. I'm not sure what Dad thinks; that we're all gonna sit around the table and sing kumbaya and become one happy family? But whatever his intentions, I'm just planning on getting through the night. I only wish I had Kenzie by my side.

MACKENZIE

After a blowout win, I ask Tiff to take me home where she helps me get ready. I style my hair while she does my makeup, then I neatly fold a little black dress into a tote bag, along with my red heels, so I can slip them on in her car. My father thinks we're getting something to eat, then hitting a movie. I caved earlier and told her about mine and Atlas's situationship—because it's neither a relationship nor a friendship—and she agreed to be my alibi. I enjoy the time we spend together, and we laugh and talk about school and boys before we get back in her car and head toward the Scotts' place.

"You ready for this?" she asks, brow raised as she glances over at me underneath the streetlamps outside their house.

I exhale and press a hand to my stomach. "Why do I tell Graham I'm here? I mean, he's gonna wonder, right?"

Tiff's soft laughter rumbles in her chest. "Heck if I know. Just . . . deflect."

"Deflect?"

She shrugs. "It always works for me. 'Hey, Tiff,'" she says impersonating someone that sounds a lot like Jenna, "'do these pants make my butt look big?' 'Oh, hey!'"—she points—"'I think I see Robert Pattinson.'" Her grin widens. "Works every time."

I laugh and lean back into the seat, suddenly wishing I *was* spending time with the girls because dinner at the Scotts sounds a whole lot more . . . complicated.

As if she can read my thoughts, she bumps my shoulder and says, "Call me when you need a ride home, okay?"

"Thanks, Tiff."

"Sure thing. It's good to have you back"—she winks—"even if you *are* stirring up trouble."

I snort and open the door, stepping into the cooling evening air and make my way up the pebbled walkway toward the grand front entrance of the Scott residence. The few dinners I've attended here previously have been cooked and served by their housekeeper, complete with crystal drinkware and linen-draped tables. Not exactly lavish like in the movies, but a solid reminder they're the wealthiest family in town.

I smooth a hand over my dress as I ring the doorbell and wait, surprised when, Sheila, Graham's mother, answers the door instead of their housekeeper. Looking stylish in a dark green dress and pearls, she pulls me in, greeting me with a warm hug before ushering me into the formal dining room. "Graham is cleaning up, so I'm sure he'll be down in a few."

I nod and my stomach ties in knots. She thinks I'm here for Graham. Of course, she does. Little does she know her son has no idea I'm even coming, and I'm clueless as to how he'll react when he sees me here.

I have no time for further contemplation because no sooner does she leave, Atlas appears from around the corner, saving me from my fretting.

I struggle to keep my jaw from hitting the floor as I take him in. The boy on a bad day is hot as sin, but Atlas in a suit? He's heart-stopping. Bring-me-to-my-knees gorgeous.

His gaze locks on mine, and he saunters toward me with the easy confidence of someone who knows how good they look. If he's uncomfortable in his dress clothes, he doesn't show it. Then again, something tells me Atlas is good at masking how he really feels, maybe even from himself.

He draws me into a warm hug the second he reaches me, pressing me against his chest where I breathe in the clean scent of his soap. My heart pounds, beating against bone, captive against my ribs. The longer he holds me, the more I melt into him, and it amazes me that I'm so affected by the embrace of a boy I've only known a few short weeks.

"Hey," I breathe, trying to ignore the way he's tracing circles on my back, turning my skin to torch flame.

"You look beautiful." The soft rumble of his voice sends butterflies rioting in my stomach. My cheek presses into the hard plains of his chest as my arms wrap around him.

If I rise on my toes and tip my head, I'll meet the warmth of his lips.

But Graham is here, I remind myself. So, I pull away just as someone clears their throat behind us, and when I shift my gaze, I see him standing there, watching as surprise brightens his green eyes to gold. The same eyes then shift, taking in Atlas's hands still gripping my waist.

I drop my arms and hold them at my sides like dead weight, unsure of what to do with myself at the same time their eyes lock. The atmosphere in the room shifts and tightens, like a rubber band waiting to snap.

My palms dampen and my breath hitches as I contemplate whether I should go to Graham or stay put, when his gaze makes a slow perusal of my body. When he grins, I sag with relief.

"Kenz . . . ?" He shakes his head like I'm an apparition. "Well, isn't this the best surprise? And that dress . . ." He bites his knuckles, and I laugh at the levity it brings. Because this is *my* Graham. My best friend. The boy I've known and loved since we were twelve.

"You're not so bad yourself," I say as he comes to my side and pulls me into a giant bear hug, dropping a kiss to the top of my head. It's familiar and comforting in a way Atlas's embrace is not. While Atlas makes my pulse race, Graham soothes my soul and smooths all my rough edges.

"I had no idea my parents invited you, but I'm so glad you're here," he whispers.

I think I might be sick as I glance over at Atlas once he releases me, nerves twisting in my stomach as I offer him an apologetic smile. I'm torn between showing affection for my best friend and the boy who's currently doing crazy things to my heart. But I'm relieved by the warmth in his gaze before it shifts to Graham, and the muscle in his jaw twitches.

"Atlas, honey, you clean up well," Sheila says as she bustles into the room, cutting through the tension.

I exhale as she offers her nephew a sweet smile and waves us all into the dining room. "Why don't you kids help yourselves to a beverage? We'll be starting dinner shortly."

"Do you want anything?" Graham asks, and I shake my head before he tugs me toward the dining room. "Come on, then."

I glance back helplessly at Atlas who shoots daggers at the back of Graham's head. When we enter the lavish dining room, I take in the table draped ivory linens. Candles, fresh flowers, and crystal all give the table a lush appearance.

I make a beeline for the first seat I lay eyes on, but Atlas walks around me and beats me to it, pulling it out for me to sit while Graham stiffens beside him. "I could've gotten the chair for her," he says, his smile tight.

"She's my—"

"What a gentleman. Thank you," I say, a little too loudly and sink into the chair. Then, pointing to the cloth napkins, I ask "Are those silk?" I glance up at Graham whose brows knit, and I motion to the chair on my right.

When he makes no move to sit, I lean closer and murmur, "I figured you'd want the one furthest from your father."

"Thanks," Graham whispers, then he offers me a private smile as he finally sinks down into the seat beside me at the same time Atlas takes the seat on my left, his hand slipping beneath the table and coming down over my bare knee.

Butterflies return with a vengeance as a zip of electricity runs up my leg, and I swallow. It takes everything in me not to pick the cloth napkin up off my plate and fan my face with it.

I risk a glance at Graham who seems unaware that my insides are turning to molten lava, and I wonder why it feels like I'm torn between these two boys beside me. Why does it feel like I can't have them both? Something more with Atlas and my friendship with Graham at the same time. It shouldn't be this hard.

Graham stretches his arm and rests it behind me on the back of my chair, while I raise my water glass to my mouth with a trembling hand and choke down a sip of ice water.

This is going to be a long dinner.

I'm almost relieved when Sheila bustles into the room, carrying a large glass of red wine, Cal following behind her as he takes a seat at the head of the table. I've always liked Graham's mom. Where his father can be overly sober and unfeeling, his mother is as warm as a ray of sunshine. I often wonder how the two stayed together all these years. Then again, maybe opposites do really attract. Maybe they make up for the qualities the other lacks.

Graham always says his mother simply likes the cushy lifestyle Cal provides, but I'm unconvinced because I see the love in her eyes every time she looks at him. The only thing I can't seem to understand is why she doesn't encourage him to go easier on Graham.

Dinner begins with Mrs. White, the housekeeper, bringing out an appetizer for each of us, and we start eating it in silence as Sheila discusses her plans for the Riverside Fall Fest this year. She's been on the committee for as long as I can remember and cares deeply about this town, however small. Graham told me the whole reason his father settled in Riverside was because of her. She'd grown up here and couldn't see herself raising a family any other place.

I give her my input when she asks my opinion on several things and offer my help in decorating the town square, grateful the topic of football has yet to come up, when Calvin finally clears his throat and directs his attention to Atlas.

"It's tradition that the Riverside MVP has a spot on the float. Think you boys are up for a little friendly competition?" He arches a brow and glances between them, and all I want to do is crawl under the table and disappear.

"Oh, now don't go putting that pressure on them, Cal" Sheila adds, and I think she's got to be kidding because of all the things Graham's father pressures him to do, the parade float at Fall Fest is the least of it.

Graham glares at his father as Mrs. White clears our plates and brings out the main course, then makes herself scarce. The table falls silent once more. Calvin takes several bites of his food before washing it down with some kind of amber liquid from a crystal tumbler. Leaning back in his seat, his gaze falls to his son. I hold my breath, because experience dictates whatever is about to come out of his mouth can't be good.

"Tonight's game was much improved from the shit show last Friday," he says between bites of steak.

"Calvin," Sheila scolds, with a little shake of the head before she returns to her meal with a smile, like he's just joking.

"Why, thank you, Father," Graham says, and it's hard to miss the sarcastic edge to his tone.

Cal nods like he did him a favor. "Your running game was there tonight, but you need to get rid of the ball sooner. You got lucky a few times. One or two scouts were watching, but they didn't seem too impressed when you failed to get rid of the ball at the end of the third quarter and you got sacked."

Graham stiffens, and my heart goes out to him. "One sack because I had shit coverage."

"Graham, language." Sheila shoots him a stern look, and I want to sink into the floor.

"Nothing about the eighty yards I threw, though, huh?" Graham says, ignoring her. "Always great with the compliments, Dad. Thanks."

Calvin shrugs. "Just calling it like I see it. Haven't heard anything from Coach about offers. At least not for you," he says meaningfully as his gaze shifts to Atlas with a smile, and my stomach sinks.

Graham finds my right hand beneath the table, and I give it a little squeeze, finding the courage to speak up. "Well, I thought he had a great game," I say, noticing the answering smile that touches Graham's lips.

Calvin makes a dismissive sound in the back of his throat. "I guess greatness is up for interpretation." He stabs his meat with his fork and takes a bite.

"Your arm was solid tonight," Atlas chimes in, but his defense only seems to make Graham angrier.

His green eyes darken as he glances from Atlas to his father. "Coach Clancy seems to think I'm doing just fine."

"Is that so?" Calvin arches his brows. "Because he pulled me aside after the game and told me that he wasn't sure what happened between preseason and now, but it seems like you're losing your edge."

Graham's eyes widen before he drops his gaze to his plate, and my heart aches for him. I understand constructive criticism, but Cal seems intent on cutting him down, no matter the time or place. Is it so hard to offer his only son even a single word of encouragement?

"He hasn't mentioned it to me," Graham mumbles as he stares at his food.

"That's because I told him I'd talk to you and get to the bottom of it. Atlas, on the other hand, couldn't have played a better game last week, and tonight was no different," Calvin says, motioning toward him. "It seems you have several schools asking about you. Keep it up, and you'll guarantee yourself a bright future. Coach said he'll direct any inquiries to me since your father isn't in a position to help."

Graham's head whips up from his plate, his expression crushed, before glancing over at Atlas, eyes narrowed to slits.

Balling his napkin in his hands, Graham tosses it onto his plate and addresses his father. "Just what is your problem with me exactly?"

Cal blinks, chewing his food. "Excuse me?"

"You heard me. I've spent my entire football career and half my childhood for that matter trying to please you, yet it's never enough."

Cal scoffs. "Oh, please. If you wanted to please me, you'd work harder, take football more seriously."

"With all due respect, Mr. Scott, Graham couldn't work harder if he tried," I say. "He's under enough pressure as it is, and he—"

"Did I ask you?" Cal cuts me off, effectively shutting me up.

"Don't talk to her that way," Graham snaps.

At the same time, Atlas shoots to his feet. "She's the best damn one of us at this table," he snarls.

Cal glares holes through his son, barely glancing toward Atlas while I watch nervously, heart in my throat.

The muscle in Atlas's jaw tenses, and just when I start to worry about what he might do or say, Sheila clears her throat and shoots me a look of apology as Atlas sits back down. "See, now this is why we don't talk sports or politics at the table," she says, as if football is the problem and not her husband. "Mackenzie,"—she smiles at me—"tell me what it's like being back at school, will you? Are you adjusting well?"

I settle my hands on my lap and try my best to offer her a smile, only to find Graham's hand sneak beneath the tablecloth again to clasp my right, giving it a little squeeze. On my left, Atlas's pinky finger finds mine. So, I sit there, tethered between them. Torn.

Somehow, I manage to make it through dinner and find myself hovering in the living room, awkwardly wondering what to do with myself as I wait for my heart rate to come back to earth. Between these boys, I have a feeling I'll be waiting a long time.

I glance at Graham as he enters the room. If this were any other night, we'd probably hang out, talking and watching movies for hours. But it's not a typical night with my best friend. Atlas is here, too, which complicates things. I'm stuck in some weird dynamic I don't even understand. All I know is the tension from dinner still lingers between us and the idea of leaving them alone in a room together seems dangerous, but I can't help myself as I excuse myself to use the bathroom. I need a moment to catch my breath, a reprieve from the rubber band currently tightening around my chest.

Head down, I hurry down the hall, toward the powder room off the den and shut myself inside. I make a beeline for the marble-topped sink, and brace my hands on the cold stone, taking a deep breath to try and clear my mind. Only a few seconds pass before the door opens behind me, and I spin toward the sound to find Atlas.

Danger glints in his eyes as he closes the door behind him and locks it.

Blood pounds in my ears as he takes a step closer, and I hold a hand out. "What are you doing? Are you insane?" I hiss. "Someone will catch us—" His finger presses against my lips, silencing me before he draws me in for a kiss.

Everything screams at me to push him away. This isn't the time or place with Graham just down the hall, but I can't seem to help myself so I part my lips.

His hands reach up to cup my face, and I sigh. His lips are soft and his mouth sweet, like the crème brûlée we had for dessert, and I want to drown in him. Forget about everything around me—my mother, the accident, my father and his rules, and Graham, furious in the other room— except him and this moment.

The soft slide of his hands drift from my face to my waist and then to my thighs where they flirt with the hem of my skirt. My breathing becomes faster as he scoots me back so my legs dig into the back of the counter, his eyes twinkling as he murmurs, "How long do you think we have until Golden Boy comes looking for us?"

I shoot him a dark look, but he only chuckles.

"He's my friend," I mutter, slightly defensive.

"Maybe. But I'm not blind, doll." His fingers brush the skin of my thighs, just above the hem of my dress and I shiver. "I see the way he looks at you."

I shake my head, brow furrowed as my thoughts drift to the field party when Graham asked me about homecoming. He's never brought it up again, and I've never asked. Maybe I don't want to know where the conversation was headed.

"We have a lot of history, that's all," I say, pushing off the sink and stepping aside so I can think, because when Atlas is this close to me with his hands on my skin, my brain shuts down and all I do is feel.

Atlas grunts, seemingly bothered by the distance between us. "Is that what you call it?"

"Jealous?" I grin.

"Maybe." He saunters toward me once more, placing his hands on my waist. "Come up to my room and stay for a while so we can be alone. I promise I'll keep my hands to myself," he says brushing his thumb over my lower lip, and I nearly laugh until he adds, "After all, I am your date, am I not?"

"Atlas, what are we doing here?" I ask, motioning between us.

"Hell if I know."

Exasperated, I sigh and step out of his grip, pivoting for the door, but not before he captures me in his arms. My back presses into his muscular chest, and all I want to do is tip my head back and press my mouth to his once more. I want to turn and trace the rigid lines of his muscles with my hands, to slide my fingers over the ink on his arm and dissect their meaning like the blind reading braille.

But I don't, because Graham is just down the hall, and the boy behind me confuses me. I have no idea where my place is in his life, and his actions only confuse me further because they don't match his words.

"I like you, Mackenzie Hart. A lot, actually."

Surprise grips me by the throat. "I like you, too," I croak.

"I wish I could say I'm that guy. The kind who makes you promises and keeps them. The kind that will never let you down. The kind that can commit and call you my girlfriend. But I'm not. I don't even know how to be that man if I tried. I'm just not built that way. Maybe it's because I can't define a functional relationship to save my life. Or maybe I'm just damaged. I don't know. All I know is I want you, even if I don't deserve you. But I can't give you what you need. All I have is this moment, right now."

I close my eyes before I blink them open and slowly turn around in his arms. "You're not damaged." I tilt my head to face him. "Don't even say that."

"It's true."

"Well, then, so am I."

He shakes his head and leans down, pressing his forehead to mine. "No way. You're absolutely perfect, Mackenzie Hart."

"You think so?"

"I know so."

We stay like that, standing with our foreheads pressed together, breathing each other in while my mind races. I want Atlas; there's no doubt about it. I just need to decide if I'm willing to risk my heart, my relationship with my father, and most importantly, Graham, to have whatever piece of him he's willing to give.

Is a chance with Atlas worth it?

My heart says yes, but my mind hesitates, too afraid to commit. "Let's just enjoy whatever this is," I say, breaking the silence.

"Yeah?"

I nod, wordless as my thoughts drift to Graham and guilt pinches my chest, but I'm strengthened by the feel of Atlas's hands in my hair.

He opens his mouth to say something before a phone rings, breaking the silence. He curses and pulls it from his pocket, glancing at the screen.

"My dad." His mouth mashes into a hard line as he tucks it away again.

"Aren't you going to talk to him?" I ask, thinking about what Calvin said at dinner.

"He wants to see me before he agrees to go to rehab. The shithead can't even pay for it himself and he wants my approval? Why? It's not like he's ever cared what I think. He's spent most of my life fucked up beyond belief, and now he wants to know what I want? Whether he should rot in jail or try and get clean? For years, I've dreamed he'd get better. For years, I've prayed he might realize I need him, and his love for me might somehow be enough to make him change."

The pain in his words wrenches in my chest. I have no idea what to say to him. Despite our differences, my father and I are close. I can't imagine what it must be like to have no one.

"Oh, Atlas, maybe . . . I mean, what if . . .?" I place my hand on his arm, and his throat bobs.

"I'm all out of hope, doll. I have been for a long time." He wraps his hand around my arm and tugs me even closer, until I'm pressed against his chest. "I'm just not capable of it anymore."

"Maybe you're looking at this all wrong," I say, sliding my hands over his muscled back.

"How so?"

"Don't call him for him. Call him for you."

He brushes a lock of hair from my face, his touch so gentle it leaves me hollow inside, when he stops. "I don't know if I can."

"Of course, you can. You're one of the strongest people I know."

His brow knits and all I want is to reach out and smooth the lines with my fingers, to ease all the broken pieces inside. "Will you go with me?" he murmurs. "To talk to him?" His eyes search mine, and I say yes before I can even think about my answer because I'm pretty sure I'd do anything for this boy. Go anywhere. Consequences be damned.

His heart beats against mine as his gaze falls to my mouth, and my breathing grows shallow because I know what comes next.

I meet him halfway, pressing my mouth against his while heat spikes my veins. I've never had this kind of connection before. It's indescribable. Magnetic. Insatiable. Every time I'm around him, all I want is more. I just wish I knew how much he's willing to give. Or how much I could take before he breaks me completely.

Chapter 22

GRAHAM

Dinner was every bit the shitshow I anticipated. But what I hadn't expected was for Kenzie to disappear into the bathroom and not return for forty-five minutes, especially as I'm 99 percent sure Atlas joined her, since he excused himself only a minute after she left to "retire to his room." A million bucks says he's with her right now.

Bested again, but I can't say I blame him. He beat me to the punch, and a part of me can't even be mad for going after what he wants.

I sink down onto my bed and bend at the waist, leaning forward with my head in my hands, unsure of whether I've ever felt quite so defeated before. I'm a senior in high school and a dang good quarterback for one of the best schools in Ohio. I should be in my prime, loving life. Yet it seems all I do is lose. My father is either an ignorant asshole or he hates me. I'm not sure which. Maybe it's both. Nothing I do ever seems to please him. If I have a bad game, I hear about it. If I excel on the field, all he does is pick apart my flaws while Atlas seems to do no wrong. He wins all of my father's praise despite the fact he's done nothing to earn it.

All I know is I've tried to please him for years and I'm at the end of my rope. I can't do it anymore and my ability to give a damn is waning by the second. Only bitterness lies in its wake.

And then there's Mackenzie. The more she falls for Atlas, the harder it will be to win her over. Even on a good day, I'm unsure whether she'll return my feelings, but now I'm even less confident because I'm competing against my cousin for her heart, while I'm still warming the bench.

"Graham?"

My head jerks up at the sound of Kenzie's voice and I take her in: red-cheeked, in a little black dress with soft waves spilling over her shoulders. She's so damn beautiful it makes my heart thud painfully in my chest. Sometimes I think if I try to become something more with Kenzie and fail, it will be the death of me. It's probably half the reason I've been too scared to give it a real shot.

I clear my throat when I realize I've been staring. "How long have you been standing there?"

"Just a minute." A soft smile spreads over her lips as she crosses the room and takes a seat beside me on my bed. "What's wrong?"

I search her eyes for a sign she's been with Atlas this whole time and find none, but I'm no fool. "Get lost in the bathroom?" I ask, trying my best to sound as if I don't care, yet unable to help myself.

Her throat bobs, giving her away, but instead of being angry, I'm transfixed by the movement. Suddenly, I don't want to know. For one shining moment, I want to pretend Atlas Scott doesn't exist. Like he didn't come barreling into our lives like a wrecking ball.

"For once in his life, why can't my father just say I played well and leave it at that?" I ask in the answering silence.

"I don't know." Her soft gaze meets mine, and she reaches out, placing her hand on my left leg while I track the movement.

"He's sure taken a liking to Atlas though. Hell, if I didn't know any better, I'd think *he* was his son and *I* was the junkie's kid."

"Graham . . ."

"What? It's the truth. All I've heard since he's moved to town is Atlas this and Atlas that. 'He outplayed you tonight, Graham,'" I say in a mocking tone. "'He'll get a scholarship, but you won't.'" I shake my head. "And Atlas just eats it up. He probably loves it when Cal shits all over me."

"That's not fair," she says, her tone irritatingly defensive.

"That's not fair?" My brows rise, along with my ire. "Atlas asks him for advice, and when Dad actually gives it to him, it's not the passive aggressive shit he gives me. It's actually useful, considerate and positive, yet even the most remote praise he gives me is laced with condescension."

"Maybe he only treats him differently because he knows how rough he's had it?"

Laughter spills from my lips. "Of course, you'd say that."

"What's that supposed to mean?"

"Nothing." I jump to my feet, unable to sit still any longer, and cross my arms over my chest as I face her. "It's just seems like maybe he has you and everyone else brainwashed. Maybe he really *is* the guy everyone says he is."

"He's not."

"Right. Because you know him so well after just a few weeks." It's amazing, in such a short period of time, how much he's gotten in her head. "Just don't expect me to be here to pick up the pieces when he breaks your heart, Kenz. Because that's exactly what will happen."

"You don't know that," she snaps.

"I do." I smirk, though there's no victory in it.

Her hands fist, but I don't care if she's mad. She needs to hear the truth.

I turn away and head to my desk where I grab my phone and text the guys. Maybe I'll go out, after all.

"What exactly is your problem?" Kenzie storms up behind me, but when I pay her no attention, she gets in my face. "Ever since the field party, you've barely spoken to me. You've been short all week. Didn't invite me to watch game tape with you on Thursday, and when I confronted you about it, you acted like it was no big deal. Like it's completely normal for you to ghost me. You say you don't trust Atlas because you don't know him, but you've made zero effort to actually *get* to know him. Instead, you're pissed at me because I might actually see something in him that others don't. So, what exactly is the problem here, Graham?"

I tip my head back and laugh bitterly, because isn't it obvious? How is it she can be so blind?

"Shit, Kenzie, maybe it's because I'm the one that's constantly here for you. I'm at your beck and call. I stayed with you every day after the accident, lifted you up, and dried your tears. I made it my personal, fucking life's mission to make you smile again. And, you know what? It was worth it. I don't regret a thing. But I follow you around everywhere like a lost puppy. I freaking watched as my cousin, and teammate, stole my spot with you at the field party and sucked your face. And I'm supposed to just be happy about it? I'm basically a boyfriend without benefits."

She stumbles back as shock rips through her features.

It feels good to stun her into silence.

Her mouth opens, but nothing comes out. She has no words for what I've just told her.

Time slows and the muscle in my jaw twitches as I stare her down, wondering what it means that she's so surprised by this admission.

"What are you . . ." She trails off, then tries again. "So, are you saying you *want* the benefits?"

I hesitate, then sigh. "Forget I said anything. Just let it go." I shake my head while my heart threatens to beat out of my chest.

What did I do?

"No, Graham." She grabs my arm, but I refuse to look her in the eye. "I want to know. What are you saying?"

I try to brush past her, but she curls a hand around my bicep, keeping me in place.

"I won't forget it," she says. "Explain it to me."

"Just stop." Emotion rises inside of me like a howling wind. If she doesn't get it now, she never will. At least if I shut my mouth, I might salvage more than a shred of dignity.

"Tell me what you mean."

"I said, drop it!" I yank my arm away, but she gets in my face.

Feet squared like a linebacker, she looks me square in the eye. "Make me."

And I snap.

I reach out and yank her to me, my mouth crashing over hers as I back her up to the desk until she's practically sitting on the edge of it.

I can taste her surprise as I lift her up, scooting her further onto the cool hard wood as I step between her legs, relishing the tiny gasp that escapes her lips. And before I can hope for it or even dream it, she kisses me back.

MACKENZIE

My lips hum from the contact while my heart threatens to rip through my ribcage.

This is Graham, my head screams. My best friend in the whole world.

His urgency softens. He slowly reaches his hands up to cup my face, his lips a tender caress while they move against mine. Butterflies flutter in my stomach, beating their wings as I try to reconcile myself with the fact that I'm kissing my best friend.

And I like it.

More than like it.

My hands tug at the silky strands of his hair until my breathing grows ragged and the world around me fades. His hands slide down my arms to my waist where he grips me like a lifeline, his fingers digging into my flesh as if he having a war with himself to keep them from roaming. I must be insane because for a split second, part of me wants them to.

He tugs at my lower lip with his teeth before placing one last soft kiss to my mouth and pulling back so his eyes meet mine, searching as I struggle to stop the world from spinning and process what just happened.

Then he smiles, and my whole world tilts on its axis.

I lift a hand to my mouth and touch my lips while he follows the movement with his gaze.

"I've been thinking about doing that for a really long time," he says, his tone gruff, and when he reaches out to tuck a lock of hair behind my ear, my heart kickstarts in my chest.

"You have?"

He nods and takes my hand in his. "Tell me what you're thinking?" he whispers, glancing down at our intertwined fingers.

The boy just blew my mind, and he's worried about me. But that's my Graham, always looking out for my best interests.

"I'm wondering . . ." I swallow. My heart is beating so fast I think it might explode. "Where this leads to. What this means."

"It *means* that you've had my heart for as long as I can remember. I'm yours, Kenz, it's that simple. And this can lead wherever you want it to."

His words hit me square in the chest, and my stomach clenches. How could I possibly go for so long without really knowing how he feels?

His throat bobs as he waits for me to respond, but my mind is struggling to play catch-up because what Graham and I have is special. No doubt about it. And his kiss . . . that kiss meant something.

I can honestly say until this moment, I've never thought about having something more with Graham. But sitting here and facing him now, our fingers and limbs intertwined like we're one person instead of two, I can see how beautiful it could be. How great we could be together.

But I can't decide anything in the moment. My mind's a mess. I need to think. Process.

As if he senses the war inside my head, he presses his cheek to mine and inhales, like he's trying to breathe me in. Like this might be the last time he gets the chance.

"Just think about it," he tells me. "That's all I ask. Take some time. Think about how great it could be. How great *we* could be. Because I promise, Kenz, I'll give you the fucking world if you choose me."

Chapter 23

MACKENSIE

TWO DAYS HAVE PASSED since the night Graham kissed me, and I'm still struggling to wrap my head around it—the way he made me feel; the way I got lost in his lips, his touch—and what that means for us.

Of course, I've noticed how, in the last couple of years, he's gone from a lanky preteen to the muscled star quarterback of Riverside. I'd have to be blind not to see that he's so heartbreakingly beautiful. All that sandy hair and those bright green eyes; he could pose for an Abercrombie and Fitch ad tomorrow, and every single girl across the nation would plaster his centerfolds over their bedroom walls.

But he's my best friend—my rock. And that's the one thing I keep circling back to because as much as I enjoyed our kiss, I can't lose him. To take what we have and move it beyond friendship, explore what could be, would mean risking everything if it doesn't work out.

Then there's Atlas. Kissing Graham, though amazing, didn't suddenly erase him from the picture. He's still in my head and my heart. And though I know feeling something for him is a huge risk, I can't help but feel it anyway. By his own admission, he's not boyfriend material.

He can't promise me he'll be here for me tomorrow, and won't define us with a label. Yet I still want him, and that has to mean something.

My phone buzzes, and I pick it up to glance at the screen. It's Atlas, here to pick me up.

Atlas: You're sure it's okay to be out here?

I quickly type back.

Mackenzie: Positive. Dad's at work. Wanna come up? Second door on your left.

It's not long before Atlas hovers in the doorway of my bedroom. His presence commands attention, and his broad shoulders fill the space as eyes, dark as an oil slick, sweep over me. "We should probably get going."

"Are you scared?" I chuckle.

"Hell yeah, I'm scared." His lips twitch in a half smile, while he grips the doorframe. "If your father comes home and finds me here, I'm not walking out alive."

I roll my eyes. "He's not that bad," I say, though he really is that bad, and Atlas knows it. "Don't you wanna see my room?" I stand up and go to him, then tug him inside by the strings of his black hoodie while his gaze heats.

"You're playing with fire, Hart."

Don't I know it.

I beckon him forward with a curl of the finger, willing him to press his mouth to mine, make me forget about Friday night. About Graham's kiss and how it's changed this between us. Because one way or another, I'll have to choose, and that choice will irrevocably change everything.

But Atlas doesn't press his lips to mine. Instead, he moves close enough that I can smell the cedar scent of his skin, yet remains far enough away, I can't touch him.

"You disappeared Friday night after you left me in the bathroom. I thought you might have come back to my room to see me." His gaze focuses on my desk while he talks, and he picks up the paperweight I have sitting on the stack of papers, testing the weight of it in his hands.

It's acrylic with a little violet inside. Graham gave it to me on my thirteenth birthday, and my chest clenches at the sight of it in Atlas's hand.

"Uh, yeah," I hedge. "Sorry about that, but after I talked to Graham, I wasn't feeling well. Since it was getting late, I didn't want Cal and Sheila to get upset with me for still being there, considering how tense dinner was."

He nods, and for a moment, I'm not sure he believes me. Sitting the paperweight back down, he lifts his head, his gaze flickering over my room, taking in his surroundings. "So, this is Kenzie Hart's lair, huh?"

I snort. "This is it."

My hands flutter around me, anxious with his assessment as he pushes off the desk and begins to roam. He reaches up to the shelf across from my bed and touches one of the trophies. "You were a dancer?"

I nod, even though he's not facing me. "For a long time, I took lessons and did competitions, but quit when I was in eighth grade."

"Why?" He glances back at me as if my answer is important. It's not.

"It was just a lot, and I wanted to enjoy high school without constantly running around on the weekends. I also wanted to do cheer instead."

He turns his attention to my dresser next and lifts up a bottle of body lotion, brings it to his nose, and inhales while his eyelids flutter closed. "So, this is why you always smell like apple blossom."

My heart kicks as he puts it back, then shifts his gaze to the mirror where he zeroes in on a strip of black-and-white photos. They're of Graham and me. We took them at a movie theater during freshman year. Then another photo, this one an action shot.

Atlas plucks it from the glass to examine it better. We're both in swimsuits and Graham has his arms wrapped around me from behind, ready to throw me in the pool. My mouth is parted in a laugh or a scream, I'm not sure. Probably both.

"You have history," he says, and something about the way he says it tells me he's heard those exact words before regarding me and Graham.

"We do," I say, because there's no denying it. "We've been friends for a long time." Nothing more, I want to add. But after Friday night, I'm not sure how true those words are.

When he turns back to me, his eyes lock on mine, and I expect him to say something else about Graham, to question me, but he doesn't. Then again, why would he if he doesn't plan on us having a future together beyond the present moment? If he doesn't want to put a label on us, what does it matter if I have something with someone else?

The thought depresses me.

His dark eyes search mine as if he can tell my thoughts are elsewhere. "You ready for today?"

It's Sunday, and we're supposed to meet his father. After I promised to go with him during dinner on Friday night, he called the next morning and told his father he'd be there for Sunday visitation. I'd be lying if I said I wasn't nervous. I've never been inside the jail before, nor have I seen a convict or a man in cuffs except for on television. Despite my father being in law enforcement, he's sheltered me from all things harmful, dangerous, harsh, or cruel in this world. Other than the accident, that is. The truth is you can't always shelter someone from the harsh realities of life, no matter how hard you try.

"Are you ready?" I ask. It doesn't matter if I'm not, it's Atlas who has to face him.

He exhales and scrubs a hand down his face. "I guess. I mean, it's not like he's never been in trouble before. This isn't his first offense. But it will be the first time I see him in prison and the last time I see him for who knows how long. He's been a crappy father, but he's always been there, in body, at least. It'll be weird not seeing him for months."

"I can't imagine how hard this is."

He shrugs. "It shouldn't be. It's not like he ever did anything to make my life easier."

I tilt my head. "It's okay to miss him, to care. He's your father."

"By blood and name at least."

"But family all the same."

He falls silent and I guide him downstairs where we step outside, greeted by a sunny blue sky. Crisp notes of autumn scent the air, reminding me of my mother—of warm apple pie, trick-or-treating, and all those fall-scented candles she used to burn.

Longing grips me by the throat and squeezes, taking me by surprise in the unique way only grief can, but I shove it down.

Atlas leads the way to his bike—he parked several houses down—and when he gets to it, he retrieves a helmet off the back and holds it out to me. But it's different from the one I'm used to. Instead of being all black, it has pink piping around the edges and a red ribbon tied in a bow hugs the sleek surface.

I take it and glance up at him in question. "For you," he says by way of explanation.

"But . . ."

He grips the solid black one that's also on the back of his bike when it hits me. He's been giving me his only helmet. Of course, he has.

I feel like a complete idiot. All along I just thought he chose not to wear one when in reality, he was merely giving it to me, putting my safety before his own even from the very first time we met, when he had no reason to. And now he's got me one of my own.

I glance back up to him to see he's watching me, and I swallow over the thickness in my throat. I have a feeling that for someone like Atlas, this is a very big gesture. At the very least, it's an acknowledgement that he doesn't plan on going anywhere anytime soon. All from a boy who claims not to be boyfriend material.

"No biggie. I saw it and thought of you." He licks his lips, and I can tell he's nervous, worried I might not like it.

"I love it. Thanks," I say with a grin, and his answering smile makes my heart swell ten times its usual size. I take the bow off and slide it on.

"Here, let me help you." He reaches out and adjusts the straps, fixing it so that it fits just right. "Perfect," he murmurs.

Without hesitation, I press my lips to his, and this time, he doesn't stop me. His hands move to my hips, and he angles his head to gain better access to my mouth, tasting me, taking his time.

My skin heats and my insides turn to liquid as he moves his hands down my arms and to my sides where he grips my waist. Lifting me up like its nothing, he spins me and places me on the side of the bike without losing contact, and I suddenly have a vision of us—all tangled limbs, hot breath, and unspoken promises—doing more than kissing.

My cheeks grow hot at the thought before he slowly pulls away with a groan. "Mackenzie Hart," he says, his voice a sexy rasp as he nips my lip between his teeth. "You're gonna be the death of me."

ele

As we drive through Riverside, I ignore the heaviness taking up residence in my chest ever since Friday night and lean into him, enjoying the feel of my body pressed to his, along with the hum of the engine beneath us.

By the time we get to the place he shared with his father, I'm able to shove what happened with Graham into the corner of my mind again so I can focus on Atlas and what he needs. Today will be hard for him, and I want to be the rock he's never had. Something tells me Atlas is used to avoiding emotional situations and shoving them in a corner, rather than facing them head-on. When you've been in survival mode for so long, you don't really have time to dwell on your feelings.

Atlas pulls into a gravel drive and slowly rounds an old Ford Fiesta. The blue paint is faded and spots of rust speckle the tire wells. An old faded yellow Class of '98 sticker adorns the rear window, and as we pass, I note the smashed back bumper.

Atlas stops and cuts the engine of his Harley when I glance up to the house and see it's not in much better shape than the car. Algae covers the siding below the gutters and the rickety stoop below the front door looks as though one good storm might rip it off.

Sitting his helmet aside, Atlas turns and helps me with mine before sliding off the bike and reaching his hands out to help me down. "It's not Pine Grove," he says once my feet are back on the ground, causing my chest to tighten.

"It doesn't need to be," I say, but he won't meet my eyes, which is how I know he's either embarrassed or ashamed. I only wish he knew I couldn't care less about his circumstances. If anything, I admire him for rising above them.

He turns on his heel, but not before he reaches back and takes my hand in his. Guiding us to the front door, he pushes it open, then hesitates as his giant body shields the inside from view.

Red-cheeked, he turns back around. "Actually, you can just wait outside if you want. I'll only be a minute."

"Atlas," I say, pressing the palm of my hand over the side of his face until he meets my eyes. "I don't care about any of this."

The muscle in his jaw twitches. "But it's just that . . . the night when I got home and the cops were here . . . I haven't had time to come back and clean up, and I forgot what a wreck it was."

I brush my thumb over his cheek, and the worry in his gaze softens the slightest bit. "It's not a reflection of you. Do you hear me? Your father, this house, you're so much more than this."

He closes his eyes and exhales and my heart aches for him. He's come so far from the cocky boy with a chip on his shoulder I met that first night.

He nods and opens his eyes. "I'll only be a minute." He takes a step backward and I immediately see what he was trying so hard to hide. There are beer cans littered everywhere and trash all over the counters and the kitchen floor. Dirty dishes sit in the sink. Even from here, the buzzing of flies reaches my ears, and despite the door being open behind me, the scent of decay is enough to make my eyes water.

His lips quirk as he eyes the sofa with a smirk, the confident boy I know returning. "I'd tell you to take a seat, but, well . . ." I follow his gaze to the giant dark stain covering one of the cushions. Several more beer cans and remnants of a bag of potato chips litter the remaining available space. "I'm sure you'd rather stand."

He points to me before he disappears down the hall, his voice trailing after him, "Don't get too comfortable while I'm gone. I hate to have to drag you out of here."

I chuckle and cup my hands around my mouth as I yell, "You're not funny!"

After he disappears down the hall, my gaze drifts across the space. Everything feels oddly cold and impersonal, there are no photographs scattering the surfaces or on the wall. There's nothing to indicate who lives here, and the absence of those personal home touches fills me with sorrow.

Atlas deserves someone who cherishes him, who proudly proclaims him as a part of their life. Someone who puts in the effort to show him they care.

More than anything I want that person to be me.

But giving myself to Atlas means having to reject Graham, and the thought of hurting him settles in my chest like a stone.

CHAPTER 24

ATLAS

Taking Mackenzie to the place I shared with my father is a whole hell of a lot like standing in front of a crowd of strangers naked, except worse. Hell, years of busting my ass in the gym and on the field count for something. I'd do that shit with pride. But the moment I pull into my driveway, I curse myself for not having the foresight to stop here first, before I picked her up.

No need to broadcast my shitshow of a home life.

But I'd been busy at practice on Saturday, working out, and then going over plays with Uncle Cal and setting up the meeting with my father today. I didn't even realize I needed to pack him a bag until my uncle told me last night that Dad wouldn't have a chance to come back home for anything. It was straight from the slammer into rehab, which is precisely how he wanted it, so that my father didn't have a chance to come home and change his mind or take off. And after practice this morning, I'd been so damned anxious to get to her, I didn't think twice about bringing her here.

This girl is just getting to my head.

I even bought a special helmet just for her, so she can ride with me anytime she wants. Because everything is better with Mackenzie—brighter, sweeter—and if I have my way, she'll be clinging to me on the back of my Harley more often.

After we leave my place, I focus on the purr of the engine beneath me and the girl behind me, currently circling her arms around my waist. The heat of her palms sear through my hoodie straight to my skin, as her breath tickles the back of my neck, and it's all I can do to keep my focus and not pull over, turn around, and take her in my arms.

I shake my head at the rogue thoughts. It's not like me to get tied up in a girl but I can't seem to help myself.

We blow through town, taking all the back roads in the hope her father doesn't catch us together. I can't imagine his reaction if he knew his daughter was not only spending time with me, but also headed to the slammer. Lucky for him, I'm making her stay outside.

When we get to the jail, I park in the furthest spot away from the building to avoid being seen, then remove my helmet as I mentally prepare myself for my visit.

"Do you want me to go inside with you?" she asks, her voice soft.

The top of her hair is mussed from the helmet, and my fingers itch to touch the silky strands, so I reach out and smooth them down with my hand, thinking how beautiful she looks with her hair windswept, skin glowing, eyes bright.

I shake my head. "Only one visitor at a time. Besides, you can't risk any of the officers seeing you. This might be a county jail, but someone inside might know your father."

Her blue eyes darken to sapphires, the firm set of her mouth tells me she doesn't like my facing it alone. Reaching out, she takes my hand in hers and squeezes. "You've got this," she says while my heart jumps in my throat.

I've never had support like this before and I'm not sure what to do with it. This girl . . . She's the most beautiful creature I've ever seen—kind and compassionate in ways I didn't think were possible, whip smart with a sharp mouth. And yet, here she is, dealing with all my crazy.

I don't deserve her.

It's a well-known fact I'm trying to come to terms with, and only one of the reasons I know this is temporary.

I smother the urge to pull her in for a kiss or a hug, because if she's in my arms, I might not find the courage to let her go and head inside. Instead, I offer her a soft smile before I release her hand and grab my father's bag from the rack on my bike, turning toward the front of the building where I quickly make my way inside.

I enter the drab interior that oddly reminds me of a less cushy bank lobby. Everything is clinical, with shades of dull gray covering the floors and walls. Heading straight for the window with the officer, I give him my name and why I'm here. A moment passes before he finds me on his clipboard, then I sign in while he reiterates the rules and instructions in much the same way they did on the phone when I called.

Afterward, he sends me to a chair in the lobby where I wait until a guard appears and motions for me to follow him.

My heart beats at a rapid pace inside my chest as I do as I'm told. I have no idea what to expect—only what I've seen on TV—and as I enter the large room with its open floor plan, it's not too far off. Faded ivory linoleum covers the floor that squeaks beneath the guards' booted feet. At least half a dozen booths are evenly spaced throughout with a large piece of plexiglass separating them down the middle, chairs on either side. One of the booths on the far right is already occupied by a male inmate and a female visitor, and when I pass, the sound of sobbing keeps me from staring.

The guard motions for me to take a seat at one of the empty booths, then leaves and returns a minute later with my father in tow. My gaze takes him in, half expecting the blitzed-out version of the man I'm used to, but that's not what I get. He looks like shit—which isn't saying much considering I've seen him in multiple states of disrepair, but his eyes are sunken in and his cheekbones are shallow. The man looks gaunter and more haunted than I've ever seen him in his life. It's almost as if he died and went all the way to hell and back to tell the tale.

Maybe it's the standard jail jumpsuit, or maybe it's his clean-shaven face—I don't know which—but his skin is the same as the sickly shade of pale gray on the prison walls. As he comes to a stop in front of the table, his eyes focus on me, dark and penetrating. Much like my own.

For a moment, I see my life play out before me and what it could be like if I don't keep my shit together and work toward a better future. It scares the crap out of me.

The officer removes my dad's cuffs and directs him to the chair, then leaves us to stand sentry in the corner of the room. When I return my attention back to my pops, I want to jump up from my seat and run. Maybe that makes me a coward, but I don't want to face him; at the moment it's hard to care.

"Atlas . . ." My father is the first to speak. The sound of his voice catches me off guard because he's not slurring his words.

I swallow, hating the way it makes me feel: longing gripping my chest and the need for him to care. So, I straighten in my seat, push my shoulders back and blurt the first thing that comes to mind. "You look like shit."

This news doesn't seem to surprise him. "Feel like it, too," he says. "I've gone through a lot these last two weeks."

"Am I supposed to feel bad?"

He shakes his head. "No. Just stating facts."

I stare at him for a moment, unused to holding his gaze for so long, slightly uncomfortable with his eyes on mine. "You clean, then?" I ask, because getting clean and staying clean in prison isn't a given.

"Either that or I died and woke up in hell." He smiles, but I don't laugh at his joke. "It was probably a good thing you didn't answer when I called. Those first few days it was pretty bad. Not sure I would've been able to talk much in the first place, but I was worried about you. Needed to hear your voice, to know you were okay."

I snort and roll my eyes, stifling the twinge of hope pinching my chest. Pops hasn't been worried about me a day in his life. And if he has, he sure has a funny way of showing it.

"How were you able to call me so many times, anyway? You're in prison and you were detoxing. Aren't there restrictions?"

"Your uncle pulled some strings," he says cryptically, and I can tell by the way his gaze darts toward the guard that it's not something he can speak about, at least not here. But this news doesn't surprise me. Cal is the kind of man that holds a lot of weight wherever he goes. Between his time in the NFL, all of his sponsorships, and the investments he's made throughout the years, he's got more money than God. Bribing a guard for special privileges is nothing to him.

But it's something to me.

Because I know why Cal did it. And it wasn't for my pops. The only question I have, the one I always have is why?

"Well, I'm here now, like you wanted. Uncle Cal's posting your bond today, and you're off to rehab, right?"

He nods. "That's the deal."

"So, what do you want?" I fidget in my seat, tired of the pretenses. All I want to do is get the hell out of here and head back to my bike so that Mackenzie can press her body to mine as we ride through town. All I want is to forget this day. My father. This moment. Everything. Because all of it's painful, and I'm so tired of living with the demons of my past when all I want is to move on to the future.

"You're angry."

"No shit."

"You should be."

I arch a brow. He's not telling me anything I don't already know. Does he think I need his approval to be pissed?

"You're damn right, I'm mad," I spit out through clenched teeth. I lean toward him, so close to the plexiglass I can see the fog of my breath on the screen. "I don't need you to validate how I feel. You've spent the last seventeen years of my life ignoring me, fucked out of your mind while I had to take care of myself when I was just a kid. So, I'm gonna ask you again, what do you want?"

He doesn't flinch, doesn't even so much as blink at the vitriol thrown his way. Instead, he holds my gaze for a long minute before he sighs and says, "When you think you're dying, then live to come out the other side, it puts a few things into perspective. I'm going to rehab, and I'm gonna try. I'm not here to say I won't give it my best shot, but I also know that I'm sober for the first time in more than sixteen years, and I don't know how long it'll last."

I laugh sardonically and flop back in my seat. The dick's already planning his relapse. Nice. Not sure why I expected any less.

"I wanted to say I'm sorry," he continues while I stare at him, trying not to feel. "I wanted you to know that you were never the reason . . ." His voice cracks, and he pauses, shifting in his seat as he composes himself.

"You and your mother were enough. You were always enough," he says, his voice thick. "But I was too far gone to realize what I had. When your mother found out she was pregnant, I knew football would provide. I had the talent and I'd already had scouts looking at me. But when I injured myself, I became lost. Suddenly, my life looked very different without it and I couldn't cope. Football was my life, everything to me. I didn't know what a future without it looked like. If I'm being honest, your mother loved me. But me? I never loved anything more than a pigskin. Everything else in my life was second best, and by the time I injured myself and started on the pain pills and drinking, I had no idea how to repair the relationships I'd already destroyed."

Is this supposed to be a pep talk? Is he giving me some sage advice? What the fuck is he trying to say? Because being told that he loved football more than me or my mother wasn't winning him any favors.

"I hear you're amazing on the field," he says when I don't respond, and I wonder where he's going with this.

I grunt. "Who told you that?"

"Your uncle."

Of course, he did. I inhale and cross my arms over my chest. I'm thankful for everything Uncle Cal has done for me—the guidance on the field, his help navigating interest from recruiters, and taking me in when there was no one else—but I can't understand why he's helping my pops or why he hasn't given up on him. I don't exactly want him updating the bastard about my life, no matter how many favors he's done for us. He doesn't deserve to know. He's had seventeen years to pay attention and get to know me, to see the man I've become, but he missed out. There are no do-overs for us.

I shrug. "I'm all right," I say, playing it off.

"He says you're more than all right. You're getting multiple inquiries from colleges."

I nod, done with the conversation. This visit is supposed to be about him, not me.

"I wish I could be there to guide you. But, son, don't make the mistake I did. Let football be your vehicle, your escape, your passion. Love it while you can, but don't let it be your all. It can't make you happy by itself because at the end of the day, it's just a job. A scholarship, going pro if you're lucky, a massive contract, none of those things can bring you the kind of lasting happiness that relationships can. Football won't last forever and when it comes to an end, you'll be left with nothing."

A bitter laugh bubbles from my chest. Unbelievable. The gall of this man.

"Are you fucking kidding me right now?" I ask, glancing around to check for hidden cameras, because this has to be a joke. "How dare you preach to me about what I should and shouldn't do with my life. About teaching me life lessons. I'm not the selfish prick staring back at his son through a piece-of-shit plexiglass. You're gonna sit here and act like it was your drive, your obsessive love of football that fucked up your life?" I tip my head back and laugh. "Like it has nothing to do with your love of booze and painkillers? I will never be like you," I say, sobering. "I will never piss my life away like that."

"And what if football ends tomorrow, what will you have?" he asks, not so much as blinking at assessment.

"I'll have my pride."

A sad smile crosses my father's lips and it makes me want to rip it off. "What else?"

"I don't need anything else. I'll figure it out, but I sure as hell don't need you to tell me." I push to my feet, the palms of my hands flat on the table as I lean toward my father. "But I can tell you this, the last thing I'm gonna do is take advice from a junkie and a deadbeat father. You're wrong about one thing, Pops; your love of the game didn't trump everything else. Your love of pills and their ability to numb away the pain did."

elle

I push outside into the open air and breathe.

Bringing one hand up to the back of my neck, I rub the tension coiled there and kick at a rock at my feet. "Fuck!"

I think of all the things my father said and I see red.

He blames his addiction on football, while simultaneously blaming his love of the game for the reason he couldn't be a better man?

What. The. Hell.

He'd been nothing more than a body, a father by blood and namesake only, and now he's giving me advice?

He's selfish. And I'm nothing like him. Just because he fucked up and couldn't cope when life got tough doesn't mean I will, too. I've been handling "tough" my whole life, no thanks to him, and I've been doing just fine without him.

I kick another rock across the parking lot, and it goes flying just as two arms slide around my waist. I stiffen before the scent of apple blossom surrounds me, soothing my black and battered soul.

"Are you okay?" Mackenzie's voice, soft as baby's breath surrounds me.

I take a calming breath and spin around to face her. Surprise flickers in her blue eyes as I take her face in my hands and crush my mouth to hers, needing to feel something—anything—to make me forget the conversation I just had.

A sigh escapes her lips as she yields to me, letting me get lost in her, as if she knows I'm hurting and she's the only balm I need.

Her body presses to mine as I tip her head, exploring her mouth. Tasting. Biting. Caressing. My fingers slide into her hair, tugging. I'm rougher than I should be, but she doesn't seem to mind, and when a helpless little moan escapes her parted lips, I take advantage.

Picking her up, I walk us to the end of the lot toward my bike as she wraps her legs around my waist, and I set her on the edge of the seat. My mouth slows, taking my time as I make my way down her jaw to her neck. My hands shift, sliding to her waist, beneath the hem of her shirt.

"Atlas..." Her voice rattles in the back of her throat, and the sound of my name reminds me of where we are, who I am—a damaged piece of baggage who has no business touching a girl like Mackenzie.

By my own father's admission, I'm not enough. I never was.

I brush my mouth over hers one last time before I lean back, soaking in her hooded eyes, still sparkling with the same desire I'm sure are reflected in my own. "We're still in the jail parking lot," she says with a chuckle.

Her cheeks flush as she presses her pouty lips together. She's so damn beautiful it hurts.

I bring a hand up to my chest and clench at the soft cotton of my shirt, over the spot where it aches for her. "Sorry. I guess I got carried away."

"How did it go?"

I sigh as I shake my head and grab her helmet from the back of my bike. Silently, I slip it over her gorgeous dark locks and snap the buckle.

I'm not ready to talk about it. I'm not sure I ever will be, so instead I meet her gaze. "Can I take you somewhere?" I ask.

She searches my eyes in the answering silence, as if she's trying to figure me out, wanting to know what I'm thinking. But I'm locked up too tight from seeing my father. My head is a mess, and there's no way she's getting a piece of my thoughts right now.

"All right," she agrees. It's all the answer I need before I grab my helmet and hop on, waiting for her to do the same because I have something I want to show her, someplace unexpected I need to be.

The clouds above thicken as we ride through town, then exit Riverside. By the time we've driven an hour and arrived at the old Shaker field, I'm happy to have shoved the conversation with my father to the back of my mind.

I get off my bike, remove my helmet, and turn to take her hand. When she steps down, she eyes her surroundings warily.

The old red brick school crumbles on its foundation, the middle caved in from a fire years ago. Whole windows are missing, black scorch marks ringing them like halos, while shards of glass glitter on the ground below.

Everything about the place is depressing, but it's not why we came here. I step closer to the chain link fence with the private property sign, my heart doing a little jig in my chest because I'm about to give her another glimpse of my world.

"Where are we?" she asks as I pull her along with me, curling my fingers into the chain link.

"This was the old Shaker middle school until a fire took it out in the seventies and they rebuilt it somewhere else. My pops and I use to live just a few blocks south." I nod down the street toward my old neighborhood, filled with dilapidated homes. "But we're not here for the school." I wink, and she frowns. "Come on. I'll help you over first."

She steps hesitantly toward the fence. "Are you sure we should be trespassing like this?"

I plant a kiss on her lips, loving how innocent she is because it's so different from anything I've ever known. "Yes, doll. It's fine. Trust me when I say, no one cares." I reach down and smooth the crease between her brow. "Now, up and over." I pat her rump.

With a chuckle, she begins to climb the fence, while I help her up, planting my hands on her ass to give her a boost and trying my best to focus on something other than how good it looks in her jeans.

The fence isn't very high, so it doesn't take her long to get to the top before she's swinging one leg over. "Hang tight, and I'll help you down," I say as I take a few steps back and get a running start, clinging to the fence and swinging myself over in one swift motion before I jump off the other side again, falling to my feet like a jungle cat.

"Something tells me you have a lot of practice with that." She quirks a dark brow, staring down at me as she straddles the fence, and all I can do is laugh.

"You'd be right." I hold my hands out. "Okay, I got you. Hop down." I grip her waist and help her to a soft landing when she jumps.

Together, we move past the old building and round the corner to the football field when I hear her sharp intake of breath, and I know we're not alone.

Grinning, I scan the muddy field where six familiar faces peer up at us, three of whom are bare chested, playing skins. "Scott?" O'Neil yells, squinting when he spies me. He shifts the football under the crook of his arm, and all the others all turn.

"You know these guys?" Mackenzie murmurs as they head over to old rickety bleachers where we're standing.

I nod and sling my arm over her shoulder. "This is where we used to come and play when we were kids." I shrug. "It was the one place we could stay out of trouble."

"Dude, is this your girl?" O'Neil finally reaches us, and I laugh. Danny O'Neil is a blond-haired Irishman and the biggest player at Shaker, so of course he'd have eyes for Kenzie.

"Yeah, which means she's off-limits so you can put your eyes back in your head, jackass."

He laughs, holding his hands up, palms out. "Damn, dude. Relax. Though I gotta say, she sure is a hell of a step up from Leah."

I roll my eyes at him. Of course, he'd mention Leah, my on- and off-again during my time at Shaker and was never anything more than a casual hookup. Anything to stir the pot.

I feel Mackenzie's eyes boring into the side of my face and make a mental note to personally thank him later.

"Guys, this is Mackenzie Hart. Mackenzie, this is Danny, Jake, Brice, Tommy, Trig, and Adam."

Mackenzie gives them a little wave, the apples of her cheeks turning a shade of pink, as she says hello while they take turns greeting her.

So damn cute.

"What brings you here, man?" O'Neil asks, spinning the football in his hands.

"Not much. We were out and I needed a breather. Thought I'd show her where I learned to play."

"We used to wipe his ass with this field." O'Neil winks at Kenz, and I scoff.

"Right. And who's the only one of us who started freshman year on varsity again?"

The guys all laugh before Trig grins and asks, "You up for a game?" He takes the ball from O'Neil's arms and tosses it to me. "Or are you just here to talk shit?"

I catch it with one hand and glance over at Mackenzie, brow raised. "What do you think? You up for it?"

"I know some football."

My brows rise. "Oh, you do?"

She nods, biting her lip, causing a warm, fuzzy feeling to hit me in the solar plexus.

"I take it Mackenzie is playing skins?" O'Neil asks, draping his arm over my shoulder as he eyes her. He's lucky he needs it to play or I'd rip it off.

I glare at him while he laughs. "I'll play skins. Kenz, you cool with going up against me?"

I'm not gonna to lie. The thought of tackling Kenzie to the ground is enticing.

Her knife-like gaze skewers me as she opens her mouth with a comeback at the same time I yank my hoodie up and over my head, and her words cut off. Swallowing, her gaze falls to my bare torso.

"Eyes up here, Hart," I point to my eyes with a grin as she snaps out of her stupor.

"Shit, Mackenzie, don't they have men where you're from?" Trig jokes.

Her cheeks turn even redder as I reach out and grab her hand in mine, moving her to the middle of the field where O'Neil explains the rules, and we get started.

An hour later, I stand there, watching as Kenz crosses the endzone, scoring the winning touchdown for her team. She spikes the ball and spins, then screams and throws her hands into the air while I watch in awe.

Dirt and grass stain her clothes while mud coats her right cheek. She's every bit as beautiful exhausted and filthy, as she was Friday night at dinner in her little black dress.

Adam and Trig run to her, offering her high fives and laughing at her excitement when O'Neil bumps my arm. I glance over to see him staring at her in much the same way I was only seconds ago. But I can't blame him. I don't know a single one of us who could keep our eyes off her if we tried.

"Damn, Scott, hold onto that one," he murmurs. Then he slaps me on the back and joins them, leaving me to stand alone, wondering how I got so lucky.

After the guys leave, Kenzie and I make a quick trip to the gas station. I'm not ready for the day to end, and she seems in no hurry, so we grab a couple of sodas, and a pizza from Mario's, then take them back to the old Shaker bleachers.

We sit at the top, both of us lounging back on the cool, hard metal.

"That was fun," Mackenzie says, putting her pizza down and picking up her soda.

I nod, taking a bite. "It's always a good time with those guys."

"They seem really nice."

I eye her over my slice. "Yeah. I think they thought you were nice, too. A little too nice. If O'Neil stared at your ass one more time, I swear I was gonna pluck his eyes out."

Mackenzie laughs and takes a sip of her soda, tightening the cap as she stares out at the field. "Do you miss them?"

I take my time, thinking about my answer. Truth is, I'm so busy with football, working and dealing with my pops, there's not much time for anything else. Except Mackenzie. Somehow, I think I could always make time for her.

"I suppose," I say, picking up a napkin. "They were my friends and my teammates. When you spend so much time with each other on the field like that, trusting one another and working together, in a lot of ways you become brothers."

"But . . . ?" She leans back on her hands, watching me, too observant for her own good.

"I don't really let anyone get too close, you know?" I watch her absorb my answer, wondering if I can really say that's true anymore. Because it sure as hell feels like I'm letting her in. "At least, not anyone but you."

Her throat bobs, and I want to reach out and touch the soft skin at the base of her throat. Wrap my fingers around her neck while I kiss her just to feel her pulse race.

"Atlas . . ." She straightens, her blue eyes darkening like a coming storm.

I sense she has something to tell me before she even starts.

"I know you said that this is just casual between us, and that you're not the boyfriend type, so this probably won't even faze you, but I feel like I should tell you anyway."

"So serious," I joke, crumpling the napkin in my hand, if only to hide the way my heart's beating like a drum inside my chest. "Okay, what is it?"

"Graham kissed me."

I bark out a laugh. I think she's joking. But when she doesn't return my humor, my smile fades. "When?"

"Friday night. He'd been upset with me all week, and we were talking after dinner—after I left you—and he basically admitted to me that he has feelings for me and wants more. I know you and I aren't serious and you owe me nothing, but we're still . . . well, whatever we are."

She motions between us, and I want to take my fucking words back. Rescind every single thing I ever said about not wanting to claim her as mine. About not being boyfriend material, because I know how this ends. She'll pick him. It's the obvious choice—the only choice—and it fucking hurts.

She's still talking when I tune back in, trying to push past the sick pit of dread sinking in my stomach.

". . . I know he's your cousin and your teammate, and I don't want there to be bad blood—"

"Let me get this straight," I say, focusing on the details or I might go mad. "I asked you to come to dinner as my date, and after we made out in the bathroom, he fucking cornered you in his room and kissed you? While you were there for me?"

I see red. Fucking red.

Leaning back, I rake my hands through my hair as my mind reels.

I asked Graham if there was anything between them, if he had a thing for her, and he denied it. Of course, I knew the fucker was lying, but I did the stand-up thing and made sure of it before I went there. He had all the opportunity in the world to set me straight, mark his territory, but he didn't. And now he has the balls to do this to me?

Mackenzie reaches out, but I want to ignore her, to brush her aside and pretend like it doesn't hurt. Instead, I just sit there like some kind of lovesick puppy. "So . . . what? Are you two a thing now? Don't you think maybe you should've told me that earlier today, before I had my hands on you? My tongue down your throat?"

My words cause her to flinch as if they've hurt her, and part of me is glad. Because I'm not a nice guy. No point in pretending. I'm a selfish bastard who wants Doll all to myself, yet I won't actually claim as mine. Because, priorities.

"We're not . . ." she starts, then stops and tries again. "Graham and I aren't together. We're"—she shakes her head—"I'm figuring it out."

I laugh, because, again, I know who she'll choose. And it's not me. My own fucking father and my mother didn't choose me. Why should she be any different?

"Okay, then," I say, my bitter tone clear as day.

"I just need some time to figure out what I want." She stares at me, but when I say nothing, she adds, "I know we're not really a thing, but I thought I should tell you in case it seems like I'm, I don't know, taking a step back."

I nod, taking in her pink cheeks, the dark hair spilling down her back, and eyes as blue as a turbulent sea. When she licks her lips, all I can imagine is Graham's mouth all over her.

It pisses me the fuck off.

I don't care if Mackenzie and I are serious or not. He knows she and I have something going. I've made no effort to hide that fact.

But Mackenzie has hidden me. She's been lying to both Graham and her father about her time with me since we started talking because she knows they'll never approve.

I swallow over the lump in my throat, but when I return her gaze, I pick up my soda and shrug like I don't have a care in the world. "It's like you said, we're casual. By all means, have at it."

Then I tip the bottle to my lips and take a long pull, hoping I don't puke because I don't mean any of it, not a single word.

Chapter 25

MACKENZIE

By the time Wednesday afternoon rolls around, I'm frustrated. Atlas seems to be avoiding me. Either that or it's a cosmic coincidence that I've barely laid eyes on him since Graham kissed me in front of the lockers Monday morning.

I walk with Graham to the locker rooms after school at his insistence, praying Atlas doesn't show until after he's inside. The last thing I want is for him to see the way Graham leans down and places a soft kiss on my cheek before straightening again, telling me he'll see me after practice. Nor do I want Atlas to see the way I blush at his touch, or the way his kiss warms me like a shot of whiskey.

It disarms me. Makes me question my own heart—my deepest desires.

Maybe I should cut my losses. Leave now. Atlas, by his own volition, admits he'll never be boyfriend material. But Graham is, and he's all in, one hundred percent. All I would have to do is say the word and I have no doubt he'd be the most doting boyfriend any girl could ask for. The more I think about everything he said the night he kissed me, the more I realize he's right. We've been skirting the line between friendship and more for a long time.

It's about time we define what we are and either step over the line or retreat.

But as sweet as Graham may be, and no matter how hot his kisses are, at the end of the day, he's not Atlas. Like it or not, I'm drawn to Atlas in a way I can't explain. He might present a woolly exterior to the world, but I'm no fool. I've seen the soft underbelly beneath, and there's no hiding it now.

I need to talk to him. I yearn to hear his voice, and I try really hard not to analyze what that means.

I'm still standing outside the lockers when the sound of footsteps echoes down the hall and my thoughts scatter. My head jerks up to find Atlas coming toward me, eyes trained on the ground as he walks. The crease in his brow tells me he's deep in thought. When he slowly raises his gaze and our eyes meet, my heart beats a little faster in my chest.

His gait slows as he closes the distance between us, eyeing me warily. "You here to see Golden Boy?"

"No. I came to see you."

"Why?"

"I haven't seen you yet this week, so I just wanted to check on you, see how you're doing," I say, hating how awkward this feels.

"Don't worry about me. I'm fine, doll." He tries to step around me, but I grab him by the elbow and stop him.

"Don't do that."

"And what is *that* exactly?"

"Avoid me. Act like we don't have something, like I don't even exist."

His jaw hardens and he meets my eyes for the second time. "Obviously, we don't have anything. I'm just giving you what you want, a little space since you two are trying things out and seeing how they fit."

I frown. While it's true I'm open to the possibility of something with Graham and giving the idea of us breathing room, I wouldn't exactly describe us as testing things out. But before I can respond, Atlas shakes his head and shifts the bag over his shoulder. "I don't have time for this."

"Atlas." My grip on his arm tightens. "Please. Graham and I are—"

"Are you really trying to say you're not officially dating Golden Boy? That you two aren't already together?

"What? No. I haven't even given us much thought yet, because it's . . . a lot." I narrow my eyes. "Who told you that, anyway?"

"Who do you think?" he bites out.

His gaze holds mine a moment longer, then he pushes through the door and disappears inside before I can stop him.

Chapter 26

MACKENZIE

I LIE IN BED, hair damp from my shower, unable to sleep. I can't stop thinking about what Atlas said. I dwelled on it all through cheer practice and on the ride home with Graham, and still, it plagues me. Is Graham telling people we're dating? That we're official? Did I somehow mislead him and give him that impression? Because as I recall, after he told me how he felt, all he did was ask me to think about the possibility of us. He's supposed to be giving me time to see what my heart wants, but how can I do that if it feels like he's plunging us into the abyss without giving my head a chance to catch up?

I need to say something to him; I know I do. But he'd been so happy when he drove me home after practice, he was practically beaming. I didn't have the heart to ruin his good mood, especially when I have no idea what I'm going to do. I'd be lying if I said I felt nothing when he kissed me. Graham's lips were an awakening. I'd felt things for him I never thought I would. Parts of me came alive at his touch.

But our friendship is at stake.

Am I really willing to risk it? Am I honestly able to set aside my feelings for Atlas?

I just don't know.

I roll over, tuck my hands beneath my face and close my eyes, willing the pit in my stomach to disappear. But I know it won't, not until this awful triangle between Graham, Atlas, and me is resolved.

A scratching sound on my window startles me, and my eyes fly open. A shiver of fear racks my body as I stiffen, staring wide-eyed at the shadow illuminated by the moon until I make out the familiar lines of Graham's face. Exhaling, I relax and get out of bed, cross the room, and push the window open, watching as he climbs inside, all long legs and lean muscle.

My heart skips a beat as he straightens, and I imagine what it would be like if he were my boyfriend. Sneaking through my window late at night once my father was asleep would hold a whole new meaning, an entirely different connotation.

"Hey." He smiles with his whole face, making his dimples pop.

The way he's looking at me, like I hung the moon, is enough to take my breath away. I've always known just how attractive Graham is, but ever since our kiss, I see him in a whole new light.

"My dad's still awake," I whisper and signal for him to keep quiet.

He nods and takes a step closer, while I take one back, and a mischievous glint reaches his eyes. "Are you nervous?"

He stretches an arm toward me, and when I swallow nervously, he laughs. Grabbing my hands, he draws me to him while my stomach does a backflip. "That's cute," he murmurs.

His gaze dips to my mouth. For a moment, I think he might kiss me.

My heart speeds up while my stomach simultaneously clenches with dread. Any further emotional vacillation, and I'll get whiplash. "Is everything okay?" I ask, hoping to keep the conversation moving, because if he kisses me again, it'll just confuse me even more.

"I couldn't sleep."

"Me neither."

His eyes search mine, and he reaches up, running a hand through my hair while I lean into him like a purring kitten. Things are changing between us; I can feel it, and it scares me.

"I wanted to ask you something. I actually meant to earlier today, but, well, I chickened out."

"You came all the way over here at midnight to ask me a question?" I joke, trying to lighten the mood.

He chuckles, causing his whole face to light up like a beacon. "I wanted to ask you if you'll wear my jersey on Friday."

I freeze while his question ping-pongs in my brain.

Oblivious to my shift in demeanor, he continues, "I know it's a pretty big deal and we're not actually together yet, at least not in that way, but I just thought, maybe you might not mind so much. I mean, we've been best friends for years. It's not really a stretch that you'd wear my jersey if you think about it."

He's trying to downplay his request to make it seem like it's not a big deal, but we both know the truth. Wearing a boy's football jersey on game day at Riverside ranks right up there with accepting a promise ring. Immediately my gaze drifts to Atlas. How he'd feel when he saw me in another guy's jersey. It would gut him, and I'd hate to think about the tension it would likely cause on the field.

I glance at the floor as my stomach swells with guilt. I shouldn't be thinking of him right now.

I open my mouth, but nothing comes out. I don't know what to say. The flame of hope burning in his eyes hurts so much I can barely hold his gaze. The longer I stand there saying nothing, the more it starts to extinguish. But my mind races. If I say yes, what will that mean? I don't want to give him the wrong impression unless I'm sure. And honestly, the thought of Atlas seeing me in Graham's jersey, with his number . . .

"It would mean a lot to me," he whispers, his thumb trailing down my cheek. "Just to know I have your support."

Wearing his jersey would mean a lot more than my support, and we both know it.

His throat bobs in the answering silence while panic fills my chest, threatening to split me in two. There is no good way out of this. If I turn him down, I wound him terribly—potentially affect our friendship. If I accept, I hurt Atlas instead.

He hangs his head, taking a step away from me, assuming my silence is rejection. The dejected look in his face causes terror to explode in my chest so I blurt out, "Of course I'll wear it."

His head jerks up, eyes bright.

"Really?"

I nod, and he grins, face glowing. To think one small request can bring so much pleasure.

He lets out a hoot and lifts me up, twirling me around, while I shush him to be quiet and laugh. "You'll wake my dad."

He sets me back on my feet, taking my face in his giant hands—the same one that wields a ball with such precision—and slowly dips his head. Impossibly green eyes search mine. "Mackenzie Hart, I think you've just made me the happiest man alive."

"Glad I could oblige." I smile up at him, but inside I flinch as my thoughts drift to the tortured boy that's held my thoughts for so long. The one who needs just one person to believe in him. And I hate myself for it. How am I supposed to figure out if there's something more with Graham if I can't even stop thinking about Atlas for a second?

"I couldn't wait another moment to ask you, but I'll let you go back to sleep now." The corner of his mouth hitches in a sly smile. "Unless, of course, you want me to stay?" he asks, backing me toward the bed. "I could keep you company."

His voice rumbles through me at the same time his finger grazes the skin at my waist, and my stomach explodes with butterflies.

Shit, I'm not ready for this...

I bark out a nervous laugh. "If you want my father to murder you when he finds you here, be my guest."

Graham purses his lips. "You're no fun," he says, but he's all tease. When my legs hit the back of the bed, he kisses my forehead, then releases me. "Get in." He motions to my pillows, so I scramble to slide under the covers, anything to smother the goose bumps dancing over my skin.

He lifts the blanket up a little higher and leans down, keeping his eyes on mine as the warmth of his breath tickles my cheek.

"Sweet dreams," he says, then smooths a hand over my hair, plants a soft kiss on my lips, and leaves with me staring after him, wondering what exactly I've gotten myself into.

Chapter 27

MACKENZIE

My father eyes me as I walk into the kitchen, his gaze making quick work of the jersey on my back, the corners of his mouth lifting in a secret smile.

It irritates me more than it should. I knew he'd be happy about the prospect of my dating Graham, but for some reason, his approval prickles. Maybe because I know if it were Atlas's number on my back, his reaction would be completely different.

"Another big game tonight?" he asks as I skirt the island and head to the coffee pot where I pour myself a small cup, then add cream and sugar.

I shrug, not in the mood to talk. "Yeah, sure."

"I might not be able to make it tonight. I work second shift."

Good, I think, then hate myself for it. Dad only wants the best for me. Can I blame him if he thinks that's Graham? He might very well be right.

"That's no problem," I say, softening my tone. "Graham will bring me home."

"No parties tonight? Straight home?"

"Uh, I think just a few people might be hanging out." It's not an outright lie. I'm not sure what Graham and I are doing after the game, and it's easier to tell my father this than answer twenty questions about the party and have him fret over my safety all night. If he's working second shift, he won't be home until after midnight, which gives me plenty of time to hang out at Crows Creek if I so choose and return home with him none the wiser.

"Well, don't forget curfew and text me to let me know where you are if you do anything," he says. I nod, then offer him a small smile as I kiss his cheek and head for the door.

By the time I step outside, Graham is already waiting. I can see his steady gaze, shaded by the dark lenses of his sunglasses as he drinks me in. If the look on his face is any indication, he likes what he sees.

He leans across the car, pushing open my door from within and whistles as I slide inside. "Damn, girl. I might be biased, but you look good in that jersey."

I laugh, shaking my head at him as he presses a quick kiss to my cheek. I can't stop the blush that spreads over my face.

"Ready?" he asks.

"As I'll ever be," I say, even though I'm not sure that's true. When we walk inside the school ten short minutes later, Graham grabs my hand, and I tense.

Despite the fact that he says he's giving me time to see if this is what I want, he seems to be pushing the envelope at every turn, and I'm unsure of what to do about it short of telling him he needs to stop.

Then where does that lead us?

I have no idea what I want any more today than I did a week ago when he kissed me. I only know what I should do—what everyone expects—but my heart won't listen. Because I can't let go of Atlas. At least not yet.

We pass Jenna and Caroline, who freeze midconversation when they see my jersey.

Jenna quirks a brow. "It's about time, girl!"

Beside her, Caroline squeals and pulls me in for a quick hug, to which Graham merely laughs.

The whole thing makes me uncomfortable. Everyone assumes we're a couple, why wouldn't they? I'm not exactly doing anything to correct this misbelief and wearing Graham's football jersey isn't exactly helping.

I'm about to pull my hand from Graham's and tell him I don't feel well, simply as my chance to escape, when we bump into Jace and Teagan.

Jace pauses and takes a slow perusal of my jersey, his blue eyes widening just a fraction. I'm not sure he's pleased. Graham, on the other hand, wears a smug smile.

"Your jersey," Jace says, rubbing the scruff over his jaw. "Man, that's . . . serious."

I swallow while my heart skips a beat. It feels like the walls are closing in on me. The oxygen in the room grows sparse and I find it hard to breathe. Everything is moving too fast, and I feel stuck, like my feet are cemented to the floor and my mouth is glued shut.

My life is one giant domino effect and I have no idea how to stop myself from toppling over.

Graham turns and glances down at me, beaming. His smug expression is gone, replaced by a gleaming pride, an unadulterated happiness I've never seen on him before. "It's about time, if you ask me," he says, repeating Jenna's sentiment.

"Does Atlas know about this?" Teagan asks. He licks his lips as if the thought makes him nervous, and my stomach drops at the sound of his name.

Beside him, Jace frowns. Their reactions are not the response I expect, considering their allegiance to Graham. It tangles my nerves in knots.

"He'll see for himself soon enough," Graham says, his voice tight. I stare up at him, dumbfounded at the venom in his voice. The only thing Atlas has ever done to him is show an interest in me.

I take a step back, tugging on his hand, and when he turns to me, I force a smile. "Hey, I'm gonna head to the restroom before I hit my locker."

"Want me to walk you?" His brows pinch, and I shake my head.

"Stay and chat. I'm fine." I motion toward the guys. Graham gives my hand a quick squeeze, then tells me he'll see me later.

My feet can't move quick enough as I make a beeline for the restroom and lock myself inside a bathroom stall. I exhale and lean against the cool metal sink, trying to collect myself and calm my racing heart before I head back into the trenches. But when I squeeze my eyes closed, all I see is Atlas, his dark gaze boring into me.

I dread the moment he sees me in Graham's jersey. Just the thought makes my knees quake, and after avoiding me all week, I'm suddenly hopeful he'll keep his distance.

I know I owe him nothing. He and I are... fooling around? Helping each other out? I don't know how to describe us, but I know none of those things suffice. It's so much more than that, at least for me, but I also know he keeps people at arm's length. Football is his number one. There's no permanent place for me in his life, he's made this clear, so why do I feel so guilty about exploring my options?

I head to the sink and run my hands under the tap, then press my cool palms against my burning cheeks before I step out into the hall.

Like a timid doe, I take a few steps, but I don't get far before my eyes lock with his. Dark like onyx, his gaze soaks me in while the muscle in his jaw twitches.

Those dark orbs focus on Graham's number emblazoned across my chest, and my throat goes dry.

His nostrils flare; his hands fist at his side. Before I can even process what he's doing, he crosses the hall, his stride quick as he wraps a hand around my elbow. Guiding me down the hall, he pauses at a supply room door and wrenches it open, then yanks me inside.

I stumble after him, gasping when he spins around and forces my back against the metal cabinet beside the door. Reaching beside me, he flips the lock in place without a single word as his eyes penetrate mine.

"What are you doing?" I choke out.

"That's *my* question, doll. Because it sure as hell looks like you're wearing a jersey, and it's not mine."

"I told you—"

"You told me that you and Graham weren't actually together." He pinches my chin with his thumb and forefinger, tipping my head so I'm forced to hold his gaze.

Like I could look anywhere else. Clearly, he doesn't realize the hold he has on me.

"Or was that a lie?" he asks.

"No."

"Then, why?"

"He asked me to wear it and I . . . it made him so happy. I figured it was a small ask, a minor gesture . . ." My voice trails off because I'm digging a hole I can't get myself out of. I have no idea what he wants me to say, but I know he doesn't believe a word that's coming from my mouth.

"So, let me get this straight. You're wearing his jersey because you feel bad? Because you didn't want to disappoint him?"

I nod, saying nothing, my throat too dry to speak even if I tried.

"Life is full of disappointment, doll, and Graham's been born with a silver fucking spoon in his mouth. He's used to getting everything he wants. His whole life has been one giant joyride. But not this time."

"You're wrong. His father—"

"His father wants what's best for him. I wish I could say the same about mine." His gaze ignites as he searches my face. "You can lie to him as much as you want, and you can lie to yourself. But you can't lie to me. Because I know what you really want. Just like I know it's not him."

"Atlas . . ." I swallow, unsure of what I want to say. *Don't make this harder than it is?* I'm the one making things hard. I'm the one that needs to choose.

His gaze drops to my chest, and his smile turns serpentine. "You can wear his jersey. But we both know who you belong to."

My heart thunders in my chest as he reaches into his pocket and pulls out a Sharpie. His eyes meet mine once more, so intense, it makes me shiver. "Take it off."

I blink. "What?"

"I *said*, take the jersey off."

My mind reels. I have no idea what he's going to do. All I know is I'm inclined to listen.

I reach down to the hem of Graham's jersey, hesitating only a moment before I lift it up over my head, letting it hang from my fingertips. Beneath the shirt, I'm wearing nothing more than a lacy white bralette.

My chest rises and falls with each intake of breath, and a gleam of light enters his eyes as he takes me, eyeing me slowly. He peruses my body at a painstakingly slow pace. The heat of his gaze travels from my waist, slowly singeing a path up my torso to my breasts where he pauses, his eyes an obsidian black, pupils flared so wide I can barely make out where they end and his irises begin.

Goosebumps break out over my exposed skin, hair on end and tingling. I'm a live wire waiting to ignite.

Before I know what he's doing, he uncaps the pen with his teeth, then steps forward and reaches one hand up to the swell of my breasts and places a palm over my racing heart while every nerve ending in my body comes alive at his touch—every synapse in my brain fires—and it's not until the tip of the marker meets my skin that I know what he's doing.

Taking his time, he painstakingly traces the number fifty-two over my breasts, branding me. Once he's finished, he leans back, his gaze drinking in the sight of his number emblazoned over my skin.

"Fucking perfect," he whispers, then his eyes meet mine. "You may be walking around with his shirt, Hart, but we both know who you belong to."

He leans into me until I feel the warmth of his breath on the side of my neck and the graze of his lips against my skin.

My chest rises and falls in a steady rhythm, and I close my eyes to fight the pressure building inside my chest as he says, "You're mine, doll. I own your heart, and there's not a damn thing anyone can do about it. Not Graham. Not even you."

I suck in a breath as cool air washes over my skin, and I hiss. But when I open my eyes, he's gone.

GRAHAM

For the first time in a long time I'm excited instead of nervous for tonight's game.

I hustle toward the locker rooms for a pre-game huddle with the team when I spot Kenzie outside waiting for me and my mood soars. Atlas passes by her first, helmet in hand as he stares her down, a possessive gleam in his eyes. His gaze slides to her chest and a smirk curls the corners of his lips.

I step forward, hands curled into fists, ready to wipe the smug smile off his face. It's one that says he knows what Kenzie looks like underneath her cheerleading uniform when I know damn well he doesn't. Kenzie's not like that. Maybe she's confused with whatever this thing is between them, but I refuse to believe she would ever entertain allowing someone like him to get *that* close.

Jace and Teagan pass, exchanging looks when they see my expression. I know what they're thinking. They're calculating all the ways in which this thing between Kenzie, Atlas, and me can go wrong. How it could affect the team. But what they don't realize is that I don't plan on losing, which means the team will be fine. As long as Atlas stays out of my way and Kenzie's with me, nothing else matters.

When I finally reach her, our eyes lock and the tension in my muscles fades. She's as beautiful as ever in her uniform, her skin glowing under the fading light. I have no idea what she'll decide about us yet, but I can't help but feel optimistic, like we're headed in the right direction.

"Hey." I reach out to lace her fingers in mine, enjoying the heads that turn our way as I step closer and exhilarated at not having to hide how I feel about her. No more pretending that I'm not completely and utterly in love with my best friend. "Will you be cheering for me on the sidelines?"

"Of course." She smiles, but it doesn't quite reach her eyes, and I know something's up. That's the thing about falling for your best friend—there's no hiding how you really feel. You know all their tells, every nuance of their facial expressions.

My thoughts immediately shift to Atlas and the way he leered at her on his way into the locker room, and I wonder if he's made her uncomfortable somehow. "What's wrong?"

"What? Nothing. I just..." She bites her lip, and I know enough about Kenzie to know she's collecting her thoughts, so I say nothing as I let her think.

"I saw your father," she eventually tells me. "Seems like he's in rare form. He was talking about the scouts that are here and how tonight will be a tough win."

I shrug. "Doesn't matter." Her eyes widen, and I reach out to stroke her cheek. "As long as I have you waiting for me, I don't care if we win or lose. I don't care about scouts. Or my father. I don't care about anything," I say, my tone soft as I dip my head, pressing a kiss to her cheek before I whisper, "Because I've already won."

When I pull away, her cheeks are a rosy pink under a furrowed brow. I wonder what has her so tied up in knots. Surely, it's not just my father.

"Listen, Graham, there's something I want to—"

"Graham!" a gruff voice calls out behind me, causing my stomach to twist with dread.

The sound of my father's voice grates on my good mood, and I can't help but wonder why he can't ever just leave me be. Let me do my job on the field without the constant criticism. Kenzie is right. I have my work cut out for me tonight. According to both Coach and my father, a ton of scouts are watching, which only adds to the pressure when all I want to do is enjoy the game.

I give her hand one last squeeze before she says goodbye and turns, leaving me with my father whose knife-like gaze bores through me.

"You're the last one out here," he barks. "Shouldn't you be huddling with your team in the locker room?"

"I was on my way in before you interrupted me," I say, making no effort to hide my irritation.

"Really? Because it looks like you were fraternizing with your girlfriend to me."

Though I love the sound of Mackenzie being referred to as my girlfriend, he makes it sound dirty, like it's a bad thing when it's the best thing in my life—better than any football scholarship could ever be.

"She was wishing me luck."

"You're gonna need it."

I chuckle, a bitter sound in the back of my throat. "Thanks for the pep talk, Dad. If that's all for tonight's daily dose of encouragement, I'll be going."

"You're making a mistake here."

I sigh, barely restraining the urge to roll my eyes. "And what mistake is that?"

"You're too invested in her, Graham. I can see it plain as day. Mark my words, it's going to come back to bite you. You're in the biggest, most important season of your life. Distractions are the last thing you need."

"Mackenzie's not a distraction."

"No, she's a complication. I can see it on your face. Don't throw your future away on a high school fling, son."

My jaw hardens. "We've been friends for years. She's a whole hell of a lot more than a fling, and you know it, so just back off."

"Get her out of your system and move on."

"Maybe you should watch your mouth." My jaw tightens, and I clench my teeth until my molars ache. He can say what he wants about me, but not Kenzie. "You have no idea what you're talking about."

"No?" He sneers, his gaze dropping to my fisted hands. "Because it looks like you're proving my point. She's already getting to you, and you can't even see it. Before too long, football will be in your rearview mirror and you'll wish you'd have given it your full attention."

"Maybe I don't give a shit," I shout, my outburst surprising us both. Dad's eyes round in surprise, so I continue. It's not too often I have his attention. "Have you ever stopped to think for one second that maybe I'm in love with her? Because I am, and there's not a damn thing you can do about it. But I can tell you this, I love her a whole hell of a lot more than I love football. This game, it's not my life. She is, and I'm not afraid to admit it. We're different, you and I."

I don't realize how true a statement it is until I voice it out loud. For years, I've focused on the sport, poured my heart and soul into it, and as I stand here in front of him, I know the real reason why. This whole time, I've been desperately searching for his approval.

But I'll never get it.

I'll never be good enough no matter how hard I try or how well I play. Dad will always want more, expect more. But I have nothing left to give, and I'm done seeking his love and acceptance.

"Have you ever thought that maybe this is *your* dream?" I continue. "I'm not like you, Dad. Maybe I don't want it as bad as you did. Maybe I don't have the skill or the talent or even the drive."

"You do. You could," he says, but I cut him off with a shrug.

"The truth is, I'm not sure I care. Because maybe you're right. Kenzie is what I really want. Everything else is just icing."

He scoffs. "You're even dumber than I thought."

"Not dumb," I say, resigned to the fact I'll never be enough for him. "I just know what I want." Turning, I push through the heavy locker room doors, my step lighter than it's been in a long time.

Chapter 28

MACKENZIE

I lean against the building, the rough brick digging into my back. I didn't mean to overhear Graham's conversation with his father. I only meant to stay here for a moment to collect my thoughts.

I'd been ready to tell Graham we needed to talk before his father interrupted us. To confront him about telling people we're officially a couple when I haven't made up my mind. I feel something for Graham, I do. If I said there was nothing between us beyond friendship, I'd be lying. I think maybe there has been for a long time, but I've just been too preoccupied with the crash, my mother's death, and everything that went along with it to realize it. But I can't deny my feelings for Atlas anymore, either. There's something between us I can't explain. Some intrinsic connection that cannot be fabricated or replicated, and I can't deny it any more than I can stay away from him, which is unfair to everyone.

The last thing I want to do is hurt Graham. Our friendship means more to me than anything. Just the thought of jeopardizing what we have scares me so much I want to curl into myself, to retreat from the world and everyone in it. Because I can't lose him. Not completely. And maybe that makes me selfish, but it's the truth.

But after the conversation with his father . . .

I press myself against the rough brick, remembering his words, letting them sink into my bones like lead. *Did you ever stop and think for one second that maybe I'm in love with her?*

I press my eyes closed. I shouldn't have expected anything different, but somehow, I downplayed his feelings for me in my mind, like they were this fleeting thing he could choose to turn off like a leaky faucet.

My heart kicks painfully in my chest.

I'm stuck.

Sinking.

I have no idea how to tell him I'm unsure about us. Because I love him, I do. Just not in the way he needs me to.

The sound of footsteps startles me, and I jerk my eyes open to see Mr. Scott round the corner. He pauses when his eyes lock with mine, sinking into all the silent places of my heart—to the truth that hides from the light.

The evening is cool and the sky is clear; it's the perfect night for a fire at Crow's Creek. But I barely notice.

I stumble as the beer sloshes from my cup, but Graham's arms steady me at the same time my gaze sharpens on Atlas across from me.

My insides twist.

Jenna sits between his legs while firelight plays over his face. Her back presses against his chest while his arms wrap around her. Every once in a while, she turns and whispers into his ear, nuzzling his neck, and kissing him, or whatever the heck it is she's doing. All I know is she's all over him, and it makes me want to puke. It fills my insides with poison, sends shockwaves through my veins.

His eyes meet mine over the glowing flames of the bonfire, and it's like someone strikes a match inside my chest. Everything ignites and a prickling awareness shimmies over every inch of my skin.

I glance away before I can get burned and take another drink of my beer even though my hands and feet already feel fuzzy. I've only had two, but I'm not used to drinking, so it's two too many. Yet it's still not enough to numb the feeling of Graham's arms wrapped around me, his hand gently gripping my waist, just below my ribs, while Atlas's gaze bores through us.

A peel of Jenna's laughter draws my attention once more, and when I risk a glance their way, I grit my teeth. She stares up at him, laughing at something he said and clinging to his every word while I wish for a distraction.

Beside me, Graham, Jace, Teagan, Knox, and some of the other guys are discussing the game and how they killed it. Tonight's game was supposed to be a hard one, but thanks to Graham and Atlas, they made it look easy. We crushed Lutton Valley thirty-five to seven, and I haven't seen Graham play that well since the year before my accident.

Of course, he gave me credit for his performance. It just adds to the pressure I've felt since overhearing the conversation with his dad beforehand.

Atlas is quiet most of the night. He doesn't join in the conversation like everyone else. An outsider might think he doesn't care, but I've come to expect his silent brooding. Of all the Friday nights I've been around him, he's never participated in post-game banter. Instead, he withdraws inside himself, preferring solitude. It's only me he seems to open up to, an observation I try not to let go to my head.

Jace belches, drawing me out of my thoughts as he glances around the circle of people sitting around the fire. "It's a small group tonight," he says, rubbing his hands together like a kid on Christmas. "Maybe we should have some fun."

"What did you have in mind?" Jenna snaps her gum, and I fight the insatiable urge to throttle her.

"How about a dip in the Black Hole?"

"No way." Jenna wrinkles her nose, and her aversion at the idea instantly intrigues me.

"What's the Black Hole?" I ask, and all eyes turn on me. It's the first time I've spoken up tonight, and I can feel a particular dark gaze boring into me.

"It's this man-made pond Jace's parents dug out last year to basically cover a bunch of old debris and junk that had been sitting on the property."

So that's why I don't know about it. They must've put it in during my time at home after the car crash.

"In other words, it's a treasure trove." Jace winks, and I can't help but laugh. "First one to find grandpa's old hay rake wins."

"Dude . . ." Graham starts.

"What?" Jace lifts one shoulder. "Live a little man."

"Who the hell knows what's in that water."

"That's what makes it exciting. Besides, Teagan, Knox, and I jumped in over the summer. It's harmless."

"Though it wasn't night," Knox chimes in. "But that makes it even better."

Jace salutes him.

"I'm down," Teagan says, tipping back what had to be his fifth beer already.

"Why not?" Knox shrugs, while Graham silently shakes his head.

"Well, you guys can jump in that mystery water all you want," Jenna says, "but there's no way I'm going near it. I'd rather stay here where it's warm," she practically purrs as she turns and tugs on Atlas's arm, batting her overly mascaraed eyes at him.

And maybe it's the sick feeling in the pit of my stomach or the hard set of Atlas's jaw when I catch his gaze, but I'm feeling dangerous. Rebellious. I want to live a little. So, I stand up, out of the canopy of Graham's arms. "I'm game."

"Seriously?" Jace arches a brow. "I did *not* peg you for a risk-taker, Hart."

"Well, I guess there are some things you don't know about me," I say.

"This is a terrible idea," Graham protests beside me.

"Okay, here's the deal." Jace rubs his hands together, glancing between Knox, Teagan, Caroline, and me. "We all jump, then race to the end of the pond. Whoever makes it first, wins."

"What do we win?" Teagan asks.

"Hell if I know." Jace laughs. "Where's your competitive spirit? Since when do we need a *reason* to win?"

"Because high stakes make everything better." Teagan shrugs. "How about your truck?"

"Hell, no."

"I don't know. I think that sounds fair," I tease as Graham slides closer.

"What do you want with my truck, Hart? You don't even drive?"

I laugh, letting the insult roll off me because I know he's just teasing. "Fair enough." I arch a brow. "How about the loser has to sprint naked through the field?"

"Now you're speaking my language." Jace beams. "Jenna, you sure you're not game?" Jace winks, and when she flips him off, he tips his head back in laughter. "Fine. Let's go."

Jace nods for us to follow, then turns and heads down the hill toward the front of their property. I take a step forward, but Graham grabs my arm before I can get very far. "Don't you think this is a bad idea?" he whispers as everyone around us heads for the pond.

"I think it's a perfect idea."

"Kenz, it's dangerous. There are old cars, broken glass, and metal and shit. If you jump in and hit the right spot, it could slice you clean open."

I roll my eyes. "It's fine. You worry too much." I move to join Jace up ahead, but the alcohol has made my movements sluggish, and Graham blocks my exit.

"I can't let you do it, especially since you've been drinking." He shakes his head. "Your father wouldn't like it, and I'm not going to risk you getting hurt."

My mouth gapes. Did he really just say he wasn't going to let me jump?

"My father's not here," I protest.

"Exactly."

I frown. "Graham, I'm jumping."

"No." His mouth presses into a firm line. "I'm putting my foot down."

A puff of air escapes my lips, conveying my disbelief. "I've spent nine months of my life holed away in my room, cooped up, wishing I could feel alive again. I don't want to be the kind of person who's afraid of everything, who's scared to take a risk, and until recently, that's who I was becoming."

"There are other ways to feel alive. You're not doing this. I'll take you home before I let you."

"Oh, yeah?" I step forward in challenge. "Just watch me."

Without another word, I sprint down the hill before he can stop me.

Maybe jumping is stupid. And maybe I am drunk.

But I don't care.

All I know is that I need a distraction from the gnawing ache in my chest. Something to numb the pieces of my heart where Atlas resides.

I hit the bottom of the hill where Jace, Teagen, Caroline, Knox and a few others are already shedding their clothes, so I push my jeans down over my hips, then slide them off.

"What the hell do you think you're doing?" Graham barks.

He grabs my arm and I'm about to bite his head off until I see the flicker of fear in his eyes, and I soften. He's genuinely worried about me.

"Graham . . ." I reach up and cup his cheek. "You don't always have to save me. Sometimes it's okay to let me go, even if it means I might get hurt," I say, wondering if he knows I'm talking about more than jumping.

I remove my arm from his grip and take a step back before I yank my shirt—his jersey—over my head in one quick motion. "I know what I'm doing," I say.

I expect the words to register, for him to say something back. Maybe even argue. But he doesn't.

Instead, he falls silent, his mouth parted in disbelief as his gaze falls to my chest. He blinks, his eyes wide, and it takes me a moment to remember the ink on my skin.

I lift my shaking hands in vain, trying to cover myself. But it's too late.

I watch the emotions play over Graham's face in torturous precision—shock, anger, and humiliation vie for dominance.

My stomach lurches. I can feel his heart breaking, smell the stench of it, and taste it on my lips as I reach for him when out of nowhere a strong hand clamps down over my arm and pulls me toward the barn.

"No way you're backing down now, Hart," Jace says, his tone hard.

I stumble beside him, glancing behind me to find Graham rooted to the spot where we left him, gaze fixed on me, jaw tense under the moonlight while I follow behind the others.

My stomach churns as everyone takes a turn climbing up the rickety ladder leaning against the old barn. I have half a mind to run back to Graham and try to explain myself. Only there's nothing I can say to make it better. And based on the way Jace is glaring holes into the side of my skull, I don't think he'll let me.

By the time I scale the roof, adrenaline grips me by the throat, and I refocus on the task at hand.

A cool wind whips my hair around my face. I'm in nothing but my white lace bralette and panties, and goose bumps cover my skin as I carefully move toward the edge of the roof.

Teagan stands on my left, while Knox flanks my right, and each of us prepare to make the jump as Jace counts down.

"Five . . ."

I stare down at the inky water.

"Four . . ."

Below me, I make out Graham on the sidelines. He's staring up at me with a look so forlorn, I second-guess my decision.

"Three . . ."

My head spins from the alcohol, and my legs begin to shake.

"Two . . ."

A surge of adrenaline pumps through my veins.

"One . . ."

I inhale a shaky breath and let go.

Arms out, I leap from the rooftop, and for a moment, I'm weightless. Suspended.

Air whistles in my ears and rushes through my hair. I'm breathless, alive in a way I only feel when I run. My heart pounds in my ears as I plummet toward the water while the others around me hoot and holler and shout.

I plunge through the inky black surface, the cold water stealing the air from my lungs. A million tiny needles prick my skin as I go down, down, down . . . until I stop, and something touches my foot and I freak.

Pumping my arms and legs, I struggle through the cold, until my head breaks through the surface and I gasp for air. My limbs go heavy, and I dip back under, wondering if maybe Graham was right. Maybe I shouldn't have jumped; maybe I am inebriated.

I shake my head and exhale through my nose, then pump my legs harder and resurface. Everyone around me cheers, as I blink through the water dripping in my eyes. Once I clear my vision, I see everyone's accounted for and beginning to swim, so I take off.

I'm not the best swimmer, but I'm decent and I hold my own until I get to the last stretch, and I start to slow. The alcohol bogs me down, and my arms and legs begin to cramp. Somehow, I make it to the end and find it's shallower. My feet sink and slip in the mud as secure my feet, enabling me to rest.

Out of breath, my pulse wild, I turn and glance around me to see everyone is already on solid ground.

Jace spreads his arms, his grin wide as he stares back at me. "Sorry, Hart, but you know what this means . . ."

I lean forward and shake my head as a chuckle escapes me because, of course, I lost.

But I'm not a sore loser, or a quitter, and I don't go back on a bet, so I pull myself out of the mucky end of the swamp.

A shiver racks my body as the cool night air hits my damp skin. I reach behind myself to unsnap my bra. It pops open, and I'm about to drop it when I'm being lifted up into the air and flung over someone's shoulder.

"No chance in hell," a deep voice growls.

Butterflies explode in my chest.

Atlas.

"What are you doing?" I ask, pounding my fists against his back.

He climbs the hill back to the fire, his long stride making quick work of the ground, until he plops me on my butt. His gaze heats as he takes me in, then turns his back to me.

"Fix yourself," he barks.

I glance down to see my bra askew, my breasts heaving with each intake of breath. But more startling is the black ink on my chest—*Atlas Scott #52*—and the reminder of Graham's tortured expression when he saw it.

My mouth flattens in to a thin line in an effort to contain my emotion. I don't recall seeing Graham when I emerged from the water. He must've left, and I know with complete certainty, this is why. Not because he was mad I jumped.

My heart leaps to my throat as I cover myself with one arm. "My clothes are back there," I snap, unsure of why I'm mad at him when I only have myself to blame for this mess I've created.

Without saying anything, Atlas retreats, and I'm left alone. Everyone else must still be back at the Black Hole, so I fix my bra, glad for the warmth of the fire as I think of Graham, off who knows where, hurting over the branding on my chest.

When Atlas returns, he tosses my stuff at me. "Here," he snaps, barely even looking in my direction. It's as if he's too disgusted to even spare me a glance.

That makes two of us.

Standing, I get to my feet, filled with the urge to defend myself. "I lost the bet. It was only fair—"

"If you think I'm going to let you run naked in front of those jackasses just so they can get their rocks off, you're wrong." He rakes a hand through his hair while the firelight plays over his face—the sharp cut of his cheekbones, his square jaw, the stubble over his chin.

"I know what I'm doing," I croak.

"Do you? Because for once, I actually agree with Golden Boy. You were too damned lit to make that jump, or the swim."

"I was fine."

"It was fucking stupid."

"You had no right—"

Atlas barks out a laugh, cutting me off. "That's the first true thing you've said all night. When it comes to you, I have zero right to take what I want, yet here I am. Somehow, I keep coming back."

I swallow, because I want what he's saying to be true. More than anything I don't want him to give up on me, to get lost in Jenna and forget me.

Without another thought, I bend down and drop my panties, then straighten.

Atlas's eyes widen, and his lips part. I grin when he can't seem to look away. It's the most powerful I've felt all week, maybe in my entire life.

"What are you doing?" he rasps.

"I'm not putting jeans on over wet underwear," I say, archly. "It'll be uncomfortable." Leaning down, I shimmy the denim over my damp skin before tugging my shirt over my wet bra.

I smirk as I stare back at him, hit with the insatiable urge to swipe the cigarette from behind his ear. I wonder what he'd do if I lit it and took a puff.

I'm about to try it just to see his reaction when Jenna crests the hill, her gaze flickering between us, making my smug smile grow even wider. Until she comes closer. Because once she reaches Atlas, she stands up on her tiptoes as she presses her body to his, whispering something in his ear.

Now I'm the one frowning. Especially when Atlas's gaze finds mine and he says, "later," before he turns and leaves me standing there alone.

A few minutes pass, and everyone returns from the pond, except for Graham, which doesn't surprise me. I don't even have to ask where he's gone. I completely understand why he ditched me.

"Well, shit, Hart," Jace croons. "You sure do know how to get those boys all riled up."

I narrow my eyes at him. Something tells me he knew exactly what he was doing when he egged me on to jump, then made the bet. "Where'd he go?"

"Graham?"

I nod.

"When your boyfriend watched Atlas throw you over his shoulder half naked like a caveman, he took off. Don't worry though. He'll be back. He just needs to cool off." Jace glances around him while the others settle in, talking and laughing. "Where'd Atlas go?" He cocks his head, waiting for my answer.

"He left with Jenna." I nearly choke on the words. I can only imagine what she'd do with him once she got him alone.

"And that bothers you?"

I stare at Jace a moment, unsure of whether he's just trying to stir the pot or genuinely wants to know. I decide on the latter. But I lie. "No," I say, rubbing the chill from my arms. "Why would it?"

He shrugs. "Just asking. It seems you two have some unspeakable thing going, that's all."

Not anymore, I think, and the thought saddens me more than it should because Atlas may have a wall up, but my relationship with Graham has done nothing to help bring it down.

I wait until Jace grabs another beer before I sneak off. Without Graham here, I doubt anyone will notice I'm gone. I need air. I need space to think. Breathe and collect my thoughts.

I need to run, but I don't have Goliath, and despite what Graham and Atlas think, I don't have a death wish, so I won't go out on these country roads, tipsy and alone. Instead, I wander through the field into the grove of trees and pause to stare up at the moonlight.

My chest tightens as I think of Graham. I love him. He's my best friend, and I can't be sure I would've made it through the darkness of the accident without him.

When I picture a future with Graham, I see how beautiful it would be. He's patient and kind, and I know him like the back of my hand. We finish each other's sentences. He means so much to me that the thought of losing him is enough to bring me to my knees. It's enough to scare me into dating him even though, if I'm being honest with myself, there's someone else taking up residence in my heart.

But that's not fair to him. He deserves someone who would kill to be with him. Someone who will worship him for the amazing man that he is. In another world and another place, maybe we could be together and work, but I can't step away from Atlas. No matter how much I want to, no matter how much I know I should because Graham would never hurt me.

With Atlas, the future is uncertain. My heart is in fickle hands, weather-beaten and pebbled and prone to flailing.

Graham is my safe place to fall, while Atlas is one giant leap in the dark.

But maybe that's what makes it worth it. Because without risk there's no reward.

I lower my gaze from the sky. When I think of Jenna in his arms, my whole body aches at the thought of them together. Knowing I pushed him there makes it so much worse.

I move further into the canopy of trees and jerk to a stop. My ears perk at a sound of something moving in the distance and a snicking sound I can't place.

I draw closer to it, wondering if maybe it's Graham when I spot someone sitting at the base of a giant oak.

Atlas. His head is down, and he's flicking a metal lighter. I don't think he notices me until his voice breaks the silence.

"Lost, doll?"

Not anymore, I think.

"Where's Jen?" I ask, willing his gaze to mine.

"Jealous?"

I shrug like I don't care. "I just find it really rich that only hours ago, you scrawled your name on my chest and claimed me, then hours later, you do whatever the hell you want. You can hook up with Jen, but if I even entertain feelings for someone else, someone I've known for *years,* it's a crime."

Atlas jumps to his feet, an angry gleam in his eye as he steps toward me. "I couldn't care less about Jen. I sent her home, if you must know. Told her it wasn't happening."

I swallow, taken aback as hope rises inside my chest. "Why?"

"Why do you think?"

My heart stills.

"I want you, doll. Only you," he murmurs, sliding a hand into my hair, his face contorted as if his admission causes him pain.

"I thought you couldn't commit? That you weren't boyfriend material?"

His gaze drops to my mouth, and he traces my lower lip with his thumb. "For you, I think I can do anything. Be anything. With you, I want it all."

My heart swells as he kisses me, until my head spins and the world around me fades to black. Until my chest fills and all the dead parts of me come alive again.

"But you'll have to choose," he murmurs against my mouth. "Graham or me. I don't share."

"It's always been you," I say, realizing at that moment it's true. I'm not sure Graham ever really stood a chance because from the first moment Atlas crested this hill, I'd fallen.

Slowly, Atlas leans in again, brushing his lips against mine, taking his time. Treating me like I'm a delicacy he must savor. Like he might die if he doesn't taste me again. Like he's lost and my mouth is a roadmap to wherever he's going.

My hands move down the hard planes of his chest, toying with the hem of his shirt when a rough voice breaks through the silence.

"I see you've made your choice."

I freeze at the sound of Graham's voice, and all the blood drains from my face as Atlas stiffens and steps aside.

"Graham . . ." Panic swirls inside me like an oil slick, smothering everything in toxic waste.

This isn't the way I wanted to tell him.

Silence settles between us as a breeze ripples through the trees, rustling their leaves with the scent of coming rain—the calm before the storm—when Graham's gaze briefly flickers to me and back.

"You son of a bitch." He shakes his head, his gaze locked on Atlas, who steps around me, muscles coiled, ready for a fight.

"You move here, join my team. You steal the spotlight and somehow fool my father into thinking you're some kind of poor lost soul looking for a fair shot, when really, you're just some juvenile delinquent who knows how to handle a ball. You move into *my* house. And now you steal *my* girl."

"Last I checked, she wasn't yours to steal," Atlas grinds out.

Graham tips his head back and laughs, a maniacal edge to the sound.

I've never seen him like this, and it kills me to know I'm the reason for why he's coming unglued.

"You don't even know her, dude."

"And *you* do?" Atlas arches a brow. "You think parading her around like a prize to be won all week is the way to her heart?"

Anger flashes in Graham's eyes like a bolt of lightning, and I hold my breath, afraid to say anything for fear I'll make everything worse.

"You think you know better? That whatever shallow relationship you can give her will be enough?" Graham bites back. "I suppose when you're done using her, you'll throw her away like a piece of trash, and I'll be the one left picking up the pieces, huh?"

"Graham," I hiss. "Stop it."

"You gonna let her speak for you now, too?" Graham chortles, stepping even closer, until he and Atlas are less than a foot apart. "It won't last, because the truth is, you've been nothing but an inconvenience since the day you were born. Your mother didn't want you. Hell, your own father would rather get high than—"

Atlas strikes before I even see it coming. His right fist crushes Graham's nose, causing his head to snap back like a bobblehead doll.

He stumbles and I yelp as his nose gushes blood. With a shaky breath, he touches the tender spot below his septum, then pulls his scarlet tipped finger away, smiling, like the pain from Atlas's fist is an analgesic for his otherwise breaking heart.

Eyes gleaming, Graham throws a punch, which Atlas quickly parries, but a hook with his left catches Atlas in the bottom of his face.

His lip splits as I scream for them to stop. My voice falls on deaf ears as they charge each other. Graham grunts and tries to land another punch, but Atlas catches his arm and spins him around, face pressed against the tree as I helplessly cry out.

Tears stream down my face as I watch Atlas tighten his hold on Graham's hands behind his back. "You done?" he asks while Graham grunts and my heart plummets to the soft earth at my feet.

"Stop!" I yell, voice thick as I bat Atlas's arm away.

When he takes a step back, I go to Graham and take his face between my hands. Dirt coats his cheek, and a sob rips through my throat. "Graham... please... I'm so sorry."

His throat bobs, and he pinches his lips together as his own eyes grow damp. Until finally, he pushes my hands away and meets my eyes.

"Don't," he says, and the sadness in his voice nearly kills me.

Then he stumbles off, back through the woods the way he came.

Chapter 29

ATLAS

I LIE IN BED, arm bent, hand tucked behind my head as the early morning sun streams through the window. My first thought when I wake up is of Mackenzie. Funny how she's also the last thing I think about before I go to bed. The girl is infiltrating my every thought, and the truth is, I'm not even mad about it. I might not drink or smoke or do drugs, but I don't need to because Mackenzie Hart is my vice. From the moment I kissed her in that field, I was hooked. Addicted. And now there's no going back.

I sigh and roll on to my side, wondering what today's practice will bring and how pissed Graham will be. It's the same reason I'm in no hurry to go downstairs. I know trouble is waiting for me when I do. The cut on my lower lip is a brutal reminder of Graham's ire and I'm in no hurry for a repeat performance of last night without Mackenzie present to keep us both in check. Worse yet, with Uncle Cal as a witness.

So, instead of breakfast, I fuel my obsession and snag my phone off the nightstand beside me, then shoot a quick text to Mackenzie.

Atlas: *think it's time we try and get you behind the wheel again. You up for a driving lesson tomorrow?*

I grin when the dancing bubbles immediately appear on my screen and smile even wider when I read her response.

Doll: *I'm up for trying. Just don't expect much. We'll need a car, though. I might like riding your bike, but I have no desire to drive it.*
Atlas: *We'll take my dad's old beater.*
Doll: *You sure?*
Atlas: *It's not like he needs it, and it's just sitting there collecting rust.*

I hit send, and then because I care about her and know how her mind works, I tackle the elephant in the room.

Atlas: *Have you heard from Graham?*
Doll: *No. He won't answer any of my calls.*
Atlas: *He will. Just give him time.*
Doll: *I'm not so sure.*

I can practically hear her sigh through the screen, and I fight the stab of guilt in my chest that I'm the reason she might lose her best friend.

I close the messaging app and reach into the drawer of my nightstand where I hastily crammed the information on my father's rehab stay, including his room and a phone number where I could reach him. Sliding the brochure out, I find the information card and dial the number listed. If we're going to use his car, I need to find the keys.

When I was a kid, I could always tell when it had been a while since Pops used. He'd get the shakes. Sometimes the sweats, too. Then came the irritability. Often, he'd ward these symptoms off with booze, but that only lasted so long before he needed a fix.

Once, when I was eleven, it had been almost a week since I'd seen him passed out on the couch, but when he started snapping at me and missing work, drinking fifths of cheap whiskey, I knew something was up, and I hid his keys because I knew what came next.

In my naivete, I thought if he couldn't drive, he couldn't get more pills. That somehow if he went long enough without using, his addiction would magically be healed. But instead, he went into a rage searching for his keys, overturning furniture and rummaging through garbage. When he couldn't find them, he left the house in the evening and didn't return until the next morning. I found him passed out on the sofa, a prescription bottle in hand.

That was the last time I hid the keys.

I have no idea if he suspected me or not. All I know is from then on, he made sure to hide them. Where he kept them, I have no idea. I never really bothered to look. But I wasn't about to go on a wild goose chase looking for them, so as much as I hate the idea of calling him, I need to. Because I'd do just about anything for Mackenzie.

I wait as the phone rings, and when a receptionist answers, I identity myself and ask for my father. When his voice comes on the line, I barely recognize it. He sounds brighter somehow—alive.

"Atlas, is everything all right?"

I grit my teeth and fight the urge to answer with a smart remark. The time to ask me that question has long since passed. I spent the better part of my seventeen years not being "all right," thanks to him, and *now* he wants to make sure I'm okay?

"Yeah, it's fine. I just needed to borrow the car. I was wondering if you could tell me where your keys are."

The line falls silent, and for a moment, I wonder if he's hung up. But then he clears his throat and says, "Unless someone moved them, they're still in the ignition. Haven't touched them in over nine months."

"What? You just left them in the ignition?" I ask, surprise, or maybe it's disbelief, lacing my voice.

Is that really where he kept them all this time?

I think back to before he was arrested and try to recall the last time he used his car, but I can't remember. I'd been too preoccupied with my side jobs, playing football, and trying to get a scholarship to notice.

"The last time I drove, well . . . I was using and I hit someone. I think it was pretty bad, though I can't be sure. Freaked me the hell out, so when I got home, I dragged myself inside where I slept it off and vowed not to drive again. Scared the shit out of me. It's probably the first time I've ever followed through on something. Hell, I waited months for the cops to show up at my door, but they never did."

A trickling awareness creeps up my spine.

My pulse pounds in my ears as I ask, "What do you mean, you think it was bad?"

I close my eyes, waiting for his answer even though, deep down I already know what he's going to say. Part of me has been waiting for the shoe to drop with Kenzie since the day I met her. Maybe this is it.

"My vision was so blurry, I was seeing double and I was going too fast. I felt the impact first. It's how I dented my back bumper, and then I heard the crash behind me. But I kept going."

Bile rises in the back of my throat while dread fills my stomach like battery acid. "When was this?" I whisper.

"Man, I don't know. It's been about nine months now. Happened early January, I think." Dad says, confirming my worst fears.

I moan as my stomach pitches, and I drop the phone.

My father's voice comes through the other line while I grip my head, my fingers pressing into my skull while Anthony Mancetti's words on the police report run through my head.

The car was blue, an older make and model . . . No doubt about it, the man driving that car killed Laura.

Chapter 30

MACKENZIE

I know I need to give Graham space. Common sense tells me it's going to take time for him to forgive me, but the fear that he won't be able to move past last night at the bonfire kills me.

I'm twisted up inside, all tangled and knotted as the look on his face when he saw me with Atlas replays in my mind. It's my own silent torture. My own punishment. Yet when I think about how I could have changed things, I have no viable answer.

The truth is, I did feel something when Graham kissed me that night. And I do love him. Just not enough. Not like he needs me to. Because there's something about Atlas I can't explain. He's magnetic—I'm drawn to him by some intangible force I can't deny—and together, we're transformative. I soften his rough edges, while he sharpens mine. He makes me stronger and helps me see the world of opportunity around me with fresh eyes, like it's mine for the taking. All I need to do is reach out and grasp the world with two hands.

In short, I couldn't stay away from him if I tried.

It's now afternoon, not even twenty-four hours since I got drunk at Crow's Creek and crushed Graham's heart, and I can't get the image of him broken and bruised out of my mind. I'll hate myself forever for hurting him if he doesn't forgive me, and the fear I may have lost him for good strikes me like an arrow through the heart.

I call him one last time, but again, he doesn't answer. Only this time, my phone pings with an incoming text after I end the call.

Graham: *Please. Stop calling. I need time.*

My stomach clenches even though his request for needing time makes perfect sense. Yet the notion our friendship will likely never be the same again, kills me.

I start to text him back, then stop because I know I need to respect his wishes.

I sit at my desk chair, staring out the window, wondering what to do with myself. My father's off duty tonight and he expects me to stay in, so there's no chance of going out. Instead, it's dinner and a movie, which basically means I'll be staring at the TV screen while my mind is elsewhere.

What I need is a distraction, an outlet for the pressure building inside my chest, filling me up like a balloon.

But I have none, so I get up from my chair, lace on my tennis shoes with a heavy heart at the reminder of Graham, and go for a run.

ATLAS

I stand in front of Anthony Mancetti's home, aware of how different it feels from the last time I was here. The quaint little house with the fenced-in yard no longer seems inviting. Instead, the walk from the side of the road where I parked my bike feels like a death march.

I pause in front of his door and knock, praying he's at home since I checked the restaurant and he wasn't working. Still, there are a thousand places he could be, but I can't face Mackenzie until I talk to him. Until I know the truth.

I glance up at the sky as I wait, noting the thick gray blanket above me.

Even the clouds are unhappy.

The door creeks open and my head jerks toward the sound.

"What are you doing here?" Mancetti asks, his wary gaze instantly shifting behind me.

"If you're looking for Mackenzie, she's not with me. I came alone," I say, wondering what connection he has to her—why he's hiding. "But I need to ask you something."

"Look, I don't know what you want, but—"

"I think I know who hit them," I blurt out.

Anthony snaps his mouth shut and his skin turns ashen. "How . . .?"

I exhale, swallowing over the ache in the back of my throat. I'm fucking petrified of what he'll tell me or what I might discover. But there's no going back. I have to know.

"The car you saw . . . the day of the accident. You mentioned there being a sticker on the back."

He shrugs. "Yeah? I didn't get a good look at it, though."

"Was it on the window or the bumper?"

"The window."

"What color was it?" I ask, my voice a whisper.

"Yellow."

I inhale and think I might be sick as I picture my father's yellow *Class of '98* sticker. My stomach churns with dread, but I know what I must do. "Do you think you'd recognize the car if you saw a picture?"

He nods, his face turning to stone as he sees where I'm headed. "I think so."

I reach into the back pocket of my jeans and pull out my phone, opening my photos to the most recent one—the picture I snapped on my way out the door this afternoon—then turn the screen to face him. "Is this by any chance the car that hit them?"

Mancetti's brows knot before he glances at the screen while I wait on rubbery legs.

A trembling hand reaches out as he takes the device from me, staring hard at the photo. For a moment, I think he might not have heard the question. But just as suddenly, he sinks to the floor as if his legs can't hold him, sitting on the threshold of his home as his throat bobs and his eyes fill with tears. A sob rips through his throat while my chest splits wide open.

"How did you know?" he asks.

Chapter 31

ATLAS

I pick Mackenzie up right on time, but when she sees me on my bike, she pauses. "Where's the car?" she asks with a frown.

I shrug, hoping I don't sound as nervous as I feel. "I thought we could just do something fun today instead? Go to lunch or take a drive on my bike. Maybe see a movie . . ." I trail off, hoping I don't sound as nervous as I feel because my insides are an earthquake, vibrating with fear and threatening to crumble from the inside out.

I need to tell her what I've discovered. I know this. And yet I have no idea how. Part of me hopes the opportunity just magically presents itself. But the reality is I know there will never be a good time to tell her my father killed her mother.

I try and rack my brain for something to entice her away from going for a drive, but my mind draws a blank. It's hard to think once fear takes the wheel, and I've been the passenger to this nightmare since yesterday afternoon.

Mackenzie chuckles. "Are you chickening out on me?"

"No. I, uh, just thought—"

"Well, we're doing this. I'm ready, and I mentally prepared myself for this since yesterday. I really feel like this might jar some memories loose."

I nod and avoid eye contact with her, but say nothing as I try and find a way out of the predicament I'm in. The last thing I want to do is take her on a driving lesson in my father's car—the car that killed her mother.

It's messed up. Beyond sick.

My face contorts in pain, and I hang my head as her smile falls. "Is something wrong?" she asks. Taking a step closer, she reaches out and wraps her arms around my neck, dipping her head to meet my gaze while I stiffen in her arms. "Atlas, talk to me. You're being weird."

Seconds pass as I try to formulate a response but fall short. Nothing I can say will make it better.

"We need to talk about something." I take her hands in mine and remove them from around my neck, holding them between us. "It's serious."

She stiffens, and like a switch being flipped, her entire demeanor changes. "What's going on?"

"Well, it's just that I found out something I think you should know . . ." My throat bobs while I run my thumb across the delicate bones in her knuckles. "It's about my father."

"Oh, Atlas." She sighs and leans into me, placing her head against my chest. "I thought you were going to say something about us—that you changed your mind. Not that I'm glad this is about your father, but whatever's happened, we'll get through it together, okay? My memory, your father, Graham . . . no matter what it is, we'll handle it together. As long as I have you, I think I could get past anything."

"Me too," I choke out.

Suddenly the air is thick, hard to breathe.

Tell her . . .

She lifts her head and meets my eyes. "Did he relapse in rehab? Is his treatment not going well?"

I hold my breath. This is it. The moment it all comes crashing down.

I exhale, and the tension drains away as I take the easy way out of the corner I've backed myself into and blurt, "Yeah. How'd you know?"

She shrugs. "I mean, what else could it be?"

The heavy burden of guilt presses down on my shoulders, but I ignore it. I may have taken the out, but the truth still waits. All I did was buy myself some time.

I'm an asshole of the worst kind. A coward.

"Nothing your father could ever do would change how I feel about you," she says, her fingers softly playing in the strands of my hair. "You know that, right?"

Her words hit home. I only wish I could believe them.

But it's easy for her to make promises she can't keep when she doesn't know what I know.

"Now, will you please take me to your father's car so I can drive?"

MACKENZIE

I eye Atlas from the corner of my eye. He's still being weird, and I can only assume the situation with his father is weighing on him. I wish there was something I could do to help, but I know there's not.

"Are you sure your dad won't mind us using his car?" I ask. Maybe that's what's bothering him.

Atlas shrugs, but there's something stiff about the movement, and instead of answering my question he asks one of his own. "Are you sure you wanna do this? We could go out instead."

I shake my head, wondering if it's his concern for me that's driving his change in behavior. Or if maybe it has to do with what happened on Friday night. It's plagues me as well. Who knows what things are like at the Scott house.

"Is everything okay at your uncle's place?" I ask. "Is Graham making things difficult?"

He sighs and rakes a hand through his hair, and I think maybe I've hit the nail on the head. "It's awkward, that's for damn sure. I don't know how much he's told my uncle, if anything. But I hardly see him, to be honest. I keep to myself, especially now, and he's never around."

"I've complicated things for you," I say, the tightness returning to my chest as remorse and guilt grip hold of me.

He glances over at me for the first time since sliding inside his father's car, and I melt under his gaze. "I'm pretty sure it's the other way around."

"Graham and my father will come around. You'll see."

Atlas nods, but he doesn't look convinced, which makes me wonder . . .

"Will it be weird for you once Graham and I start talking again, if we're friends?"

"As long as I have you, nothing else matters." His throat bobs. "As long as you're mine, I think I could navigate just about anything."

A slow smile splits my face in two. "Me too."

Emotion flickers in his eyes before he leans forward and pulls me in for a kiss. It's warm and soft and tender, everything Atlas hides away from the world, so different from the razor-sharp front he puts on. And when he pulls away a moment later, I'm stronger. Less afraid.

"Let's do this." I lift the keys and stick them in the ignition, hating the way my breath hitches or how my hand shakes and my heart pounds as I crank the engine alive. The act is simple, yet terrifying. But I want to be strong. Brave.

Once it's running, I exhale, trying to ease the bubble of anxiety ballooning in my chest but it doesn't work. Every nerve stands to attention, my whole body lit like a livewire.

"Sit for a minute," Atlas murmurs, breaking through my thoughts. "What's something that you like talking about? Something that has a way of relaxing you?"

"Um . . . running," I say, which only makes me think of Graham and how he's currently not talking to me.

"Okay, why don't you lean your head back against the headrest," he says, pausing for me to do so. "Now close your eyes, and picture yourself running. The soles of your shoes crunching over gravel. The way your breath goes in and out of your lungs in a steady rhythm. Imagine your muscles warming up, coming alive. Your calves burning from the exertion."

I do as he says, listening to the sound of his soothing voice and concentrating on the feeling I get when I run. The rush. The wind in my face. The rhythm of my feet pounding on the pavement. My pulse hums in my neck—in time with my breath—and after a while, I relax into the seat. The tension in my grip loosens, along with the vice around my chest.

"Okay, now open your eyes," Atlas's voice soothes, "and put the car in drive."

I blink my eyes open and reality returns, but panic doesn't come rushing in like it always does. Instead, I hold it at bay as I pull the gear shift into drive.

"Take your foot slowly off the brake and just let us drift to the end of the driveway."

My heart kickstarts in my chest and sweat prickles my forehead. I know what's coming. How it only takes a moment to spiral.

A wave of emotion swells inside of me, and any moment it will come crashing down. Still, I do as he says, slowly lifting my foot from the brake, trying not to panic when the car lurches forward and we begin to roll.

The breath rushes from my lungs, and suddenly, I can't breathe. I can't catch my breath. My heart does a handstand inside my chest while the car careens down the driveway as I cover my face with my hands.

Atlas reaches across me and grabs the wheel as a guttural moan escapes my parted lips, and I brace for impact.

"Mackenzie . . . Doll . . ." Atlas shakes me, but I don't respond. I merely shake my head.

I can't open my eyes any more than I can grip the wheel and stop us from plunging to what I'm sure is our imminent demise.

Suddenly, I'm no longer in Atlas's fathers rusted-out Ford. Instead, I'm back in my Jeep Wrangler.

I'm yelling—shouting—at someone to get out of the way when I feel a jolt and my whole body flies into the dash. A shrill scream pierces my ears as I see the telephone pole. We're careening toward it, and I realize with complete clarity we're going to hit.

We're going to die.

My thoughts race faster than the car.

I wish I could tell my parents I love them. That I'm sorry I was mad. But I can't seem to open my mouth.

The crunching of metal coincides with an indescribable pain. It's like metal spikes hammering into every inch of my body. It's shocking and sudden, and the acrid scent of gunpowder fills my nostrils.

My head throbs. Pounds. Pain gnaws at my bones and clouds my thoughts as a scream curdles from my lips.

Out of nowhere Atlas's voice breaks through my thoughts. It's pacifying, yet slightly frantic, and as I come back to the present, I realize I'm in his arms, clinging to him as tears stream down my face.

Somehow the car has stopped.

And when I blink around me, I'm no longer back in my Jeep.

My heart thumps. I urge it to calm down, to come back to earth as I try to compose my thoughts. I must've had a flashback, but before I can further analyze it, Atlas squeezes me tighter while he runs his big, strong hands down the length of my hair, whispering over and over again, "It's okay. It's okay."

I swallow and close my eyes again, letting him mollify all the pain running through me. Because I want to believe him, I really do.

CHAPTER 32

GRAHAM

Coach blows the whistle at the same time Atlas rips his helmet off and storms the field until he's in my face. "What the hell was that?"

He's mad. Good. That makes two of us.

Ever since Friday night, anger has been my best friend, which is a good thing considering I'm down one.

"Looks like you missed the ball," I say, my tone impassive.

"That's bullshit and you know it. That was an impossible catch," he spits out, teeth bared and eyes glaring.

"Jace caught the one before it on the same play," I say, smirking as I meet his heated gaze.

"Yeah, because you threw it right into his fucking chest."

"Is that what you need? For me to throw it right into your hands? Because this is football, *son*. It doesn't always work that way."

"What did you call me?" He steps closer. No doubt his blood is boiling, and I'm loving every minute of it. Goading him is probably foolish, but I can't seem to help myself.

Grinning, I catch sight of Mackenzie on the sidelines with the other girls and my resolve strengthens. I'm glad she's watching. I want her to see the pain she's caused.

"I know the game," Atlas snaps. "You're messing with me."

He comes closer until his face is only inches from mine, the mask of my helmet nearly touching his nose.

I laugh and his fists clench.

Go ahead. Throw a punch, and you'll get benched so fast . . .

"Ladies, if you're done bitching, can we get on with it?" Jace appears and shoves the ball in my arms while his gaze darts between us.

I've been tight lipped about what went down at Crow's Creek after I found Kenz with Atlas, but I'm sure he knows. Word has a way of getting around in Riverside. Not to mention, I'm sure he and every other soul there that night saw Atlas's name and number scrawled across her chest. He's got to know how much it gutted me, how the sight ripped me to shreds. I've spent every night since thinking about how it got there. Did he initiate drawing on her chest, or did she? Did they laugh about it, knowing she'd wear my jersey with his name and number inked on her skin beneath mine?

I take one last lingering look at Atlas before I spin on my heel and go back to my position on the field. Beside me, I nod to Knox, our best linebacker and murmur, "Let's teach the new kid a lesson, huh?"

He gives me a tight nod before lining up with the defense.

The ball snaps. I take a couple steps back, finding my man—Atlas. He's nearing the end zone when I throw it just as Knox breaks through the line and smashes into him, completely annihilating him.

Atlas rolls on his side with a moan, and it's a moment before he gets to his feet, but once he does, he roars and all hell breaks loose. Several of my men come to Atlas's defense and get in Knox's face while I stay put, watching the scene unfold before Atlas turns to me and we lock eyes.

He charges toward me, his face contorted with rage as he places his hands on my chest and shoves while I smirk, taunting him, when Coach blows the whistle and appears between us. "Do we have a problem here?" he asks, glancing from me to Atlas.

Silence settles over us, and the tension grows.

Atlas's chest heaves as his knife-like gaze hardens on me. "No. No problem."

MACKENZIE

On Wednesday, I do something I haven't done since the day of the crash. I decide to skip class.

The flashback I had in Atlas's father's car is eating away at me. Nothing about it was revolutionary. But it *has* confirmed something I previously thought to be true. I *was* angry with both of my parents, particularly my mother, prior to the crash.

And now I'm dying to remember why. It feels crucial, somehow. Like if I can just remember that one piece of information, I'll remember everything.

Which is why I fake being sick this morning.

When I don't come down for breakfast my father comes looking for me, finding me in bed with the covers drawn to my chin. I groggily blink my eyes up at him, a manufactured rasp in my voice when I say, "I'm not feeling well this morning."

My father frowns and places a hand on my forehead. "You feel a little warm. Should I get the thermometer?" He starts to turn for the bathroom, but I stop him.

"No. I'm sure it's just a cold." I reach up to my throat, giving the impression it hurts to talk. "Do you think it would be okay if I stay home?"

My father's forehead creases in concern and I push back the wave of guilt. "Sure, sweetheart. Do you want me to take a personal day and stay home with you? I can get you some soup and we can watch a movie."

I shake my head, squeezing my eyes shut. "No, Daddy. You've taken enough time in the last year. I'll be fine. I'm just going to sleep anyway." I roll over on my side, facing away from him in the hope he'll listen. "Go ahead to work. I'm just going to rest."

"Okay. If you're sure..."

"I'm sure," I sigh and focus on my breathing, steadying the rise and fall of my chest as if I'm already falling asleep when he reaches out and gives my shoulder a little squeeze.

A minute later, I hear the click of my bedroom door close shut, and I roll on to my back, staying in position in case he comes in one last time to check on me.

Ten minutes later, when I hear the engine roar to life outside my window, I jump up out of bed and head to my window where I stand to the side, lest he see me, and I watch as he backs his cruiser down the driveway and heads away from home.

I quickly change, then head to the kitchen where I pour myself a cup of the remaining coffee in the pot and doctor it to my liking before I make my way upstairs to his office.

I hover outside the doorway as my conscience kicks in and I think through what I'm about to do. I know I shouldn't snoop in here; it's where my father keeps all the bills and files and anything personal. Ever since I was little, it's been sort of an unspoken, yet known fact that this was his domain and I'm not to enter.

Which is exactly why it might hold answers.

I take a step inside and head straight for my father's desk. A framed photograph of the three of us sits on the surface of the gleaming mahogany.

I reach out and pick it up, holding it in my hands as I stare at the image of my mother, and I'm hit with an overwhelming sense of longing. I remember when it was taken. We'd gone on a trip south. Drove from Ohio to Virginia. We stayed several days before heading on to Florida where we spent a week at the beach and a day at Disney.

My father's arms are wrapped around Mom's waist while my mother and I gaze at each other, our smiles wide. There's so much love in her eyes it hurts.

I swallow as a familiar thickness clogs my throat. Tears sting my eyes and grief swells inside of me, threatening to drown me if I don't rein it back in.

I put the photo back down and take a deep breath. Closing my eyes, I wait until the aching subsides and the tightness in my chest loosens. Then I remind myself of my mission and blink my eyes open as I search his desktop.

Everything is neat and orderly, which is just like my father. I open the filing cabinet beside me and see alphabetized bills and other files such as the deeds to the house, insurance paperwork, tax documents, and receipts.

I slam the cabinet closed and search the narrow desk drawer next, only to come up short. Then I move to the drawers on the left side of the desk. On top is a brochure with a gorgeous stone building on the front. Bold font boasts, "Piedmont Academy, America's Oldest and Most Prestigious Private School." Frowning, I flip the brochure over to find an address on the back for a city in Virginia.

Glancing down at the desk drawer, something else catches my eye that I missed—a realtor's business card for the same Virginia town.

I put them back and shake it off.

There could be a million reasons my father has those, all of which I'm sure means nothing. My father would never think of leaving Riverside. This is where he grew up. Where my mother and father met and fell in love. We have a million memories here, all of them good.

But one of them bad. Very bad, I think.

I shake my head, pushing the prospect of moving aside because it's ridiculous.

Flipping through the rest of the drawer, I find little else. Old magazines, pamphlets and brochures—nothing of importance, so I move onto the bottom one.

I sort through a stack of papers on the top and some office supplies, again thinking I'm going to come up empty when a manilla envelope catches my eye. The front is blank and as I slide it out, a chill creeps up my spine. There's no label or writing on it and when I peek inside, I make out a small stack of photos and papers.

Wasting no time, I dump them out on the desk and gasp.

My hands fly to my mouth and my heart leaps in my throat as I stare at the photographs in front of me. They're of my mother and Anthony Mancetti. He's holding her in his arms in one of them while she gazes up at him, smiling. In another, they're caught in a passionate embrace, their lips locked, eyes closed. Another shows them holding hands across a table and I'm sure it was taken at Manja, Manja because it matches the image from the flashback I had the day Atlas took me to the scene of the crash.

The world as I know it tips on its axis.

My mother and Anthony Mancetti were lovers, that much is clear. And obviously, my father knew about it.

I swallow and my hands tremble as I pick more photos up. All the pictures were taken at odd angles from an outsider's perspective. So, either my father hired someone to follow Mom, or he followed her himself.

I sit there a moment, waiting for this revelation to sink in before I move to the papers, pick them up, and suck in a breath. Divorce papers.

Another blow.

"Oh my gosh," I murmur.

Tears sting the back of my eyes and my throat grows tight. My mother was having an affair and from the looks of these documents, she'd asked my father for a divorce.

I flop back in the desk chair while the air hisses from my lungs like a deflating balloon.

I sit there, shell shocked, wondering where I go from here. My parents were unhappy. My mother was unfaithful, and I must've found out about it, which was why I was angry at her. It's why I went to the restaurant that day.

My hands tremble as I slide my phone out of my pocket and text Atlas.

Come quick. I found something, and I need you.

Chapter 33

MACKENZIE

By the time Atlas arrives thirty minutes later, he finds me curled up in a ball on the couch, fighting for air.

His eyes widen as his arms come around me at once, and when he asks me what's happened, I blurt out everything—all the sordid details. "It has to be why I was mad at her, at both of them. I must've found out about either the affair or the divorce."

"Or both," Atlas says, and I nod.

"I always held my parents' relationship in such high esteem, like they were the pinnacle of a happy couple. They always seemed so strong together, so in love. I would never have suspected otherwise." I close my eyes and bring my hands up to my forehead. "I wish I could just remember how it all went down. Maybe they told me about the divorce and I got suspicious, so I skipped school and followed my mother. Or maybe I found out about the affair first and went there in the hopes of catching them." The thought twists my stomach, and I grimace. "Either way, it all makes more sense, even if I don't know all the details."

Atlas pulls me tighter, until I'm pressed into his chest. "I'm sorry."

"I always thought they were so in love."

"I'm sure at one time they were," he says.

"So, what happened? I don't understand."

He's silent for a moment because we both know he can't answer my question. Neither of us can.

"Are you going to confront your father? Tell him that you know?" he asks after a moment.

I shake my head. "I don't think so, but I don't know." My head spins, my thoughts an endless merry-go-round. "I guess we can understand why Anthony Mancetti acted so weird and didn't want to talk to me." I straighten, meeting his eyes. "It certainly explains why he referred to my mom by her first name, and it definitely gives more credence to his story about there being a second car involved."

Atlas stiffens, but I continue, on a roll.

"If my father knew about the affair, which he obviously did, it makes sense he wouldn't want to talk to Mancetti. I'm sure he despises the man. So, he shrugged him off, glossed over the eyewitness report. Which means it's likely Mancetti is right."

"Maybe. But I wouldn't rule anything out," Atlas says, clearing his throat. "For all you know, your father had another officer look into it and nothing turned up."

I frown. "I doubt it. I mean, there was hardly even anything about the accident in the report." His gaze drops to mine, and my eyes prick with tears. "Which means he ignored evidence that could've brought my mother's killer to justice. If we hadn't gotten struck by another car, we wouldn't have crashed that day. To think he could've relieved all my guilt, taken away the pain of thinking I killed her." My throat thickens, my voice tight. "He knew, yet he let me believe . . ."

A sob rips through my throat, and I trail off, trying to rein in my emotion while Atlas presses a kiss to my cheek.

"Everything's gonna be okay," he murmurs. "I'm sure he had a reason . . ."

"What reason could he possibly have that would justify keeping this from me and not investigating it further?"

"Maybe he was scared."

"Fear is not an excuse."

"Kenz, he's your father . . ."

Sniffling, I sober as my mouth presses into a thin line. "Which is precisely why his betrayal hurts so much more. He's supposed to love me like no other, yet he lied to me. He put his own hatred and pride before the truth. And he did it all at the expense of his own daughter's happiness."

ATLAS

If my heart beats any harder, it will pump right out of my chest.

My thumb strokes her cheek as I try to play it cool, but inside I'm screaming.

My gaze soaks her in, radiant even with her mussed hair and damp cheeks, pink from crying, and I want to puke. If Mackenzie can't forgive her own father for keeping this from her, how can I expect her to forgive me?

I open my mouth to confess, to tell her what I know. That I, too, have a secret. I know she didn't kill her mother in that crash—my father did. But I can't do it. I can't bring myself to say the words and single-handedly destroy the best thing that's ever happened to me.

I rake a hand through my hair, vacillating between the truth and keeping it to myself when she dries her eyes and turns more fully toward me.

"I found something else in his desk that was weird. A brochure to a private school in Southern Virginia, along with a card for a realtor in that area."

I freeze, then drop my hand. "What do you mean?"

"What if he's thinking about moving us?" Her eyes search mine. "I can see the appeal. Part of me doesn't blame him for wanting a fresh start after what happened."

I swallow. The thought of Riverside without Mackenzie doesn't sit well with me. "He can't do that, right? He'd ask you first, make sure you wanted to go."

"That's the thing. I don't even know anymore. Apparently, he does whatever he wants."

I shake my head, refusing to believe it.

"He won't do that," I say, even though I know that's not true. I'm certain Chief Hart would do anything to keep Mackenzie safe and away from the likes of me, even if that means uprooting and moving her to another state. "I can't lose you," I croak, barely recognizing my own voice.

Which is precisely why I can't tell her what I know, because it will change the way she looks at me. Even if she doesn't blame me, how can we be together, knowing my own flesh and blood is the reason her mother no longer lives and breathes?

The fact he hit them and killed her would remain a dark cloud hovering over us forever, a stain on our relationship.

She reaches out and takes my face in her hands, and I try to find comfort in it, but it's hard because I don't deserve it.

I'm not worthy.

"I won't leave you. I'll refuse to go," she says, though we both know it's not true. If her father wants her out of Riverside, there's not a damn thing she can do about it.

She leans into me, pressing her forehead against mine. "I know this sounds crazy, and we've known each other only a short time, but I've fallen for you, Atlas Scott. The world and everything in it can be against us, and I'll still love you."

My heart thunders in my chest as I grip her waist and pull her to me, drinking in her words. They're so sweet I could drown in them. Hell, maybe I already have. All I know is I feel like I'm sinking, headfirst into the abyss.

Because I love her, too. I think I've known it since the first moment I laid eyes on her.

But I can't seem to push the words past the thickness in my throat—through the fear I might lose her.

Instead, I pull her even closer and take her mouth with mine while my hands roam, tracing the shape of her curves beneath the thin cotton of her dress and memorizing them like I might never get the chance again.

With a moan she yanks it over her head, then pulls me toward her, until her back presses into the sofa and I cage her with my arms.

Before I moved to Riverside, football was all I thought about. It was the only thing that mattered, and I was fine with that. I was happy with my singular world.

But now?

Now I crave so much more. I still want football, but I want it alongside Mackenzie Hart. The girl I call doll—the one everybody treats as though she's made of porcelain, when really she's made of stone.

My hand slides down her sides to her waist, and finally, her legs where I splay my hand over the outside of her thigh, feeling the rough edges of a scar I've never noticed.

Pulling my mouth from hers, I move to the raised flesh, tracing the thick, silvery-pink lines with my fingertips, like highways on a roadmap, as she sucks in a breath.

I glance up at the sound to see her staring. "It's from the accident," she says, though I need no explanation.

"They're beautiful," I whisper. Then I dip my head, tracing the puckered flesh with my tongue in reverence, grateful like hell she's alive; that the same crash that claimed her mother spared her. Grateful for the ridges over her leg which prove she's still living, breathing.

I move up her body once more and meet her mouth with mine, her kiss feverish as she grips the hem of my shirt in her fingertips. I help her with it, tossing it to the ground as my eyes drink her in: Lips pink and slightly swollen from our kisses. Hair rumpled. Creamy skin glowing in her silky pink bra.

The girl beneath me has gotten under my skin, and I can't imagine my world without her.

My mouth moves to her jaw, teeth scraping against the delicate skin of her neck, kissing my way back to her plump lips.

Who needs words when I can show her how I feel?

Her back arches as I slide my hand beneath her bra, unsure how far I should take it when she reaches behind herself and unclasps it, then moves to the button of my jeans. "You sure?" I rasp, and she nods.

Then, I get lost in her.

Chapter 34

GRAHAM

I take the familiar turn into Pine Grove. Mackenzie wasn't at school today, and I haven't spoken to her since Friday night at Crow's Creek where I got my nose bloodied and bruised, along with my ego.

I hope she's not sick, just like I hope she understands why I didn't show up on Monday morning to pick her up. Or any of the mornings after. I couldn't bring myself to face her, not when all I keep picturing is Atlas's name and number scrawled over her chest in black ink.

My hands clench over the steering wheel and my throat tightens as I remember the scene in front of the Black Hole. How afraid I was when she jumped. How devastated I felt when I found her with him.

I've spent all week avoiding Atlas, with the exception of practice, which has been even more tense since the dirty tackle I pulled with Knox on Monday. Yet I still feel like a fool.

I practically threw myself at Kenzie, but I was just so relieved to finally have my feelings heard. Part of me wonders if she felt anything at all, or if she felt trapped. Maybe she pitied me and that's why she entertained the idea of us. Or maybe she felt guilty the whole time for wanting someone else.

I'm not sure which is worse. All I know is I'm a fool for ever clinging to the idea of us, and thinking she'd suddenly want me when I've been here for the past six years. I've been right in front of her this whole time and she's never once looked at me as more than a friend.

And though I haven't had the courage to face her before now, I can't just shut off the little voice inside my head—the one that's worried about why she might've missed school. My feelings haven't changed just because she wants someone else. I can't just cut them off.

Besides, I might still love her, but I also promised myself that no matter what happened between us, we'd stay friends. Even if she flat-out rejected me. Even if we tried and didn't work out. Or if she chose someone else.

And I would honor that.

Because when you love someone, all you care about is their happiness in spite of your own. And if she is happy with Atlas, well . . . I'd just have to learn to live with it.

In the meantime, I just need a little time and space to try to numb my feelings and find a way to move on once and for all. I just hope she understands it'll be a gradual process jumping back into our friendship.

I slow as I approach her house and turn into the driveway when my stomach sinks.

A black Harley is parked in her father's spot.

I want to puke. Bang the steering wheel. Or scream. Maybe all three.

Of course, he'd be here with her. They're together now. She's his to take care of, not mine, and I need to learn how to be her friend without crossing boundaries like I've been doing for so long.

There's only one problem.

I have no idea how the hell to do that.

The pressure in my chest grows as I stare up at her house picturing them together. I should go up to the door, knock, and check on her like a normal human being. Friends check on friends when they're sick, right?

But I can't do that. Not with Atlas inside. I'm just not there yet.

Decision made, I back out of the driveway and head away from her house, wondering how long it will be until Atlas hurts her as I white-knuckle the wheel.

Resentment grows inside me like a bitter seed, sprouting to life.

Everything was fine until he showed up. Hell, if he hadn't, Kenzie and I would probably be together right now. She would've given me a real chance without him in the picture, I'm sure of it.

Anger grips me like a vice, and without forethought, I'm back on the main road, heading toward the center of town. To the precinct.

I pull into the parking lot of Riverside PD and turn off the ignition, only hesitating a moment before I make my way inside. Cindy, the office manager who works for the department, is the first face I see. She sits at her desk, a broad smile on her face when she sees me, and greets me warmly.

"Well, hey, there, Graham. What brings you here? Everything all right?"

I nod and force a smile. "Everything's fine. Thank you, ma'am. But, actually, is Chief Hart in? I have a personal matter I want to discuss with him."

"Well, he sure is. Hang on one second, honey, while I give him a ring." Cindy picks up the phone, dials his extension, and waits. It's only a minute before I hear her tell him I'm here and another couple minutes before he appears from the hallway, his mouth drawn down like a bow, his forehead knotted in concern.

"Graham? Come on back." He motions for me to follow as Cindy waves and tells me to say hello to my mother for her.

Once we're in his office, he motions for me to take a seat. My gaze makes quick work of my surroundings while I sink down into a chair across from him, lingering on a framed photograph of Mackenzie. I recognize it as her school picture from freshman year.

"So, how can I help you?" Chief Hart says, wasting no time. "I hope everything's okay. You're, uh, face looks a little . . ." He motions to his nose, and I instinctively reach a hand up to my face.

"Oh, uh, yes, sir." I rub my damp palms on the front of my jeans as doubt start to slither into my subconscious. "That was Atlas Scott."

"He hit you?"

"We got into an argument, and he lashed out. Doc said I'm lucky he didn't break it."

Hart runs a hand over his face. "You know you can press charges for assault. Do you want to leave a report, get it on record?" he asks, shuffling through some papers on his desk.

"Well, that's not really why I'm here," I admit to him.

"If he laid his hands on you . . ."

"I'll think about it, but I came toda

Hart's expression turns stony, my busted nose forgotten. "Has something happened? Is this about her being sick today?"

"No, sir." I shake my head. "I mean, not exactly. It's just . . . I guess she's dating my cousin"—I squint, unsure of whether I'm going about this the right way—"and I guess I'm just worried about the impact he might be having on her."

The color drains from his face. "I thought . . . but she wore *your* jersey Friday night."

I nod but say nothing.

He rises to his feet and begins to pace behind his desk. "I explicitly told her to stay away from him. That he's a bad influence."

"I can't say I disagree. Even last Friday, she was acting a little reckless. She had a couple of beers, then went swimming in this old pond at Crow's Creek—"

"She *what*?" His eyes widen. "And she was drinking?"

I swallow. "Just now I went to see her, and he's there."

His face reddens and a vein in his forehead flickers to life. "You're sure?"

"I saw his bike in your driveway with my own two eyes."

The chief's expression turns thunderous as he swipes a set of keys off his desk and points them in my direction. "I'll take care of this."

Chapter 35

MACKENZIE

The soft press of Atlas's lips on the side of my face wakes me. I blink up at him, my vision bleary with sleep. "I'm sorry. I must've drifted off."

"It's okay. It's been a stressful week," he says, pressing a kiss to my temple.

He's wrapped around me from behind, my back pressed into his muscled chest, and as consciousness returns, I remember what we did, and my cheeks burn.

"No regrets?" he asks, noticing and searching my gaze for the truth.

"No regrets," I say, biting my lip in an effort to hide my smile.

"Good."

I roll on my back, finding his mouth with mine and kissing him until he pulls away with a sigh. "I should probably go."

"Do you have to?"

"It's getting late, and I need to be gone when your father gets here."

I nod and say nothing because I know he's right.

Propping myself up on my elbow, I watch as he gathers his things when the door bursts open and my father stands in the doorway. His eyes widen as he takes in the scene before him.

I can only imagine how it looks. Me on the couch, with my hair rumpled. Atlas standing before him, his T-shirt dangling from his fingers.

A murderous gleam flickers in his eyes as the bottom drops out from under me. I've seen my father countless times in his uniform, but never before has he looked so menacing. For the first time in my life I'm scared of what he might do.

"Dad!" I get to my feet and cross the room, but he ignores me. He doesn't even glance in my direction as he takes a step toward Atlas.

His gaze makes quick work over the ink on his arm as he points to the door. "You have one second to get the hell away from my daughter!"

Atlas squares his shoulders and the muscles in his forearms flex as I scramble to stand, pressing myself into his side and taking his hand in mine.

"Dad, he's my boyfriend. I asked him to come."

"I don't care who the hell he is. He's not welcome in my house, and he has one minute to vacate the premises before I arrest him for trespassing." My father's face reddens as his nostrils flare, a vein pulsing at his temple.

I stare at him, dumbfounded. "You can't be serious?"

"Try me."

Swallowing, I turn to Atlas to find his eyes already on me. "I don't wanna leave you with him like this," he says quietly.

My father scoffs and starts to protest when I whisper, "I'll be okay." I reach out and squeeze his hand. "Just go."

Atlas brushes past my father and moves toward the door, jaw tense, mouth a flat line. At any moment he might snap and judging by the tense set of my father's shoulders, he's ready for it.

Once he's at the door, Atlas shoots me one last lingering look before he opens it and steps outside, disappearing from view.

"What are you doing here?" I spin around, pinning my father with a look. He wasn't due home for a couple more hours.

"I come home and catch the two of you in a compromising position, and you want to know what *I'm* doing here?"

I roll my eyes. "It wasn't *that* compromising," I mumble.

You should've seen us an hour ago.

He arches a brow, and for a moment I think I've stunned him into silence, until he says, "I thought I told you to stay away from him."

"Looks like I didn't listen."

I cross my arms over my chest as we face off, containing the swell of anger rising inside of me. How dare he hide the truth about my mother, then reprimand me for not following orders. Respect goes both ways.

I make a move to pass him and head for my room, done with talking to him, when he grabs my arm and stops me. "We're not done here."

I rip my arm from his grip. "I think we are."

"This is exactly what I was afraid of," he seethes. "You've known him a month and already he's getting to you. Dismissing my rules, drinking at parties with friends, swimming in some pond at night while drunk, and now—"

"Who told you that?" I narrow my eyes on him, but he doesn't so much as flinch.

"He's trouble, Kenzie."

"Oh my gosh." My eyes widen as it hits me. "Graham told you, didn't he? He went to you?"

"Now that's a young man with his head on his shoulders. He cares about you. He's not some trash kid with a—"

"You know nothing about Atlas!" I snap. "You judge him, but he's good and genuine and kind."

"His father—"

"He's nothing like his father. He's a good man. And I love him."

My father stumbles back, his expression stricken. "You're seventeen. You know nothing about love."

I chuckle bitterly. "And you do?"

"Of course, I do. Your mother and I were happily married for twenty—"

"Was the happy part before or after her affair?" I interrupt him.

He pales. "What?"

My resolve hardens. Deep down, I'm sure there's a part of me that feels for him—the betrayal, the loss of a marriage and best friend—because if there's one thing I know about my father, it's that he loved my mother fiercely. But right now, the part of me that's angry with him for hiding the truth is stronger than my sympathy.

"You lied right to my face. That morning, I remember being angry. I just couldn't remember why. But it's because I found out, didn't I? About the divorce? Maybe even the affair? And you knew this, but you told me you had no idea what happened that day, why I might've skipped school or been upset."

His throat bobs. "There was no reason to tell you. No point in ruining the memories you had of her."

"It was the truth," I say, unable to believe what I'm hearing.

He steps forward, hands out, his tone pleading. "I just thought it would be easier for you if you remembered us as being a happy family. That nothing was wrong and she hadn't gone outside our marriage. You never should've found out about it anyway."

"But I did. And what's worse, you let me believe that *I* killed Mom. All because you refused to talk to Anthony Mancetti about what he saw that day. You could have relieved me of all of that guilt," I say as a tear slips down my cheek. "All that pain."

His mouth rounds, his face drawn. "I didn't . . . How do you know . . . ?"

"I spoke with him myself and it took all of two minutes for him to convince me another car struck us before we went off the road."

"You shouldn't have spoken with him. There was zero evidence that day another car was involved."

"There was an eyewitness!" I scream, throwing my arms in the air. "He was there. Or doesn't it count because he was banging Mom?"

"Watch your mouth." He lunges forward, hand drawn back, and it's the first time in my life I think he might lay his hand on me.

I flinch and take a step back while guilt registers in his dark gaze.

But I refuse to back down.

I have far too much to say.

"Maybe I can understand hiding the divorce and the affair. I get why you would want to forget that. And I can believe you wanted me to remember only the good things about Mom, about us. But letting me live with the guilt that I drove us off the road and killed her? That"—I point at him—"is unforgivable."

I spin on my heel and run for the stairs, my father's voice sounding out behind me as I shut myself inside my room, sink to the floor, and let the tears fall.

Chapter 36

MACKENZIE

I throw my pompoms in the air as the ball sails into Atlas's hands and Riverside pulls ahead in the last few seconds of the game. Fans roar behind me and the squad launches into one final cheer before screaming and celebrating with the rest of the crowd. At twenty-eight to twenty-one, Riverside takes another win, leaving us undefeated. Atlas and Graham are the stars of the game.

I turn and glance into the stands, even though I know my father isn't there. At my request, he stayed home tonight. At his insistence, however, I'll be joining him afterward. I'm still not talking to him since I discovered he lied, which means I basically live in my bedroom most days since I've been grounded all week. It's his last-ditch effort to keep me away from Atlas, but it's not working. We see each other at school and afterward at practice, and we talk on the phone every chance we get. He can't keep us apart no matter how much he wants to, and this lack of control eats him alive.

The boys race off the field as the cheerleaders line up, forming a barricade against the crowd toward the entrance of the lockers. Once they disappear inside, I take my time, wandering through the stands and the endless sea of faces, biding my time until Atlas returns and I can have at least a few minutes before Caroline drops me off at home.

I make small talk with a couple seniors, sheepishly ducking my head as I say hello to the Scotts, unsure of what he's told them when I spot Graham leaving the locker room, and my chest squeezes. I miss our friendship, our long talks, and our carefree banter. I itch to tell him what I discovered about my parents and the accident. For years, he's been my sounding board, so it feels weird to keep this from him now, but even if he weren't still heartbroken and not speaking to me, I'm angry at him for ratting me out to my father.

There's an ocean between us, and I don't see either of us bridging it anytime soon.

He turns as Tiff appears at his side and glances down at her. The smile he offers her is timid, shy almost, and it makes my heart clench. I remember a time when he looked at me with the same warmth in his green eyes, and I can't help the spike of jealousy running through me, even if I have no right to feel that way.

Tiff laughs at something he says, and when he lifts his head, his eyes lock on mine. I expect him to instantly sober and frown, but he doesn't. Instead, he offers me a small wave, and I wonder if maybe I'm wrong. Maybe not all is lost between us.

My answering smile says it all—I miss you, forgive me—but I don't say any of those things. I'm still upset with him for running to my father, so I say nothing and watch his retreating form when a warm embrace envelops me in their arms, and I smile. The scent of cedar and sandalwood drifts toward me, a scent I'd know anywhere.

"Hey," his deep baritone rumbles through me as he presses a kiss into my hair, and I turn around to face him.

Stretching onto my toes, I fist a hand around the collar of his shirt and pull him toward me. Our lips meet and a familiar warmth radiates through me.

"I suppose you're still grounded?" he asks against my mouth.

"Unfortunately." When he frowns, I add, "But why don't you go to the creek? Maybe it'd be good for you to hang with the guys."

I don't miss the way his gaze shifts behind us to where Graham is standing.

"Nah. Better not."

My shoulders sink. "You guys have to make up eventually. You're cousins and you're still living together. I hate that I'm the reason you're fighting."

"Don't fool yourself, doll. We weren't exactly besties before either."

I grin. "Did you just say besties?"

Atlas laughs. "Maybe."

He leans down, pressing his forehead against mine. "I wish I could see you tonight."

"Why don't you come over after dark. Just climb up and knock on my window."

"Mackenzie Hart, what a rebel you are. I'll have to think about it." He grins. "I'm afraid you might steal my virtue."

"Like anything about you is virtuous," I tease.

He growls, and I laugh at the same time a pleasant shiver dances over the surface of my skin.

"Hey, Kenz, you ready?" Caroline calls out.

"Coming," I yell back with a sigh. "So, I'll see you tonight?"

I back up slowly, my hands still in his until only our fingertips are linked.

"Tonight," he confirms.

I spin around and yelp as I smack into someone passing by when a gush of something wet and cold splashes down the front of my shirt.

I blink at the girl across from me as she gapes. "Oh my gosh." She covers her mouth with her hand, her empty soda cup in the other. "I am so sorry."

"No. No, it was my . . ." I trail off when a wave of vertigo hits me, and I stumble. "It was my fault," I whisper as my head spins.

I reach up to grip my skull while an image bursts inside my head like a firecracker. With an explosion of light, I'm back in Manja, Manja.

Tomato sauce and garlic scents the air. The chink of silverware surrounds me as I stand there, staring at their table—Mom and her lover. I'd overheard them on the phone together the previous night, and then this morning my father told me Mom's job was making her move, so she'd be getting an apartment out of town, as if it was perfectly normal—us living apart. But I knew the truth. Mom was having an affair, and they were getting a divorce.

And now here I am, watching her share a meal with this man.

They lift their glasses of red wine to their lips as they talk and when Mom tips her head back and laughs, I'm filled with the desire to know what's so funny. What could she possibly find humorous about this situation when she already has a husband—someone she's pledged her life to.

I start for their table, ready to confront her. I want to let her know how awful she is and how much this hurts when I hear my name and pause in my tracks. I stand there, only yards away, my mother's back to me as I strain to hear.

"Telling Kenzie will be the hardest part. I just don't want to hurt her."

"I know." The man reaches out and takes her hand, brushing his thumb over her knuckles. "But you deserve to be happy, too."

Nausea bubbles from my gut into my throat while my stomach churns, and I think I might be sick.

Spinning around, I make a beeline for the door when a waitress steps into my path, tray in hand, and we collide. The tray tips on impact and despite her effort to stop it's fall, a glass of ice water drenches me. Plates fall with a clatter to the floor. People gasp around us.

"I'm so sorry," the waitress says, hands fluttering as if unsure how to help me.

"No. No, it was my fault." I risk a glance over my shoulder and when I do, Mom's eyes lock on mine.

She knows I know.

I dart for the door.

My shirt is soaked and I'm sure I look crazy, but I don't care.

The minute I burst outside I sprint for my car. I jump in and start it, hands trembling as I turn the keys in the ignition.

Mom appears on the sidewalk, searching the lot for my car, and when she finds it, she heads my way.

I put the car in drive and press the gas pedal pausing only a moment before I pull out onto the road, but it's just enough time to allow Mom to open the passenger door and jump inside.

"Get out," *I scream at her as I pull out of the parking lot.*

"Not until you talk to me." *Her voice is thick, and I'd bet anything that if I glance her way, tears will be glistening in her eyes.*

An engine roars behind me and I check the rearview mirror to find a small blue Ford Fiesta coming dangerously close to my bumper. I flinch, sure they're going to hit me from behind when they go to pass. Something dangles from their rearview mirror, and I try to make out what it is only to realize with disgust that it's a lucky rabbit's foot.

"I don't want to hear anything you have to say," *I tell her once my eyes are back on the road.*

"Mackenzie, please—"

They're the last words that come out of her mouth because the blue car comes back in our lane too early, cutting her off. Their backend smashes into the front of my car, sending us careening off the road straight toward a telephone pole.

A scream curdles in my lungs seconds before impact, and the last thing I remember is the yellow sticker on the back window before the lights go out.

"Mackenzie. Kenz!" Atlas shakes me and his voice startles me back to the present.

I blink, dazed as I glance down at myself to see I'm curled into a ball on the ground. A crowd of people gather around me, staring.

"Kenzie," a familiar voice calls out, before the comforting embrace of his arms support my weight.

Graham.

"No." I shrug him off. "No!" I say, louder this time as I turn on Atlas.

"It was him," I say, a tremor in my voice. "Your father."

"What?" Atlas pales, but he doesn't flinch. His eyes don't even so much as widen in surprise, which is how I know he knows.

"You know already, don't you?"

"I don't know what you're talking about," he whispers, but there's nothing convincing in his words.

My throat tightens until it feels as though it might close shut entirely. "How long have you known?" I croak.

He swallows but says nothing, and then it dawns on me. "You already knew the day I drove your father's car. It's why you tried to change our plans and talk me out of it. You knew, and yet you still let me drive it? You let me drive the car responsible for killing my mother?"

My stomach pitches and I have to clamp my mouth shut against the bile rising in the back of my throat.

Tears sting my eyes as they fill, remembering the last words I shared with my mother; none of them were good. We never got a chance to make amends.

"Mackenzie . . ." he reaches out to me, clasping my arm in his hand, but I shrug him off.

"Don't touch me! What kind of sicko lets their girlfriend drive the car that killed her own mother?" I sob.

"I didn't . . ." His face goes ashen. "I wanted to tell you. I tried. I didn't even suspect anything until I called my father for the keys."

"That was days ago!" I say through my tears. "This whole time you've been lying about it. Even after everything I discovered that day in my father's office. The whole time you knew there was more, but you said nothing. And then we . . . and then you . . ."

I bend forward at the waist, thinking about what we did, what we shared together, all while he knew the truth.

Oh, God. This can't be happening. It's not real. Please, let it not be real.

"Please. Can we just talk about this?" His hand encircles my bicep, and I think I might be sick. "Doll?"

"Don't call me that!" I straighten, tears spilling down my face. "We are over," I force out with the slash of a hand.

"No!" he shouts. "Mackenzie, no. Please. I love you."

I gasp, his words detonating like a bomb inside my heart, sending shrapnel everywhere.

"You don't," I say.

"I do. I love you." His eyes darken, his tone fierce as he takes both of my arms in his hands, looking me straight in the eye. "I was too scared and too stupid to tell you that day. But I do. I love you a million times over."

"Don't say that," I whisper. Then I shake my head and cover my ears, unable to listen any longer.

"It's true."

"Even if it were true, you and I"—I point between us—"we can't get over this. I can't ignore the fact that you knew something so huge and kept it from me. I can't forget that you took me in his car after you knew what happened. We can't overcome this. Because your father is sitting in rehab somewhere, safe and warm and cared for. While my mother is rotting in her grave."

I'm stunned; numb as I sit in the passenger seat of Graham's car as he drives me home.

The scenery outside my window blurs, a watery landscape of colors behind my glistening gaze. I have no idea how I get to my bedroom or what he tells my father. All I know is the minute we step inside, I fall to my bed and weep.

Graham was right.

So was my father.

In the end, Atlas hurt me, just like they said he would.

Pain envelopes me. It chews me up and spits me out, and the little voice inside my head—the one that warned me every time Atlas and I got close—awakens and grins, displaying her claws as she tells me how stupid I am. Atlas himself warned me away, yet I didn't listen. This was probably just another game to him, a chance for revenge. Maybe all he wanted all along was to get me into bed and see how far he could take it—the chief's daughter.

Like a fool, I fell head first into love.

And now I'm paying the price.

Graham's arms come around me, holding me tight, his hands stroking my hair in a soothing rhythm. Only a short time ago, he vowed he wouldn't stick around to pick up the pieces of my broken heart, yet here he is. The only person in my life who's never lied to me, who's been there for me with unwavering devotion.

So, I lean on him with a heavy heart as the pain of betrayal sinks its teeth into muscle and bone and sinew, and I let myself come undone, knowing he's my soft place to fall.

Chapter 37

ATLAS

THREE WEEKS LATER...

A camera flash blinds me while I sit at a table with Coach Clancy, Jace, Graham, Teagen, and a handful of guys from our team. Several news outlets rally in front of us, snapping pictures and lobbing out questions about the state championship. Last Friday, Riverside secured their spot alongside a team from southern Ohio.

I scan the faces in the crowd, recognizing fans from their presence in the stands on Friday nights, hoping to find her face among them.

My stomach sinks when I don't.

Sorrow clings to me like a second skin. I miss the sound of her voice, the high tinkle of her laughter. I hunger for her smart mouth, her soft lips. And the scent of apple blossoms.

The last few weeks, I've driven myself crazy thinking about her. I even found myself sampling all the lotions at the drug store the other day just to try and satisfy my craving, only to leave disappointed and longing for her even more than before.

I've replayed the days after I spoke with Anthony Mancetti in my mind and how I'd do it differently if I could. When I imagine it this time, I go straight to Mackenzie and tell her what I discovered, then we work through it together.

But those are merely dreams—fantasies—and it's no surprise she's not here. I haven't spoken to her since that night. She refuses to answer my calls and ignores me at school. I even risked showing up at her house when her father was home only to find myself quickly ushered off the property.

My eyes lock on Uncle Cal's, beaming with pride as his gaze shifts between both Graham and me, but the moment doesn't feel nearly as momentous as I thought it would. Then again, nothing does since Mackenzie.

"Atlas Scott, rumor has it after a short relationship, you're newly single."

The sound of my name draws me up short, and my head jerks in the direction of the reporter. A middle-aged blonde holds a microphone below her mouth.

"That doesn't sound like a question," I say in response.

Laughter rumbles through the crowd.

"Here's a question," she grins. "It's what every girl out there wants to know. What's it going to take to win your heart?"

I swallow and my gaze darts around me as my mouth fills with sand. I don't want to answer her question. Instead, I want to shrivel up, sink into the ground and disappear. But all eyes are on me. Everyone's staring. Waiting.

"Uh, I'm sorry," I choke out, saying the first thing that comes to mind. "You must've misheard. I'm not single."

The woman frowns. "Oh. Well, can you tell us—"

"Mackenzie Hart," I say, staring straight into the video camera. Several flashes go off, their shutters snapping. "Doll, if you're watching, I'm not giving up on you. We're not done yet, not even close."

I stand as several reporters lob follow-up questions my way.

Ripping my mic off the collar of my shirt, I descend the stairs of the makeshift stage. I need to get the hell out of here, away from all these people and their questions.

My throat tightens as I burst outside the double doors into the hallway behind the gym. It's dark and quiet, hidden away from the commotion behind me.

I lean against the cool, hard wall and take a deep breath in an effort to collect myself when I hear the sound of my name.

"Atlas?"

I wheel around at the high soprano and frown at the tall brunette before me.

Great. Another reporter come to ask me more questions about my love life. Like that has anything to do with how well I handle a ball.

I straighten as I turn to face her. "Look, I'm done with questions. If you have anything you want—"

"Atlas, it's me..."

I blink at her, and a vague recognition trickles into my subconscious when she adds, "Your mother."

Find out what happens next for Mackenzie, Atlas, Graham, and the rest of the Riverside boys in

Love How You Love Me !

Acknowledgments

I wanted to give a special thank you to my husband, who put up with my writing this book and the chaos that comes with deadlines, even when he was down and out with a broken pelvis. I also want to give a special shout-out to my editor Yvette Rebello, who truly helped make this the best book it could be. Thank you for all of your input and suggestions. Also, thank you to my beta readers! I was so worried about getting this story right and you helped ensure I did just that.

Printed in Great Britain
by Amazon

464e8076-5180-403b-b529-0e32d23f590bR01